AF207309

Studien zu Lateinamerika
Latin America Studies

edited by

Prof. Dr. Dr. h.c. Kai Ambos,
Georg August University of Göttingen

Prof. Dr. Manuela Boatcă,
Albert Ludwig University of Freiburg

Prof. Dr. Hans-Jürgen Burchardt,
University of Kassel

Prof. Dr. Olaf Kaltmeier,
Bielefeld University

Prof. Dr. Anika Oettler,
Philipps University of Marburg

Prof. Dr. Stefan Peters,
Justus Liebig University of Gießen

Prof. Dr. Stephanie Schütze,
Free University of Berlin

Volume 40

Pedro Alarcón

The Ecuadorian Oil Era

Nature, Rent, and the State

 Nomos

© Cover illustration: www.pinterest.de: Artist: Joaquin Torres Garcia (Montevideo, Uruguay, 1874–1949); Title: América Invertida, 1943.

Funded by the DAAD from funds of the German Federal Ministry for Economic Cooperation (BMZ).
SDGnexus Network (grant number 57526248), program "exceed – Hochschulexzellenz in der Entwicklungszusammenarbeit"

DAAD Deutscher Akademischer Austauschdienst
German Academic Exchange Service

 **SDG** nexus network

The Deutsche Nationalbibliothek lists this publication in the Deutsche Nationalbibliografie; detailed bibliographic data are available on the Internet at http://dnb.d-nb.de

a.t.: Facultad Latinoamericana de Ciencias Sociales (FLACSO) sede Ecuador, Diss., 2020
Original title: "Rent and the State: An Approach to the Ecuadorian Oil Booms and Their Impact on Social Formation"
Directed by Prof. Dr. Stefan Peters of the Justus-Liebig-Universität Giessen

ISBN   978-3-8487-7985-7 (Print)
            978-3-7489-2115-8 (ePDF)

British Library Cataloguing-in-Publication Data
A catalogue record for this book is available from the British Library.

ISBN   978-3-8487-7985-7 (Print)
            978-3-7489-2115-8 (ePDF)

Library of Congress Cataloging-in-Publication Data
Alarcón, Pedro
The Ecuadorian Oil Era
Nature, Rent, and the State
Pedro Alarcón
245 pp.
Includes bibliographic references.

ISBN   978-3-8487-7985-7 (Print)
            978-3-7489-2115-8 (ePDF)

1st Edition 2021

© Pedro Alarcón

Published by
Nomos Verlagsgesellschaft mbH & Co. KG
Waldseestraße 3-5 | 76530 Baden-Baden
www.nomos.de

Production of the printed version:
Nomos Verlagsgesellschaft mbH & Co. KG
Waldseestraße 3-5 | 76530 Baden-Baden

ISBN (Print):   978-3-8487-7985-7
ISBN (ePDF):   978-3-7489-2115-8

DOI: https://doi.org/10.5771/9783748921158

Onlineversion
Nomos eLibrary

This work is licensed under a Creative Commons Attribution
– Non Commercial – No Derivations 4.0 International License.

Table of Contents

List of Figures

List of Tables

List of Abbreviations

AfDB	African Development Bank
BCE	Banco Central del Ecuador
BEV	Banco Ecuatoriano de la Vivienda
BIESS	Banco del Instituto Ecuatoriano de Seguridad Social
BNF	Banco Nacional de Fomento
BMZ	Bundesministerium für wirtschaftliche Zusammenarbeit und Entwicklung
CAN	Comunidad Andina
CEPAL	Comisión Económica para América Latina y el Caribe
CEPE	Corporación Estatal Petrolera Ecuatoriana
CEREPS	Cuenta Especial de Reactivación Productiva y Social, del Desarrollo Científico Tecnológico y de la Estabilización Fiscal
CES	Consejo de Educación Superior
CFN	Corporación Financiera Nacional
CGY	Certificado de Garantía Yasuní
CIADI	Centro Internacional de Arreglo de Diferencias Relativas a Inversiones
CNE	Consejo Nacional Electoral
CONADE	Consejo Nacional de Desarrollo
CONAIE	Confederación de Nacionalidades Indígenas del Ecuador
CONAM	Consejo Nacional de Modernización del Estado
EAR	Ecuadorian Amazon Region
ECLAC	Economic Commission for Latin America and the Caribbean
ECORAE	Fondo para el Ecodesarrollo Regional Amazónico
ENAC	Empresa Nacional de Almacenamiento y Comercialización
ENE	Emisiones Netas Evitadas
ENPROVIT	Empresa Nacional de Productos Vitales
FEIREP	Fondo de Estabilización, Inversión Social y Productiva y Reducción del Endeudamiento Público
FEISEH	Fondo Ecuatoriano de Inversión en los Sectores Energético e Hidrocarburífero
FEP	Fondo de Estabilización Petrolera
FETRACEPE	Federación Nacional de Trabajadores Petroleros Estatales de CEPE
FETRAPEC	Federación Nacional de Trabajadores de la Empresa Estatal Petróleos del Ecuador
FLOPEC	Flota Petrolera Ecuatoriana
FONADE	Fondo Nacional de Desarrollo

GDP	Gross domestic product
GFCF	Gross fixed capital formation
GNI	Gross national income
ICSID	International Centre for Settlement of Investment Disputes
IEA	International Energy Agency
IERAC	Instituto Ecuatoriano de Reforma Agraria y Colonización
IESS	Instituto Ecuatoriano de Seguridad Social
IFI	International Financial Institutions
IMF	International Monetary Fund
INECEL	Instituto Nacional de Electrificación
ISI	Import-substitution industrialization
ITT	Ishpingo Tambococha Tiputini
JUNAPLA	Junta Nacional de Planificación y Coordinación Económica
KSA	Kingdom of Saudi Arabia
LPG	Liquefied petroleum gas
LRSE	Ley de Régimen del Sector Eléctrico
MDG	Millennium Development Goals
MIT	Massachusetts Institute of Technology
MITI	Ministry of International Trade and Industry
NIC	Newly industrialized countries
OCDE	Organización para la Cooperación y el Desarrollo Económicos
OCP	Oleoducto de Crudos Pesados
OECD	Organization of Economic Cooperation and Development
OLADE	Organización Latinoamericana de Energía
OXY	Occidental Petroleum Corporation
OPEC	Organization of Petroleum Exporting Countries
PAIS	Movimiento Patria Altiva i Soberana
PdVSA	Petróleos de Venezuela S.A.
PETROECUADOR	Empresa Estatal Petróleos del Ecuador
PETROECUADOR	Empresa Pública de Hidrocarburos del Ecuador
REDD+	Reducing Emissions from Deforestation and forest Degradation
SAP	Structural adjustment program
SDG	Sustainable Development Goals
SENESCYT	Secretaría Nacional de Educación Superior, Ciencia, Tecnología e Innovación
SENPLADES	Secretaría Nacional de Planificación y Desarrollo
SOTE	Sistema Oleoducto Trans-Ecuatoriano
TFP	Total factor productivity
TRANSNAVE	Transportes Navieros Ecuatorianos
UNCTAD	United Nations Conference on Trade and Development
UNDP	United Nations Development Programme
UNEP	United Nations Environment Programme

UNESCO	United Nations Educational, Scientific and Cultural Organization
UNFCCC	United Nations Framework Convention on Climate Change
WC	Washington Consensus
WCED	World Commission on Environment and Development
WTO	World Trade Organization
YNP	Yasuní National Park

Abstract

By focusing on half-century of recent Latin American economic history, this book presents a multidisciplinary approach to the relentless quest of development in the Global South and aims at revitalizing the academic debate if natural resources abundance is a blessing or a curse. The pioneering diachronic comparative approach of two Ecuadorian oil booms, 1) 1972-1980, and 2) 2003-2014, shows processes of continuity and change in the capacity of the peripheral state to intervene in the national development process and its consequences on social formation framed by the contemporary forms of global capitalism and the irruption of environmental thinking into development policymaking.

The Ecuadorian state's struggle with multinational corporations for the appropriation of a larger portion of oil rent became a landmark of the 1970s; henceforth, oil rent has been central to modernization. Since the dawn of the twenty-first century, social environmental awareness is deeply entrenched in the Ecuadorian sociopolitical arena and increasingly contributes to expose the flaws of the prevalent natural resources-based development model. Together with environmental thinking, social environmental awareness strives for further influencing development policymaking and advocates for the reconstruction of the concept of development itself.

The study of either Ecuadorian oil booms through the viewpoint of nature, rent, and the state allows a historical-structural approach to the process of development. Such methodological strategy converges upon the heritage of Latin American development studies, which takes into account a scenario framed by 1) external constraints (the insertion of the country into the broader international division of labor) and 2) domestic circumstances (different development policymaking strategies and common debatable outcomes regarding economic diversification and temporary improvements in socioeconomic indicators).

Keywords: Latin America, development studies, neo-extractivism, environmental discourses, buen vivir, peripheral state

Acknowledgements

This book is the culmination of my PhD studies at FLACSO under the direction of Prof. Dr. Stefan Peters of the Justus-Liebig-Universität Giessen. Its publication is possible thanks to the SDGnexus Network funded by the German Academic Exchange Service (DAAD) from funds of the German Federal Ministry for Economic Cooperation (BMZ).

I could not have formulated this book without guidance and criticism of fine scholars, among them my wife María Augusta Espín. I also found a mentor in my dissertation director, who closely supervised my thesis and enriched it with bright comments at every step of the long journey. His intellectual contributions greatly improved this manuscript. Now I happily can count Stefan as a friend.

I am grateful to Daniele Benzi, Julio Oleas, William Sacher, and Alberto Acosta for their academic contributions during the early stages of this book. Jan Ickler proofread some sections of the manuscript, thereby he openhandedly offered thought-provoking criticism. Carmen Diana Deere, Anita Krainer, and Myriam Paredes ensured stimulating environments for the elaboration of this book as they invited me to join their academic projects and to teach in their courses. My fellow researchers Virginia Villamediana, Lucía Yamá, Claudia Arce and Paulina Quisaguano provided greatest joy from comradeship and put their vast knowledge of the social sciences at my disposal. Thanks for generosity and goodwill. My debt of gratitude goes also to all my reviewers, especially Sebastian Matthes, Juan Pablo Pérez Saínz and Rafael Domínguez Marín for their erudite and enriching comments.

FLACSO Ecuador funded my research during three years from February 2015 until February 2018. Between March and August 2018, European Union Erasmus+ funds financed my doctoral stay at the Freie Universität Berlin. Another rich source of academic exchange was my participation in conferences and congresses. I was granted financial support from the University of Kassel, the Latin American Studies Association (LASA), and the Maria Sibylla Merian Center for Advanced Latin American Studies (CALAS) to participate in academic events abroad, where I exposed the progress of my research and received constructive feedback. Last but not least, during the long journey of my PhD studies, my family welcomed me

Acknowledgements

to take shelter (and warm meals) in Quito, Conocoto, Tonsupa, Adliswil and Kew Gardens.

22

Introduction

After an interlude of low international prices, raw material markets boomed at the dawn of the new century and carried renewed hopes for natural resources-rich countries. Accompanying the favorable external conditions, the internal circumstance of many Latin American countries renovated. The state reclaimed a principal role in defining the shape of the national development process after being relegated during the last decades of the twentieth century; a significant portion of the region experienced the rise to power of democratically-elected governments that declared their intention to fill the gaps left by the state's withdrawal from key economic and social arenas. Economic planning epitomized the state's efforts aimed at fighting dependence on natural resources rent.

The end of the twenty-first century commodities boom cast a shadow over the optimism that reigned during a decade. Only a few years after international prices of commodities plummeted, the region's domestic circumstance seems to be reshaping again. Governments that ruled during the long commodities boom ended their periods or were replaced by others that aim to take distance from their predecessors in Brazil, Uruguay, Argentina, Ecuador, and Bolivia. Amid skyrocketing fiscal deficits, traditional lenders such as the International Monetary Fund (IMF), returned with their well-known impositions to Argentina and Ecuador.

During 2019 Latin America went through a wave of social protests; people in Chile, Ecuador, Venezuela, Colombia, Bolivia are taking to the streets. The roots of the protests are not monocausal; though, a common thread is recognizable, disappointment with the outcomes of the prevailing natural resources-based development model and the insight into the lack of alternatives. The gloomy sociopolitical atmosphere reminded of that of the last decades of the twentieth century, when the region was heavily indebted and prices of commodities reached historical minimums. In such context, the state stepped aside from key economic decisions in favor of the prevalence of global market rules.

The pursuit of exorcising dependence on natural resources became a common theme in contemporary Latin American economic history; in order to cope with the volatility of international prices of commodities, individual Latin American states deployed extensive planning efforts aimed at diversifying national economies. Significant efforts coincided with periods of high international commodities prices. Though, in the eyes of the rest of the world, Latin America is a traditional raw material provider; natural products are still topping the region's export portfolio, especially in South America (UNCTAD 2019; WTO 2014).

The legacy of (or the hangover from) the youngest commodities boom invites not only to revisit the question if natural resources are "a blessing or a curse" in natural resources-rich countries, but also revives the discussion on development itself. The irruption of environmental thinking into development theories introduced a new ontological perspective that insists on overhauling the concept of development in the twenty-first century. This book aims to converge upon these contemporary academic debates by delving into the legacy of half-century Ecuadorian oil era.

Hence, the contribution of this book is directed to present an interdisciplinary approach to recent Ecuadorian economic history with emphasis on an unique at this time diachronic comparative approach of two oil booms 1) 1972-1980, and 2) 2003-2014. Thereby, this work aims to shed light on the question how the state's efforts to exorcise dependence on natural resources during oil booms impacted on Ecuadorian social formation in the long run. The developmental endeavor of the Ecuadorian state is discussed within a historical-structural approach that takes into account the country's traditional position in the international division of labor. Alongside, the diachronic comparative approach to the oil booms seeks to identify processes of continuity and change by focusing on the interrelations between the concepts of nature, state, and development. It is argued that the incorporation of environmental thinking into the state's logic during the last decades of the twentieth century contributed to the articulation of the national development project and to the reformulation of the notion of development itself, in which more social actors became involved. The hypothesis from the case study and the theoretical implications aim to contribute to further research on the quest of development in natural resources-rich countries in the Global South.

Development in Latin American Social Thought: The Mobility of a Concept

Economic growth has been central to the concept of development. In an analogous fashion as the role of money in the economy, orthodox development economists traditionally believed that economic growth made development possible and mostly pretended to legitimize their particular stance through abstract mathematical and statistical models. Whereas Rostow

(1990 [1960]; 1959) blindly believed in the "magic" of economic growth, Kuznets (1973; 1971) posited that economic diversification is central to development. Within this particular *weltanschauung*, industrialization functioned as the barometer for progress. The idea underlying the prioritization of industrial development was that more advanced sectors of the economy (such as the manufacturing sector) might lead to a more complex division of labor and hence to a higher standard of living (Sachs and Warner 1995, 5). This main postulate of development economics[1] fits perfectly well in modernization theory, where economic growth is essential to cause a collection of social and cultural changes, including occupational specialization, urbanization, and higher levels of education, which in turn might even catalyze democracy (Ross 2001, 336).

An evolutionary perspective, in which every country might attain development through economic growth, was displayed in Rostow's 1960 classic *The Stages of Economic Growth: A Non-Communist Manifesto* (Rostow 1990). In line with modernization theory, the author presented the transit from traditional societies to mass consumer societies as a process to take place during the history of capitalism; the Rostownian transit entails successive stages: 1) the traditional society, 2) the preconditions period, 3) the takeoff, 4) [technological] maturity, 5) the period of diffusion on a mass basis of durable consumers' goods and services (Rostow 1990, 3). This orthodox vision that predominated in development economics also permeated the international political arena since the end of the Second World War. During his inaugural address (nicknamed "the Point Four Program"), Harry S. Truman, the thirty-third president of the United States, invoked the "vital forces" of capitalism, namely, capital, technology, and international cooperation (Escobar 1995a, 36; Alarcón 2020, 217) in order to launch the pursuit of development as "a new world order" (Rist 2008, 72):

> I believe that we should make available to peace-loving peoples the benefits of our store of technical knowledge in order to help them realize their aspirations for a better life. And, in cooperation with other nations, we should foster capital investment in areas needing development (Harry S. Truman, inaugural address, January 20, 1949).

The quest of development as a world order imprinted the political practice in Latin America as well. When governments managed to increase their ex-

---

1 For an economics orthodox perspective, see: Rosenstein-Rodan (1943); Solow (1957); Nurkse (1960 [1953]), Lewis (1954b); Rostow (1990 [1960]; 1959); Hirschman (1961); Kuznets (1973; 1971).

penditure for development purposes (support of domestic industry, construction of infrastructure to promote industrialization, among others), the state's action converged in an "ideological current known as *desarrollismo*" (Kay 1989, 28). Though, the mainstream stance on development presented in the "Point Four Program" was promptly called into question. Latin American social thought advocated a more comprehensive approach to the national development process, which included the switch of the unit of analysis from individual nations or regions to global interdependence. On the one hand, the pioneering perspective implied by the Latin American theoretical schools of (under)development evidenced the influence of international hierarchies on the national state's (under)development path. On the other hand, it opened the gates to the analysis of state's agency (i.e. its capacity to intervene in the national development process) within the cycles of the capitalist world-economy.

Hence, contrary to modernization theory, that centered its analysis on societies' characteristics, Latin American theoretical schools of (under)development postulated the thesis of the leading role of the state in the national process of development[2]. Essential to the more global perspective opened by Latin American social thought was the exposition of the outward-oriented development model, which rests on exports of raw material and imports of manufactured goods (and capital) and traditionally tied the region to the Global South. Hence, the state's developmental endeavors have been regarded in Latin American social thought as attempts to climb up the hierarchy of the international division of labor by establishing an "*autocentric* national economy" (or an inward-oriented development model), i.e. an economy in which the relations with the exterior are subject to the logic of internal accumulation and not the reverse (Amin 1990, 11).

---

2 German economist Friedrich List is regarded as a pioneer in discussing an active role of the state in the national development process (Acosta 2004a, 82; Schuldt 2004, 191). Schuldt (2004, 191) argued that Germany's successful development model during the end of the nineteenth century was based on "state-led selective openness to globalization", which was inspired by List's 1841 opus The National System of Political Economy (*Das Nationale System der Politischen Ökonomie*). In his work, List (1955) advocated 1) the prioritization of industry over agriculture, 2) state's protection of national industry, 3) the durability of state's institutions and laws, and 4) state's regulation of trade (List 1955, 9-29 in Schuldt 2004, 212-214).

Natural Resources Rent and the State: A Global South Perspective on Development

Development economics also shares with modernization theory the idea of the centrality of natural resources to the process of development[3]; natural resources are venerated as a "development motor". Therefore, a strong argument is that European industrialization indeed benefited from natural resource endowments (Peters 2017a, 47). Though, in order to bankroll its developmental endeavor, the Latin American state first faced the challenge of the appropriation of natural resources rent. This problem turned particullary evident during boom periods, which were triggered by improvements in the terms of trade with the Global North or by discoveries of new endowments. In classical Political Economy, rent refers to the kind of surplus generated by mere property over natural resources as opposed to the income obtained from the exploitation of labor/capital (profit) or the selling of labor (wages). Theoretically, rent is put straightaway at the rentier's disposal, since it is not gained on a basis of competition or profit. Though, an initial bargaining between the state and private actors (domestic or foreign) took place as a requisite to the control over a larger share of natural resources rent in Latin America. This antecedent decisively impacted on the forthcoming state's agency. On the one hand, the initial bargaining between the state and private actors left a legacy of "overly-centralized political power" (Karl 1999, 34). On the other hand, the appropriation of natural resources rent caused many Latin American states' proneness to rent dependence. This, in turn, was accompanied by a pessimistic vision of the possibilities of economic diversification, since industrialization efforts indeed require a basis of competition and profit that is not commonplace in rentier state configurations.

Thus, rent contributed to the construction of a negative vision of natural resources abundance in countries in the Global South. Rent transfer, or the international transfer of surplus from consumer states towards extractivist states (Peters 2017a, 48), enabled the latter to increase their import capacity of manufactured goods from the Global North through mere nat-

---

3 Though, Hirschman (1961, 110), a development economist, already questioned the too few "backward linkages" of the natural resources sector with other sectors of the economy and advocated for industrialization, since it provides with more "backward and forward linkages". According to the author, every country ought to identify and support the domestic economic sectors that are likely to be most interdependent, i.e. the sectors that hold the most "linkages with other sectors of the economy.

ural resources extraction, i.e. without the need of promoting other more productive sectors of the domestic economy (Baptista 2010, 153). Consequently, natural resources rent was central to the perpetuation of the outward-oriented development model. The concept of rent itself was assigned a negative load, which was charged up during boom periods as windfall revenues poured generously into natural resources-rich states. Saad-Filho and Weeks (2013, 19), defined windfalls as "economic gains realized without sacrifice, or without the expenditure of resources"; the authors emphasized that the term windfall is used to imply that the gain is temporary, and suggested that it results from "luck rather than effort". This added a further argument to link rent to an "unearned, temporary, and undeserved" revenue[4] (Saad-Filho and Weeks 2013, 4). In a contemporary definition of rent, Mayer (1999, 4) argued that it corresponds to any revenue "in excess of production costs and a normal return on capital"; inherent to the nature of rent is the way how it might be collected, either from "power-based means" (Wilcock et al. 2016, 12), or from privilege-based means. In this vein, Becker (2008, 15) recapped that rents enjoyed by natural resources-exporting countries stem from "special natural production advantages".

However, in many Latin American countries, state's appropriation of natural resources rent led to economic growth, which in turn mirrored in the improvement of socioeconomic and development indicators (e.g. the Gini index, the Human Development Index, the multidimensional poverty index). Such positive advances were particularly evident during boom periods and contrasted with the negative vision of natural resources that prevailed in Latin American social thought, thus updated the academic research question if natural resources abundance is a blessing or a curse.

Nature and Environmental Awareness: Latest Guests on Development Thinking

During the last decades of the twentieth century, Latin American states embraced the official environmental discourse inspired by United Nations' sustainable development (United Nations 1992; 1987). The discourse relies on the utopia of combining the polar opposites of natural resources extrac-

---

4 Elsenhans (1986, 32) argued that due to this origin, the use of rent is not subject to economic control mechanisms. In the same vein, Ross (2012, 27) argued that oil revenues are marked by their exceptionally large size, unusual source, lack of stability, and secrecy.

tion and environmental protection on the basis of technology, capital, and international cooperation[5], hence, it rests on green capitalism. Together with the state's construction of an official environmental discourse, environmental awareness mushroomed among society. Whereas states advocated for natural resources and environmental management, society bet on conservation of nature. Increased social environmental consciousness was central to the denouncement of the destructive socioecological consequences of extractivism, i.e. the "intensification of natural resources' extraction for commodification in the global market" (Burchardt et al. 2016, 7). Hence, the rise of social environmental awareness in Latin America stacked up a strong argument to the "resource curse" thesis, which affirms that natural resources-based development models hinder economic diversification and industrialization (Auty 1993).

The irruption of environmental thinking into Latin American social thought thus had an ambiguous impact on the approach of the outward-oriented development model. On the one hand, the official environmental discourse of sustainable development further legitimized the reliance on natural resources. On the other hand, widespread social environmental awareness was central to the incubation of further arguments to the critique against the natural resources-based development model. The construction of antagonist environmental discourses, 1) an official discourse that stemmed from green capitalism, and 2) a discourse that was rooted in the cultural critique of modern society (Hajer and Fischer 1999, 3), is founded on different meanings of nature. Whereas states hold the notion of natural resources available for commodification, civil society defends the concept of natural heritage. These antagonist environmental discourses became, in turn, central to the construction of different concepts of development during the first decades of the twenty-first century.

Environmental thinking and social environmental awareness enriched the interdisciplinary academic approach of (under)development and added up a new set of challenges to the study of the process of development in natural resources-rich countries. The developmental role of the Latin American state was not immune to the irruption of environmental thinking and social environmental awareness. On the one hand, the state was compelled to revisit its logic in order to include an official environmental

---

5 The reiterated allusion to the "vital forces" of capitalism (Escobar 1995a, 36) in the environmental discourse of sustainable development (United Nations 1992; 1987) suggests a continuity with the orthodox perspective of development economics as it is displayed in the Point Four Program of 1949.

discourse. On the other hand, social environmental awareness proved to be capable of steering the relationship between state and society during the first decades of the twenty-first century.

Structure of the Book

The theoretical section (chapters 1 to 3) begins with a discussion on the role of the state in the development process of natural resources-rich countries. The developmental state theory has prevailed in academic literature approaches to the problem of the state's leading role in successful industrialization. Chapter 1 *Eighty Years of "Sow the Oil": A State's Discourse* argues that the developmental state theory cannot be easily transplanted to approach the Latin American state's effort to break dependence on natural resources. Alternatively, the chapter presents the concept of the Latin American *desarrollista* state and advocates for the inclusion of region-specific particularities, such as natural resource-abundance and Latin American populism, into the study of the state's capacity to intervene in the national development process. The discussion on the irruption of nature into development thinking during the last decades of the twentieth century and its consequences for today's Latin American social thought is presented in chapter 2 *Bringing Nature Into the "Sow the Oil" Discourse*. The chapter argues that the irruption of environmental thinking, which led to the incorporation of different meanings of nature into development studies, represents an ontological and epistemological challenge to the contemporary academic approach to (under)development. Chapter 3 *Nature, State, and Development: A Dissection in Three Acts* is the core of the theoretical section and elaborates the triad nature-state-development as a theoretical tool to analyze the process of (under)development in Latin America with a leading role of the state since the end of the Second World War. The critical review of literature showed that Latin American development thinking treated the problem rather unconnectedly. Alternatively, the triad nature-state-development opens the gates for a more thoroughgoing approach to the role of the state in the development process within region-specific external conditions and domestic circumstances.

The methodological section (chapter 4 *Ecuador 1972-2017: Case Study and Methodological Approach*) begins with an explanation of the conditions that make Ecuador a most relevant case study within Latin America. Then, the chapter highlights the interdisciplinary perspective needed to carry out the historical-structural approach with emphasis on the diachronic comparative approach of its oil booms. Finally, the methodological section 1) exposes the research categories, 2) describes its operationalization for the country study, and 3) explains the methods for gathering relevant information.

The empirical section entails two chapters where half-century of recent Ecuadorian economic history is observed through the lens of the triad nature-state-development. Chapter 5 *"Sow the Oil": The Ecuadorian Classic* Desarrollista *State* approaches the developmental endeavor of the Ecuadorian state and its outcomes during the 1970s' oil boom with an emphasis on the period 1972-1980. Chapter 5 highlights the struggle of the Ecuadorian state for the appropriation of a larger share of oil rent and its further influence on capitalist modernization. Chapter 6 *"Sow the Oil" Revisited: Nature and the Ecuadorian Neo-Desarrollista State* focuses on the twenty-first century commodities boom (2003-2014) and its assimilation by the Ecuadorian state during the period 2007-2017. The inclusion of environmental thinking and social environmental awareness into development policymaking resulted in the particular discourse of *buen vivir* that was built upon the indigenous weltanschauung of *sumak kawsay* (good living). The rise and fall of the discourse of *buen vivir* is epitomized by the Yasuní-ITT initiative, a failed plan to save the Yasuní National Park (YNP) in the Ecuadorian Amazonia from oil drilling.

The last chapter (*Conclusion: Beyond the Ecuadorian Case*) summarizes the research's principal empirical findings and proposes some theoretical implications for a further academic approach to the (dis)connection between natural resource-abundance and development. The closing discussion presents a further research agenda that emphasizes on pending research questions, which are motivated by the approach of the concepts of nature, state, and development in natural resource-rich countries in the Global South.

Chapter 1: Eighty Years of "Sow the Oil": A State's Discourse

"Instead of a curse, which turns us into a parasitic and idle nation, may oil be the fortunate circumstance that allows us, with its sudden richness, to boost and strengthen the productive evolution of our peoples" (Uslar Pietri 1936).

"Sow the Oil": Oil Booms and the State's Developmental Endeavor

Latin America has traditionally attracted the attention of scholars worldwide, who became fascinated by the quest if natural resources boost or hinder development. Venezuela has been the region's case study par excellence since the country relies on one natural export product since the early decades of the twentieth century: oil. Though, already by 1936 the potential negative effects of long-term reliance on oil concerned Arturo Uslar Pietri, a Venezuelan writer and politician. In an editorial to a local newspaper, the author pointed out the necessity of exorcising natural resources dependence by means of economic diversification. The metaphor used by Uslar Pietri (1936) to address the problem of Venezuela's economic diversification is well-known until present day as "sow the oil". Otherwise, so the author, oil was to "curse" the country and turn it into an "immense parasite [...], unproductive and idle". Hence, Uslar Pietri's prescription applied particularly to avoid that "black gold" turned into the "devil's excrement" (Pérez Alfonzo 1976). For many years, this vision imprinted development thinking in Latin America as industrialization was regarded as the epitome of successful economic development.

Such a view was soon integrated into a more global perspective. Two oil shocks (1973-1974 and 1978-1979) dramatically multiplied international oil prices and confirmed that oil appraisal was governed by geopolitical criteria[6]. The first shock was provoked by the embargo that major members

---

6 From the viewpoint of macroeconomics, oil price might be estimated in the ground of supply and demand. Whilst, the recognition of a portion of surplus (i.e. the rent) for the owner of the subsoil resource, or the landlord, would play a main role in the microeconomic estimation of the price of oil. During the global oil shocks (1973-1974 and 1979-1980), supply of oil was disrupted due to political rea-

of the Organization of Petroleum Exporting Countries (OPEC) issued against the biggest oil consuming countries that supported Israel during the Yom Kippur War. As a consequence, international oil prices nearly quadrupled. The second shock, which doubled prices again, was triggered by the overthrow of the regime in Iran, a main member of OPEC[7], and the fears of new supply interruptions in Western countries. The shocks provoked an unprecedented oil boom that triggered distinct reactions around the globe. On the one hand, the oil boom disquieted major consuming industrialized countries grouped under the Organization of Economic Cooperation and Development (OECD)[8]. On the other hand, the extraordinary rise of oil prices gave national states in exporting countries the foretaste of nationalist control of natural resources rent. Yet, a new keyword was envisaged to link oil with development in exporting countries: Optimism. The boom fertilized the discussions on "sow the oil" and even the attempts to turn it into reality in exporting countries.

On the other side of the coin, in industrialized consuming countries[9], the end of cheap oil triggered discussions on the alternatives to deal with the break of flows and even on the possible options for the downfall of

---

sons. The interruption of the flow of oil put pressure on importing countries to recognize a higher value of rent for exporting countries, the owners of the subsoil resource.

7 The Organization of Petroleum Exporting Countries (OPEC) was established in 1960 in response to the previous international governance scheme for oil which was dominated by multinational private corporations. Current OPEC members are Algeria, Angola, Ecuador, Equatorial Guinea, Gabon, Iran, Iraq, Kuwait, Libya, Nigeria, Qatar, Saudi Arabia, United Arab Emirates, and Venezuela.

8 In 1974 the Organization of Economic Cooperation and Development (OECD) established the International Energy Agency (IEA) as a political counterweight to OPEC. Main duty of the IEA was the assurance of energy supply for OECD member countries.

9 OECD countries demand about one half of current overall oil consumption of nearly 100 million barrels of oil per day. Oil has been the world's leading energy source for about the last hundred years; though, about 15 percent of worldwide oil consumption is linked to non-energy uses, i.e. oil is raw material for most diverse industrial processes.

stocks[10]. Already by 1956 the matter of the finiteness[11] of oil was implied in Hubbert's peak oil theory, which affirmed that US oil extraction (excluding Alaska) was about to reach its peak around 1970. This breakpoint supposed the start of progressing decline of oil fields productivity until exhaustion. M. King Hubbert, a geologist at Shell Oil Company, further predicted global peak oil for 2010 (Eccleston 2008, 25). Beyond questionable outcomes and methodology, the theory exposed a real concern: the fact that ahead of peak oil, "prices rise unless demand declines commensurately". As big consumers relied on fresh Alaskan and North Sea oil (Campbell and Laherrère 1998, 78), international oil prices followed a decreasing trend which began in the early 1980s and continued even after the end of the twentieth century, thus closing the boom period of the 1970s.

As oil prices plummeted, the external debt burden became tangible in former prosperous exporting countries, principally in Latin America. OPEC's quota system[12] revealed politically insufficient to halt the falling-off of oil prices, and rather caused the separation of member countries Ecuador in 1992 and Gabon in 1995. Exporting countries replied to low prices typically by trying to increase national oil extraction hand in hand with multinational corporations. Under such a scheme, privatization of state oil companies was not automatically a collateral effect, but an alignment with the policies of the Washington Consensus (WC) that sponsored state's withdrawal from key arenas of the economy during the height of neoliberal globalization.

However, in 1988, the World Bank assessed six oil exporting countries[13] in Africa, Asia, and Latin America. The title of the study seemed to reflect the zeitgeist of the epoch: *Oil Windfalls: Blessing or Curse?* (Gelb 1988). By and large, the assessments focused on the way how national states assimilated the global oil shocks, i.e. the way how the positive external condition

---

10 Research on alternative energy sources was boosted in industrialized countries during periods of high international oil prices. Energy saving initiatives were also set into force, Germany and Switzerland, for example, enforced the plan *Autofreie Sonntage* (Car free Sundays) between November and December1973, a ban on family cars' use on Sundays.

11 Oil extracted nowadays took millions of years to be produced under high pressures and temperatures within the planet's subsoil. Since the rate of world's consumption of oil greatly exceeds its rate of production inside the Earth, oil is considered non-renewable.

12 OPEC monitors the global oil market and assigns member countries quotas to raise or lower oil extraction in order to control overall supply. Hence, the organization aims to influence oil prices from a macroeconomic perspective.

13 Algeria, Ecuador, Indonesia, Nigeria, Trinidad and Tobago, and Venezuela.

influenced domestic circumstances in individual countries. The problem of economic diversification was by far not exhausted, though, its approach involved a new main actor: The state. Regardless of the success of the enforced "sow the oil" strategies, oil windfalls allowed the state in oil exporting countries to improve its possibilities of intervention in the national development process, i.e. its agency. The enhanced state's agency materialized mainly as 1) the establishment of state-owned industries, 2) the support of nascent industrial enterprises with subsidies and tax exemptions for industrialists, and 3) the protection of domestic industry through import tariffs.

The twenty-first century commodities boom was triggered by increasing demand from non-industrialized countries, especially China (World Bank 2018, 52). "Sow the oil" seemed possible (again) as assessments ordered by multilateral organizations[14] reported particularly high economic growth rates based on natural resources rent. Moreover, economic growth frequently mirrored in key development indicators and even in social achievements in oil exporting countries. A renewed feeling of euphoria impregnated the atmosphere of the 2003-2014 boom, this time accompanied by the deliberate negation of the volatility of international commodities' prices. The state, which was kept to the minimum at the shadow of the market for the last two decades, reemerged (Peters 2019, 2; UNDP 2013, 66) and became the main actor of the domestic circumstance within oil exporting countries. This was the *"renaissance"* (Peters 2017b; Peters and Burchardt 2015, 7) of the state's developmental endeavor. A renewed tide of oil nationalism accompanied international high prices. Exporting countries rejuvenated strategies to better appropriate swollen oil rent: Ecuador resumed OPEC in 2007 and Gabon in 2016. In 2006, Ecuador, Venezuela, Bolivia, Chad, and Russia expropriated assets in the oil sector thereby restaging the trend of nationalizations that prevailed throughout exporting countries of the Global South between the 1960s and the mid 1980s (Arbatli 2018, 103). The *déjà vu* seemed complete when national states increased their investments in the primary sector of the economy in order to back state-owned oil companies.

Along with the youngest commodities boom, academic debates on resource nationalism, i.e. the state-led efforts to increase national control

---

14 The United Nations Development Programme entitled its 2013 Human Development Report "The rise of the South" (UNDP 2013), the World Trade Organization, in its 2014 World Trade Report, highlighted "the rise of the developing world" (WTO 2014, 5).

over natural endowments and to enhance state's influence over the primary sector of the economy at the expense of foreign participation, mushroomed (Arbatli 2018, 101; Pryke 2017; Haslam and Heidrich 2016; Childs 2016; Wilson 2015). Resource nationalism is rationalized by the idea that the enforcement of market-led strategies might not lead the state to fully benefit from the richness of its national (sub)soil. However, different from resource nationalism of the 1970s that was triggered by foremost ideological and political reasons, during the twenty-first century, pragmatism is regarded as a main driver of national states intervention. In the light of swollen natural resources rent income, exporting states pursued to increase their participation in the oil sector in order to leverage extraction for concrete economic goals and even developmental purposes. State ownership, state intermediation in the private sector and tax measures count as intervention strategies regarding state's different objectives of rent distribution, industrial transformation or market-based investment promotion (Arbatli 2018, 105; Wilson 2015, 412).

In Latin America, nationalism was propelled by the democratic "left turn" of a significant portion of the region (Levitsky and Roberts 2011; Beasley-Murray, Cameron, and Hershberg 2010). Either adherents of the 'pink tide' or not, Latin American states revisited the "sow the oil" imperative, as did other natural resource-dependent economies around the globe. The creation of market niches, preferably with the participation of the domestic industrial sector, was the preferred option of economic diversification within the blatant evidence of market predominance. Hence, the updated "sow the oil" strategies advocated for a more selective integration into globalization based on "competitive rather than comparative advantages" (Kay and Gwynne 2000, 58).

Nevertheless, nearly eighty years after the appearance of the "sow the oil" discourse, the long twenty-first century commodities boom ended. According to the World Bank (2018, 51), the dramatic[15] decline of international oil prices was triggered by a combination of 1) surging United States shale oil production, 2) receding geopolitical risks involving some key exporters (e.g. Iran), 3) shifts in OPEC's policies, and 4) weakening global growth prospects. The legacy of the youngest oil boom in natural resources-rich countries was rather the re-primarization of the exports' portfolio, i.e. the reinforced reliance of the economy on natural resources rents

---

15 Oil prices dropped in such a dramatic way between mid-2014 and early 2016 that the World Bank (2018, 51) characterized the period as "one of the largest oil-price shocks in modern history".

(CEPAL 2014, 29; Bárcena and Prado 2015, 19; Burchardt et al. 2016, 8). Despite the modest improvement of international oil prices since 2016, the worldwide trend indicates that boom prices are far to be reached. Though, fostering economic transformation remained a "classic" contemporary task of national states (Evans 1995, 5), and fighting against oil dependence further topped the agenda in natural resources-rich states for economic, political, and environmental reasons. Venezuela's "changing industrialization strategies since 1920" (Di John 2009), or Ecuador's heralded *cambio de la matriz productiva* (transformation of the productive structure) add to further contemporary "sow the oil" endeavors in Sub-Saharan Africa and the Middle East: Nigeria's promotion of local participation in extractive activities (Ovadia 2014, 143; Ovadia 2013, 322), Angola's state efforts to encourage economic diversification (Peters 2019, 361) and to establish a fund to insulate the economy from volatile prices (AfDB et al. 2013, 192), or the *Saudi Vision 2030*, that aims to raise the share of non-oil exports (KSA 2016, 61) and to increase private sector's contribution to the economy of the Kingdom of Saudi Arabia (KSA 2016, 53) in order to deal with common concerns about reliance on volatile revenues (Ulrichsen 2017, 210).

New and old sets of policies to "sow the oil" are publicized, despite former partial successes or even sound failures. The way how oil booms shaped internal circumstances within oil rent-dependent states resembled Sisyphus' efforts to push the boulder to the top of the hill. Though, throughout eighty years "sow the oil" evolved from a particular view of economic diversification into the epitome of the relationships between the state and development in natural resources-rich countries; thus, functioned as a discourse where "concepts, theories, and practices were systematically created" (Escobar 1995a, 39).

Lost in Translation: Developmental State vs Desarrollista State

The developmental state theory provided a particular explanation to successful industrialization with a specific role of the state in East Asian countries. It emerged to make sense of the "meteoric rise" as economic powers of the so-called 'Asian Three', namely Japan, Taiwan, and South Korea, during the late 1970s (Thurbon and Weiss 2016, 637) and echoed during the very years of neoliberalism supremacy. Even though detractors of the developmental state theory argued that the extraordinary socioeconomic performance of the newly industrialized countries (NICs) was due to the benefits of free market and liberalization associated to state's retraction of key economic sectors (Lal 1983; Balassa 1981 in de la Cruz 2014, 28), further analysis appeared as a "counter- critique" and advocated for a certain developmental role played by the state (Johnson 1999; Öniş 1991, 109). In the context of the Cold War, the concept of the developmental state disclosed a third way that differed from free-market capitalism or state-directed communism and, hence, challenged the prevailing state-versus-market paradigm in an empirically informed way (Thurbon and Weiss 2016, 638). However, economic success of East Asian NICs contributed to further draw attention to the role of the state in development policymaking.

Following the pathbreaking study of Chalmers Johnson (1982), *MITI and the Japanese Miracle: The Growth of Industrial Policy, 1925-1975*, which researched into the Japanese Ministry of International Trade and Industry (MITI) as a "pilot organization that controls industrial policy through its influence over [economic] planning" (Johnson 1982 in Stubbs 2009, 2), other scholars conducted pioneering studies in South Korea and Taiwan (Amsden 1985; Amsden 1989; Evans 1995), which exemplified the process that took place in East Asian newly industrialized countries (NICs) "of moving from a set of assets based on primary products, exploited by unskilled labor to a set of assets based on knowledge, exploited by skilled labor" (Amsden 2001, 2). Two key factors were regarded as essential to the economic success[16] of the developmental state in East Asia: 1) the role of bureaucracy in catalyzing domestic industrialization, and 2) the significance of market's realm to economy and society within the East Asian developmental state.

First, despite industrialization in East Asia was undertaken by the private sector, state bureaucracy occupies a leading position in developmental state theory due to the role it played in the creation of strong links with national industrial elites (Evans 1998, 142; Evans 1995). Two main characteristics of the bureaucracy in connection with the developmental state were already exposed by Johnson (1982), namely, 1) the existence of a small, inexpensive, but elite state bureaucracy staffed by the best managerial talent available, and 2) a political system in which the bureaucracy was given sufficient scope to take initiative and operate effectively (Johnson

---

16 Success of East Asian NICs might also be connected with inflow of foreign capital in form of development cooperation during the Cold War. Up to the mid-1960s, Northeast Asian states received "huge amounts" of US financial, technical, and even military support (Wade 2018, 530). "According to geopolitics, those countries built a frontier. Beyond that border, there was the *other* part of the world. Welfare and progress had to be exhibited to that *other* part of the world" (Víctor Bretón, interview, August 8, 2016).

1982 in Stubbs 2009, 2). However, the developmental state managed to maintain autonomy from industrial elites due to the weakness of the private capital in the aftermath of the Second World War (Evans 1998, 142); such a configuration of state's autonomy in a context of strong connections between industrial elites and state bureaucracy was termed by Evans (1995) "embedded autonomy".

Second, besides the role of the state bureaucracy, the significance of the market (or of competence) to economy and society was central to the East Asian developmental state theory. The state was expected to cultivate certain "market-conforming methods" (Johnson 1982 in Stubbs 2009, 2) or "developmental capacities" (Leftwich 1993a, 620) in order to "influence the course of economic and social change" (Evans 1995, 18). Efforts undertaken by the East Asian developmental state to "tame domestic and international market forces and harnessing them to national ends" (Öniş 1991, 110) or, in Wade's (1990) words, to "govern the market", mostly materialized in state's protection of national industry (particularly infant industry) within a market-led, outward-oriented development model[17]. The state's hand manifested in a series of incentives and rewards to persuade domestic capitalists to undertake investments in targeted sectors of the national economy (Nem Singh and Ovadia 2018, 1038); among the principal mechanisms enforced were directed credit, fiscal incentives, trade protection, and hard bargaining with multinationals intending to channel foreign investments into the national economy (Wade 2018, 527). Though, many authors coincide in arguing that the East Asian developmental state implemented a carrot and stick policy in which time-limited support was conditioned by performance requirements measured in international competence standards (Nem Singh and Ovadia 2018, 1038; Wade 2018, 528; Thurbon and Weiss 2016, 640). In this line, de la Cruz (2014, 38) argued that penalizations consisted in reducing incentives, such as tax rebates, and in cancelling bail-ins in order to force fusions. A developmental state's measure, which is highly unlikely to be enforced in Latin America, is the implementation of mechanisms to "restrain non-productive wealth accumulation and luxury consumption" (Wade 2018, 528).

---

17 When approaching development, Leftwich (1993a, 620) advocated for the return of politics. In the author's vision, politics was expected to give rise to a state with certain "capacities" to generate "positive developmental consequences" (Leftwich 1993a, 620). Though, the envisioned kind of state was only to be found in "a few societies (mainly Southeast and East Asia) with anything comparable to the strong or long state traditions of the West" (Leftwich 1993b, 57), i.e. the East Asian NICs.

Based on 1) the role of state bureaucracy in the national industrialization process, and 2) the relationship between state and market (or even between the state and the private sector), it is argued that the developmental state theory could not be easily grafted onto the Latin American context. On the one hand, whereas a state bureaucracy that catalyzed industrialization by building strong links with domestic industrialists was at the East Asian developmental state's disposal, strong personal leaderships that overshadowed weak political institutions[18] traditionally regulated the relationship between the Latin American *desarrollista* state and local economic elites. On the other hand, the recognition of market's supremacy and the East Asian developmental state's orientation towards "market-conforming methods" also diverges from the pro-statist stance of the Latin American *desarrollista* state.

In order to rationalize the developmental success in East Asia during the post-Second World War period, another widely explored field, besides 1) the role of state bureaucracy in the industrialization process and 2) the significance of market's realm to economy and society, was the relationship between the agrarian and the industrial sectors of the economy. Kay (2002, 82) argued that there is widespread consensus among development economists upon the necessity of surplus transfer from the agrarian sector to the industrial sector, especially during the earlier stages of industrialization in order to support industrial capital accumulation. Central to the developmental state's successful transference of surplus from the agrarian to the industrial sector was the scenario left by the Second World War and the enforcement of land reform prior to industrialization; Japan, Taiwan and Korea carried out expropriative land reforms (Wade 2018, 529; Evans 1989, 575). As a result of this particular historical cocktail, the landowner class was practically absent, peasants' pressure was heavily reduced, industrial groups were disorganized and undercapitalized, and foreign capital was channeled through the state apparatus (de la Cruz 2014, 45; Kay 2002, 54; Evans 1989, 575). Kay (2002, 54) argued that a repressive state appropriated peasants' agrarian surplus in order to bankroll the national industrialization process. The latter has been further associated with the authoritarian vein of the developmental state (Nem Singh and Ovadia 2018, 1034). Regarding the majority of Latin American countries, Cueva (2013, 167) argued that the economic expansion of the United States after the Second

---

18 For a brief rationalization of the social construction of the figure of the leader in Latin America, see the section *Latin American populism: Desarrollismo's (un)invited guest*.

World War deeply influenced their actual domestic industrialization process. Latin America's insertion into the capitalist world-economy was reinforced through raw material and natural resources exports as the primary sector confirmed to be the most dynamic sector of the economy (Cueva 2013, 166; Fajnzylber 1990, 15). Hence, a key problem regarding industrialization in Latin America was the transference of surplus from the primary sector of the economy (not only the agrarian sector) to the industrial sector (Cueva 2013, 162-166).

However, Kay (2002, 52) argued that land reform in Latin America (with the exception of Mexico) was enforced subsequently after the industrialization process of the aftermath of the Second World War; according to the author, this fact negatively impacted on the capacity of the Latin American state to appropriate agrarian surplus for the industrial sector[19]. Different from East Asia, land reform in Latin America (with the exception of Cuba) had a meager impact on redistribution (de la Cruz 2014, 44). Big landowners outlasted land reform until the 1970s (except for Mexico and Bolivia) and adamantly opposed the process to the point of reverting it in Guatemala (from 1954 on) and in Chile (after 1973) (Bretón 2006, 61). Hence, the higher degree of autonomy of the East Asian developmental state of the aftermath of the Second World War, which enabled the transference of surplus from the agrarian to the industrial sector, blatantly contrasted with the efforts of the Latin American state to content powerful domestic propertied classes.

Despite an alleged demise of the developmental state theory, academic research on the role of the state in the national development process never lost momentum. De la Cruz (2014, 31) argued that the end of the twentieth century witnessed the "collapse" of developmental states due to 1) external conditions such as the 1997 financial crisis of the Asian markets, and 2) internal circumstances within Asian developmental states related to capitalist cronyism between government officials and big corporations. Though, the developmental state adapted and evolved, and even "moved in a neoliberal direction" during the "gestalt shift" of the rise of market globalization policies (Wade 2018, 531-535).

During the beginning of the twenty-first century, attempts to transplant the East Asian developmental state mindset to the study of the role of the

---

19 The process of land reform in Latin America has been rather related to a process of migration from the countryside to urban areas. According to CEPAL (1977, 20), migration was central to the region's social change during the period 1950-1975.

Latin American state in the national development process resulted largely in academic approaches to governance strategies aimed at creating globalization with a "human face". However, as the conceptual framework of the developmental state further stretched to fit Latin American perspectives, it overlapped other concepts, mainly post-neoliberalism, neo-structuralism, neo-developmentalism, and neo-extractivism (Nem Singh and Ovadia 2018, 1039). In order to contribute to shed light to these contemporary academic debates, the next section focuses on region-specific analytical characteristics of the Latin American *desarrollista* within conditions imposed by the capitalist world-economy.

The Classic Latin American Desarrollista State: A "Poulantzas' Reformulation"

The peripheral capitalist state has been widely approached in academic literature through its extraversion and its socio-structural heterogeneity. On the one hand, the idea of extraversion emphasizes on the integration of the peripheral state into the capitalist world-economy through its outward-oriented development model. On the other hand, socio-structural heterogeneity makes reference 1) to the prevalence of pre-capitalist modes of production (which are shaped by personal dependence relationships) within capitalism, and 2) to the growing urban marginal population that, away from the agrarian sector, fails to integrate into the urban labor market (Becker 2008, 18). Whereas the concept of extraversion reminds of the external conditions imposed by the capitalist world-economy on peripheral states, socio-structural heterogeneity recalls the domestic circumstances within Global South countries. Other theoretical constructions have also contributed to understand the peripheral state, such as rentier theory and the already mentioned developmental state theory. Rentier theory provides rationalization to the consequences of the enforcement of the rentier state's political regime, which is bond to the transfer of surplus from states in the Global North to extractivist states in the Global South and, hence, might cause dependence of the latter on rent generated by the sales of natural resources overseas. Besides, the developmental state theory focuses on states' agency, i.e. their capacity to intervene in the national development process, through the role of state bureaucracy and the relationship between the state and the market (or the private sector of the economy). Though, the mainstream of rentier theory, which rests on neoclassical and institutionalist[20] theoretical backgrounds, and the developmental state theory, which provides a particular explanation to successful economic development in East Asian countries[21], conflict with the approach of this book that aims to highlight 1) the prevailing role of the Latin American state (over the market and over social classes) in the domestic decisions on the national development process during commodities boom periods, and 2) weak national political institutions that are overshadowed by strong leaderships.

Thus, this section delves into the traditions of state theory in order to propose an adequate rationalization for a natural resources-rich peripheral state that strives to "sow the oil". Two concepts become key to the approach proposed in this book: State bureaucracy and state's autonomy. *First*, the Marxist and the Weberian traditions of state theory have in common the idea of the state as a domination form that exerts authority through bureaucracy. Whereas the Marxist tradition considered the state as an instrument of the dominant class, or as an instrument that aimed to mirror the balance of powers between social classes (Cantamutto 2013, 103), the Weberian tradition focused rather on "how the state works" (Leftwich 1993b, 56). Hence, scholarly approaches to the state bureaucracy had been mostly backed by the Weberian tradition[22]. *Second*, discussions on the concept of autonomy, which are shared by both traditions, the

---

20 The climax of new institutional economics took place in 1993, when the institutional theorist Douglass North was awarded the Nobel Prize for Economics. Then, the notion that "getting the institutions right is the key to successful economic development" (Harris 2014, 558) became widely accepted among orthodox analyses of less developed countries. In such period, when "good governance" was the keyword to approach the economic as well as the sociopolitical sphere, the state was considered a mere actor under the umbrella of the market.

21 "Market-conforming methods" (Johnson 1982 in Stubbs 2009, 2) and "developmental capacities" (Leftwich 1993a, 620) cultivated by the East Asian developmental state in order to "govern the market" (Wade 1990) comply with the idea of a "strong but limited government" prescribed by New Institutional Economics (Bardhan and Udry 1999, 222).

22 Pablo Andrade (2015) deployed the Weberian baggage in *Política de industrialización selectiva y nuevo modelo de desarrollo* (Selective industrialization policy and new development model), in order to research into industrial policy in Ecuador during Correa's government between 2009 and 2013. Andrade (2015, 15) used the questionnaire to "measure the degree of *Weberianity*" designed by Evans and Rauch (2007) to conduct interviews with an ample range of high-ranking government officials (from ministers and state secretaries to intermediate managers), i.e. the "state's bureaucracy in charge of industrialization policy". In his conclusions, Andrade (2015, 82) argued that government's internal struggles hindered the cre-

Marxist and the Weberian, stem from the *Manifest der Kommunistischen Partei* that regards the state as "a committee for managing the common affairs of the whole bourgeoisie" (Marx and Engels 1848, 4).

Neo-Marxist authors further developed the concept of state's autonomy from social classes or dominant social factions. In line with the idea of the state as an instrument of the dominant class, Miliband (1969, 15) argued that economic elites and state elites "can be assimilated". Hence, the project of economic elites may result in the project of the state since the state is considered as "the only social institution with capacity to achieve that interests of specific groups appear as interests of the whole society" (Osorio 2014, 71). Poulantzas (1978, 122) contested such a vision and posited that the state strives to impose its capitalist project on society, not as the politics of a dominant faction, but as "the politics of the political elites or the politics of the bureaucracy". Thus, contrary to Miliband (1969), Poulantzas (1978) implied that state elites are not necessarily saturated with economic elites. This position was central to the idea of the "relative autonomy" of the state in capitalist society (Poulantzas 1978). Leftwich (1993b, 56) argued that "considered strictly from a developmental point of view", a vision of the state that focuses on its relative autonomy is "essentially a conception of a modernizing state, active and pervasive in the promotion of capitalist development". Hence, the state might be regarded, in Poulantzas' Neo-Marxist reformulation, as the subject of development (Poulantzas 1978, 121) instead of a mere agent of the politics of the dominant classes.

Though, neither the Weberian nor the Marxist tradition of state theory integrated the role of natural resources rent into the analysis of state's relative autonomy. As mentioned before, the endeavor of economic diversification in natural resources-rich peripheral states recalls the original problem of the transference of surplus from the primary sector of the economy to the industrial sector, which in turn evokes the challenge of state's relative autonomy from social classes. In order to approach this theoretical gap, this book aims to sustain that the appropriation of natural resources

---

ation of an "autonomous bureaucracy" capable of heading economic development. Andrade (2015, 83) identified two antagonist positions regarding industrialization within Correa's government. On the one hand, a faction that grouped together ministries and governmental organizations in charge of planning and higher education prioritized a vision of industrialization based on science and technology. On the other hand, the Office of the Vice President headed the group of governmental agencies that promoted petrochemical industry and energy infrastructure.

rent endowed the Latin American *desarrollista* state with relative autonomy from dominant social factions. Whereas the East Asian developmental state managed to maintain autonomy from industrial elites due to the weakness of the private capital in the aftermath of the Second World War (Evans 1998, 142), the Latin American *desarrollista* state was able to gain autonomy from dominant social factions on the basis of the appropriation of natural resources rent. Therefore, the Latin American *desarrollista* state struggled with the private capital (domestic and foreign) in order to appropriate a larger portion of rent. Relative autonomy not only improved Latin American states' agency (their capacity to intervene in the national development process), but also was central to the imposition of a rentier capitalist developmental project on society.

The conception of the Latin American *desarrollista* state proposed in this book highlights the state's relative autonomy on the basis of rent appropriation and aims to mirror the dispute between the state and (foreign) private actors for the appropriation of natural resources rent[23]. It is argued that an imperative of the Latin American *desarrollista* state was to assume the role of a "effective landlord" (Coronil 1997, 65), i.e. a state that exerts control over the rents generated by the natural resources of its national (sub)soil. The role of landlord was fulfilled when the state was also able to determine the allocation of natural resources rents among society. Then, the state assumed the role of "arbiter" of the natural resources' surplus (Conaghan 1988, 48). The purpose of presenting a landlord-arbiter state configuration is to open the gates to a wider understanding of the capacity of the Latin American *desarrollista* state to steer the interest of even antagonist social classes to follow its developmental project. Conaghan (1988, 48) stated that during the first Ecuadorian oil boom, "the locus of decisions on the distribution of the surplus shifted from the market into the heart of the state bureaucracy". Hence, state bureaucracy played a key role in the landlord-arbiter state configuration, not the role of cultivating links with the private capital (like in the East Asian developmental state), but the role of supporting the imposition on society of the developmental project of the Latin American *desarrollista* state.

Following this logic, this book regards governments as the head of the state apparatus that give direction to the whole state-administrative activi-

---

23 A balance of powers between social classes that materialized in the struggles of the modern Latin American state to overthrow the oligarchical state during the twentieth century is also mentioned; though, presenting an analysis of the balance of powers between social classes is beyond the scope of this book.

ty. The emergence of so-called *progresista* governments with a strong anti-oligarchical or anti-elite discourse during natural resources boom periods is compatible with the afore mentioned premise of the possible separation between economic elites and state elites (Poulantzas 1978). Regarding the character of the imposition of the state's project on society, two main outcomes are considered. On the one hand, developmental politics can be regarded as "the politics of the bureaucracy", when the state and society coincide in a common vision of development. On the other hand, when the imposition of a developmental project provokes a break between state and society, developmental politics can be regarded as "the politics of the political elites".

Latin American Populism: Desarrollismo's (Un)Invited Guest

According to Cueva (2013, 158), populist politics was the preferred mediation between *desarrollismo* and society. Hence, an approach to populism becomes central to any theoretical rationalization of eighty years of "sow the oil" attempts across the region. Latin American populism, understood as a political strategy that "vacillating, deviously, and incompletely accomplished several essential missions for the transit from the oligarchical society to the modern bourgeois society" (Cueva 2012, 232), coupled with *desarrollismo*, provides a comprehensive perspective to assess the sociopolitical processes linked to economic diversification and its attempts. Since *desarrollismo* advocated the departure from the established natural resources-based development model, it adhered to one of the main objectives of Latin American populism: To seize the state in order to take control over the national economy. The alternative proposed by *desarrollismo* is a more autonomous (and less rentier) development model, which relies on the domestic market and on internal accumulation rather than on "the gambles of the world market and its international price policy" (Baran 1968, 101), i.e. the so-called inward-oriented development model. Hence, the *desarrollista* proposal was doomed to come into conflict with the domestic *status quo* since an alliance of local agro-exporters, landlords, and banking and financial oligarchy traditionally profited from the natural resources-based outward-oriented development model.

The *desarrollista* state summoned an ample developmental coalition, headed it, and challenged the power of local oligarchy (Malloy 1977, 13). Hence, the Latin American classic *desarrollista* state emerged as a response to the previous natural resources-based development model that was enforced within feeble national states. The developmental coalition that challenged the local oligarchical elite was held together[24], not without tensions, by "policies that combined state support for import-substitution industrialization with social and economic concessions to the urban middle and working classes" (Conaghan 1988, 22). Cueva (2013, 158) identified opposition to the oligarchy as a seminal characteristic of Latin American populism. In order to summon an ample anti-oligarchical coalition, populism did not appeal to class (Malloy 1977, 13), but invoked 1) peoples' sovereignty as "the incarnation of authentic nation that antagonistically confronts the oligarchy, which represents the foreign-dominated antination" (de la Torre 2000, 141), and 2) citizenship as a hypothetical tie between society and state[25]. Once in government, populist regimes aimed for a "more effective and directive governmental decision-making" (Malloy 1977, 13) by mobilizing popular support on the basis of the promise of distributive policies.

In line with the aim of taking control over national economic activity, the anti-oligarchical coalition (i.e. the developmental alliance headed by the state), cultivated a nationalist[26] discourse, which rejected the influence of external actors in domestic economy and politics. The nationalist discourse reminded of the fact that natural resources rents had to be disputed with foreign capital. Defense of natural resources against foreign interests and the claim that natural resources would mainly serve for national interests converged upon a key notion of the nationalist discourse: 'strategic resources', i.e. natural resources rent to be used to boost the national development process. Besides the anti-oligarchical vein, the ideology of *desarrollismo* entailed also an "anti-feudal" component (Kay 1989, 28). The establishment of an inward-oriented development model required the creation of an internal market, such endeavor meant the consolidation of the capi-

---

24 The developmental coalition and its partakers are approached comprehensively in the section *The Challenges of Latin American Social Thought*.

25 Malloy (1977, 13) connected the concept of citizenship with "the nation", which was incarnated by the state. Alternatively, de la Torre (2000, 145) argued that central to the concept of citizenship is the promise of "access to constitutionally prescribed but unmet rights" in a context of prevalence of economic, social, ethnic, and status inequalities.

26 Kay (1989, 14) recapped that in contrast to Eurocentric academic debates, that often associate nationalism with imperialism and right wing political ideologies and movements, in the context of Latin America "nationalism acquires a progressive connotation, being the expression of anti-colonial, anti-imperialist, or even anti-capitalist struggles".

talist mode of production, thus, the removal of the traces of feudalism. Import-substitution industrialization was in the core of the capitalist developmental endeavor; though, even industrialization, the emblem of development for the classic Latin American *desarrollista* state, depended on natural resources, since they dispensed the only mechanism of capital accumulation within the region (Cueva 2013, 96).

By placing natural resources in the center of its industrialization project, *desarrollismo* emulated modernization theory and its idea of natural resources as a prerequisite, and industrialization as the core of economic development. Though, while modernization theory centered its analysis of the development process on societies' characteristics, *desarrollismo* rather focused on state's agency. The Latin American *desarrollista* state mirrored another key feature of *desarrollismo*: its "technocratic" (Kay 1989, 28) imprint. *Desarrollismo* also shared with modernization theory its faith in economic planning. Therefore, the establishment of the inward-oriented development model relied on an "administrative machine that can do the work of planning" (Lewis 1954a, 122), which materialized in the creation of specific governmental organizations. In *desarrollismo*, as in modernization theory, popular support was central to governmental decision-making. Lewis (1954a, 128) argued that "popular enthusiasm was the lubricant of planning and the fuel of economic development".

Despite the fact that comprehensive economic planning in *desarrollismo* entailed the enforcement of distributive policies, *asistencialismo* was the norm rather than the exception (North 1985, 452). Patronage or *asistencialismo* comprises the set of measures that are intended to benefit lower income classes, such as subventions and subsidies, but mainly conditional cash transfer programs. The enforcement of such measures might fall under the wide scope of clientelistic practices, which offer certain social groups privileged access to state services or benefits in exchange of political loyalty to a certain political group (Becker 2008, 19). However, populism was present in Latin America before the outbreak of *desarrollismo* as a political force, and outlived the end of *desarrollismo*'s nationalist and distributive state policies (de la Torre 2000). Notwithstanding modernization theory argued that populism was predestined to be a temporary phenomenon, Latin American populism transfigured and populist politics were recognizable throughout time across the region. De la Torre (2000, 140) identified four prevailing characteristics of Latin American populism: 1) its "Manichaean discourse" of people versus elites, 2) the building of coalitions of "emergent elites with the popular sectors", 3) its "ambiguous relationship with democracy", and 4) the social construction of a leader "as a symbol of redemption".

The possibility of a Manichaean construction of the categories *peoples* and *elites*, due to their inherent vagueness as concepts and their mutable nature throughout time, might be a powerful reason to explain the adaptation of populism in most diverse moments of Latin American contemporary history, in which coalitions of social forces were summoned to challenge (domestic or foreign) traditional elites. Whilst, the "ambiguous relationship" of Latin American populism with democracy not only refers to (military) dictatorships, but also to authoritarian regimes. Malloy (1977, 4) identified authoritarian state configurations with the intention of "impose on society a system of interest representation". Hence, the Latin American *desarrollista* state fits well into Malloy's (1977) definition of authoritarian states with its intention to impose on society a representation of development linked to the establishment of an inward-oriented development based on industrialization. Undoubtedly, the social construction of a leader "as a symbol of redemption" has been a landmark in recent Latin American history. Cueva (2012, 229) argued that populism "materialized in *caudillista* movements", instead of in sound political parties. One important consequence of this statement is that strong leaderships appear in the forefront of the narrative of eighty years of "sow the oil".

Chapter 2: Bringing Nature Into the "Sow the Oil" Discourse

"[Marx's] account of the productive engagement of Monsieur le
Capital with Madame la Terre unwittingly serves to confirm
dominant representations of a world polarized into a masculine
and creative order which is the home of capital in the metropolitan
centers and a feminized and subjected domain where nature
passively awaits capital's fertile embrace in the periphery"
(Coronil 1997, 57).

A Prelude: The Pathway to the Farewell of the State

Throughout the 1980s, Latin American countries faced payback time for
the "sow the oil" attempts of the previous decades. External debt triggered
a severe economic and social crisis known as the Latin American lost
decade (*década perdida*). Hettne (1987, 14) argued that the "time bomb" of
debt grew out of unprecedented international lending by private banks in
the latter part of the 1970s. Subsequently, several countries reached a point
where they lost capacity to repay their external debt obligations[27] (mainly
Mexico, Brazil, and Argentina). In 1982, Mexico defaulted on its external
debt. Like Mexico, other Latin American countries had increased their external debt for purposes of industrialization and infrastructure during the
previous decades. Table No. 1 depicts 1) the multiplication of Latin American external debt between 1970 and 1982, 2) the growth of the private
banks' share of external debt, and 3) the increase of the ratio of service payments to exports, i.e. the proportion of export earnings required to pay
interest and amortization on the debt. Latin American external debt nearly
quadrupled between 1970 and 1975 as the banks' share of debt doubled
during the same period. Debt quadrupled again between 1975 and 1982 as
the banks' share of debt continued increasing. Whilst, the ratio of debt service to exports jumped from a "feasible" 26.6 percent in 1975 to an "impos-
sible" 59 percent in 1982 (Bulmer-Thomas 2003, 351).

---

27 Herrero (2019, 85) argued that main ingredients of the "bomb" were 1) the rise of
    the real interest rate, and 2) the appreciation of the U.S. dollar, which reduced
    the value of the region's exports.

Remarkably, Mexico, Brazil, and Argentina (countries that defaulted on their debt) had relied on an industrialization strategy, in which "firms were encouraged to exploit opportunities provided both by the protected domestic market and by the growth of world trade" from the 1960s onward. Colombia, Haiti, and the Dominican Republic also prioritized the protected industrialization strategy (Bulmer-Thomas 2003, 316). Though, in the 1970s, Argentina switched to a market-oriented strategy, which aimed at reducing protection in order to move domestic prices more closely in line with international prices. Such strategy was pursued by Chile and Uruguay; a main consequence of the enforcement of a market-oriented and less-protected environment was "the replacement of high-cost local industrial production by less expensive imports", i.e. negative industrialization (Bulmer-Thomas 2003, 323).

Table No. 1: Latin American external debt indicators 1970-82

	Total public, private, and short-term external debt, in billions of US\$	Banks' share of public external debt (percent)	Ratio of service payments (interest and amortization) to exports (percent)
1970[28]	20.8	19.5	17.6
1975	75.4	42.9	26.6
1979	184.2	56.0	43.4
1980	229.1	56.6	38.3
1981	279.7	57.6	43.8
1982	314.4	57.6	59.0

Source: Bulmer-Thomas (2003, 352)

The Latin American *década perdida* was the prelude to the enforcement of neoliberal policies across the region. During the last decades of the twentieth century, the leading role of the Latin American *desarrollista* state in the national development process was challenged by the Washington Consensus (WC) and its intention to force the prevalence of market rules within national borders and international free trade. The enforcement of market-led policies across the region reached a peak during the 1990s, while the neoliberal agenda demanded state's withdrawal from key arenas of the economy on the basis of the blatant consequences of the lost decade, and

---

28 External public debt only.

on the pretext of state's incapacity and corruption[29]. As an overall framework for the enforcement of the neoliberal agenda, the Washington Consensus anticipated structural adjustment programs (SAP), which pursued cutoffs of social benefits and the reduction of the state apparatus thus in different degrees imprinted the economies of the Latin American countries. Though, far beyond a range of economic measures, the WC "deserved to be endorsed across the political spectrum" (Williamson 1993, 1329), since it implied a set of governance devices in which the state's role in the development process was meant to change drastically, not only vis-à-vis domestic circumstances, but also on a global scale.

The establishment of the World Trade Organization (WTO) in 1995 inaugurated a new global governance scheme[30] that sought the elimination of barriers to trade based on a renewed bet on the Ricardian classical doctrine of comparative advantages. Under such a regime, state's enforcement of policies to protect or support non-competitive domestic industry looked at least provoking, if not bluntly blasphemous, against neoliberal globalization and free market gospels. State's intervention was considered as the main source of free market distortion, and even as the principal cause of corruption (Nederveen Pieterse 2010, 7; Todaro and Smith 2012, 482). Under such a regime, Latin American states devoted to keep globalization's gates open by sharing natural resources rents with (foreign) private interests[31]. The enforcement of market-led policies in Latin America resulted in an overall increase of the volume of exports of goods. By 1998, half of the Latin American countries exported at least about a third of their GDP; only four countries exported less than a fourth: Brazil, Argentina, Peru, and Bolivia, while the Dominican Republic, Panama, and Costa Rica (the most open to external markets) showed export coefficients larger than fifty percent (Benavente 2001, 19).

---

29 In this line, Kaufmann (2019) asserted that "corruption is not the disease that erodes the system in the Global South, it is the symptom of a weak sociopolitical and economic system".

30 In 1994, during the economic hegemony of neoliberalism, 123 states signed the Marrakesh Agreement on international trade, thus founding the World Trade Organization (WTO).

31 Daly (2019, 13) argued that among the perils of globalization are 1) tolerance of corporate power in domestic markets in order to be big enough to compete internationally, and 2) intensified specialization with the consequence of reducing the range of choice of ways to earn a livelihood, and increasing dependence on other countries.

Most economic diversification attempts supported by Latin American states during the last decades of the twentieth century resulted in an ampler portfolio of raw material exports. Whilst, some increase of exports of manufactured goods was correlated to *maquiladoras* (assembly plants) located in Central America, mainly in Mexico (Bulmer-Thomas 2003, 316). Table No. 2 depicts the volume of exports of goods and the net barter terms of trade for the period 1980-2000. Whereas the volume of exports of goods nearly quadrupled between 1985 and 2000, the net barter terms of trade followed a steadily decreasing trend that began in 1980 and ended in the last years of the twentieth century. The latter speaks for an increase of exports of raw material in a context of low international commodity prices.

Table No. 2: Volume of exports and net barter terms of trade, Latin America 1980-2000

	Volume of exports of goods (**1995 = 100**)	Net barter terms of trade (**1995 = 100**)
1980	n.a.	161.6
1985	44.7	125.5
1990	65.3	94.4
1995	100.0	100.0
2000	159.8	103.6

Source: Bulmer-Thomas (2003, 364-369)

The upsurge in the overall volume of exports mirrored in an improvement in the economy after the *década perdida*. Though, the growth of GDP per capita, in turn, did not correlate with a reduction of poverty measured in the percentage of households below poverty line. Table No. 3 shows the growth of GDP and the percentage of households below poverty line for the period 1980-2001. Whereas the growth of GDP per capita from -0.9 in the 1980s decade to 1.2 in the following decade speaks for a recovery of the economy, the fluctuation of the percentage of households below poverty line between 35 and 41 percent during the last decades of the twentieth century speaks for the prevalence of household poverty in Latin America. Hence, the enforcement of the WC neoliberal agenda revealed insufficient to deal with the Latin American debt crisis of the last decades of the twentieth century[32].

Table No. 3: Growth of GDP per capita and percentage of households below poverty line, Latin America 1980-2001

	Growth of GDP per capita (US$ at 1995 prices)	Households below poverty line (percentage)
Circa 1980	n.a.	35
1981-1990	-0.9	n.a.
Circa 1990	n.a.	41
1991-2001	1.2	n.a.
Circa 2000	n.a.	35

Source: Bulmer-Thomas (2003, 383-387)

The other side of the coin was the increase in the volume of imports. Even during the period of apparent prevalence of international free trade and market liberalization, within the reign of the WTO, "a formidable arsenal of weapons" was required to control the demand for imports and to ration available foreign exchange (Bulmer-Thomas 2003, 365). On the one hand, in order to support domestic production, countries in the Global North imposed "intense protectionist pressures" that affected both traditional and nontraditional exports from Latin America. On the other hand, Latin American countries relied on quotas, licenses, high tariffs, and other mechanisms to decelerate nonessential imports, which conspired against the achievements in the balance of payments done by the outstanding increase in the volume of exports (Bulmer-Thomas 2003, 365).

Revisiting Development Thinking: From the Environment to Nature

With the retraction of national states, the agency of multilateral organizations gained momentum. The height of neoliberalism "interfaced with the international environmental discourse of sustainable development" (Lewis

---

32 Besides the crises "in the real world" and the "institutional crisis of the nation state", Hettne (1987, 5) drew attention to a crisis in development theory. The author based his contention on the "incapacity" of the social sciences, in general, and development studies, in particular, to correctly understand the phenomenon of crisis in the context of the development process (Hettne 1987, 7).

2016, 77), which was originally outlined in 1987 by the World Commission on Environment and Development (the Brundtland Commission) of the United Nations. The Commission's Report, *Our Common Future* (United Nations 1987), called for the inclusion of an environmental component into development planning. Hence, the United Nations' sustainable development discourse advocated a permanent position for the environment within further debates on the development process of national states (Alarcón 2020). However, before the emergence of the sustainable development discourse, discussions on development included *natural resources* rather than the *environment*. In 1972, the United Nations Conference on the Human Environment was held in Stockholm; member states agreed upon a give-and-take relationship between natural resources and development: Development was considered in the conference's declaration as a requisite to preserve the environment (United Nations 1972). That same year, *The Limits to Growth: A Report for the Club of Rome's Project on the Predicament of Mankind* (Meadows et al. 1972) was published. This milestone of environmental thinking warned of the consequences of the finiteness of the resources that had been sustaining global economic growth. Meadows et al. (1972, 15) approached five global concerns, which illustrated the relationship between natural resources and development at that time: 1) accelerating industrialization, 2) rapid population growth, 3) widespread malnutrition, 4) depletion of non-renewable resources, and 5) deteriorating environment.

Twenty years after Stockholm and five years after *Our Common Future*, Rio de Janeiro hosted the United Nations Conference on Environment and Development (the so-called Earth Summit) in 1992. Representatives from 172 nations signed their adhesion to the environmental imperative outlined in the discourse of sustainable development and thus the rise of the concept of the environment. The Agenda 21 action plan (United Nations 1992), a main outcome of the summit, placed the imperative of environmental policymaking at national and subnational levels. As national states assimilated the mainstream environmental discourse of sustainable development[33] into domestic political institutions, the Latin American re-

---

33 Outcomes of the 1992 Earth Summit were 1) the Agenda 21 action plan, 2) the Forests Principles, and 3) the Rio Declaration with 4) the Convention on Biological Diversity, 5) the United Nations Convention to Combat Desertification, and 6) the United Nations Framework Convention on Climate Change (UNFCCC). Together, this arrangement encompasses the master narrative of the discourse of sustainable development.

gion experienced a wave of creation of environmental national authorities, such as ministries, and promulgation of new environmental legislation during the 1990s. The states' official environmental discourse backed the natural resources-based development model and evoked the faith that environmental problems might be solved by technology, capital, and international cooperation, the "vital forces" of capitalism (Alarcón 2020, 217; Escobar 1995a, 36). Hence, the states' official environmental discourse explicitly alluded to progress and modernization.

With the embracement of the official discourse of sustainable development and the adoption of the concept of the environment, national states accepted the necessity of investing in 1) environmental protection and 2) natural resources management. For natural resources-dependent economies, this imposed a constraint on the free availability of natural resources rent, when it implied reinvestments in the state-owned natural resources sector. However, capitalism promptly outlined the narratives of the green economy and the circular economy[34] in order to match environmental management with economic growth, and to convey that investing in the environment is certainly a good investment (in monetary or chrematistic terms).

While Latin American national states configured an official environmental discourse that rested on progress, environmental consciousness of the negative socioecological consequences of extractivism mushroomed among society. Environmental movements embodied society's increased awareness, and claimed a permanent place in national politics. Since the environmental discourse appealed by social movements was rooted in the cultural critique of modern society (Hajer and Fischer 1999, 3), it was antipodal to the official discourse held by national states. Criticism was directed mainly at 1) the instrumental perspective, which considered nature as mere natural resources required for modernization, and 2) the dialectic subject-object that deemed nature to be subjugated by a detached subject: man[35]. The evidence of socioecological degradation and depletion of natu-

---

34 Green economy and circular economy are strongly criticized in ecological economics. Herman Daly (2019, 9), the champion of ecological economics worlwide, argued that both, green economy and circular economy, are based on "growthism", i.e. the belief that economic growth is the costless solution or at least the necessary precondition for any solution to socio-environmental problems such as poverty, environmental destruction, climate change, etc. Ecological economics rather advocates the subordination of the economic system to the size of the ecosphere (Daly 2019, 10; Martínez-Alier and Roca 2001, 15).

35 Critical stances entail a gender perspective that also denounces patriarchy.

ral resources as a consequence of extractivism added arguments against the possibility of catching up with the consumption standards of the Global North.

Whereas the concept of nature appeared in the state's official discourse as mere natural resources available for commodification, social movements defended alternative meanings of nature related to natural heritage and to ancient peoples' habitat and means of existence. These stances on the relationship between society and nature became central to the construction of the concept of development in the twenty-first century. When environmental movements denounced the disastrous socioecological consequences of the natural resources-based development model, they pointed at the rentier state as the political regime that legitimized it. Antagonist meanings of development, that derived from these alternative visions of the society-nature relationship promptly acquired the capacity to shape the relationship between state and society in the twenty-first century (Alarcón, Rocha, and Di Pietro 2018, 66). Leff (1999, 94) recapped that the reasons for socio-environmental movements[36] to mobilize not only stemmed from cultural and symbolic values, but also from material and social interests. Nonetheless, the agency of socio-environmental movements became central to the understanding that socioecological problems are eminently political and hence any techno-economic treatment of the relationship nature-society is doomed to be insufficient (Leff 1986, 145 in Martínez-Alier and Schlüpmann 1991, 318). Central to the construction of the environmental discourse of the social movements that highlights nature (as opposed to natural resources and the environment) is the defense of land and peoples' cultural rights (as opposed to capital investments in environmental protection and natural resources management). According to Leff (1999, 94), these "values" are capable of "driving new social actors and conducting political actions towards the construction of a new social order". The exposition of natural values in the discourse of the social movements indeed contributed to the critique of the state's developmental project during the twenty-first century commodities boom (2003-2014).

---

36 The movements that Leff (1999) refers to as "socio-environmental movements" are sometimes called in this book plainly "social movements" in order to emphasize the antagonism toward the official environmental discourse held by the state. However, the designation aims to stress on the social movements that embraced environmental awareness of the negative socioecological consequences of extractivism.

The Legacy of the Youngest Boom: The Triad Nature-State-Development

The end of the "idyllic decade" (Ocampo 2015a, 8) of the twenty-first century commodities boom marked a watershed in the development process of natural resources-rich countries. With the benefit of hindsight, it might be argued that efforts done by Latin American states to diversify the productive structure during bonanza periods, i.e. efforts to "sow the oil", contrast with the enduring dilemma of an insufficiently diversified export portfolio accompanied with a heavy external debt burden at the end of natural resources boom periods. Transient development achievements accomplished during bonanza periods, as improved socioeconomic indicators, correlate with the ongoing re-primarization of the economy and the intensification of natural resources' extraction. This paradox might lead to the conclusion that state's commitment with economic diversification was reaped outside the economic arena, elsewhere in the social formation. Hence, the study of the legacy of the oil booms and its outreach is a contemporary task of development thinking.

During the twenty-first century commodities boom, contemporary scholars and authors approached the process of development in natural resources-rich countries, mainly in Latin America, through the lens of neo-extractivism. According to Svampa (2013, 30), the reigning "economic and political-ideological" order in Latin America during the youngest boom, was the "*consenso de los* commodities". Under such a regime, Latin American neo-extractivism was the favored development strategy of states across the region. The dissection of Latin American neo-extractivism shows, on the one hand, a socioeconomic ingredient that stresses on the leading role played by the state in 1) the appropriation of swollen natural resources rent, and 2) its distribution among society. Hence, the economic parameters of Latin American neo-extractivism do not differ from the arguments of the rentier state theory. On the other hand, the assessment of the neo-extractivist development strategy reveals a political-ideological component, which emphasizes on the states' struggles to impose the natural resources-based development model on society despite the apparent consensus on the centrality of natural resources rent to the achievement of development goals. These struggles manifest in socio-environmental conflicts on natural resources in territories affected by extractivist activity. Hence, two characteristics of the youngest natural resources boom become central to open the gates to a deeper understanding of the development process in Latin American natural resources-rich countries: 1) the incorporation of the state's agency, i.e. its capacity to intervene in the national development process, not only by appropriating and allocating natural resources rent during a specific international juncture, but also by shaping a domestic environmental discourse, and 2) the emergence of society's environmental awareness of the negative socioecological consequences of the prevalence of the natural resources-based development model.

In order to assess the role of the state in the development process and its outcomes on society in Latin America since the end of the Second World War, this book proposes an interdisciplinary approach named the triad nature-state-development. The triad might be visualized as a triangular pyramid (Figure No. 1). As any tetrahedron, it is composed by three side faces and a triangular base. Figure No. 1 depicts an analogy between the triad nature-state-development and a triangular pyramid, where the side faces of the pyramid correspond to the components of the triad, namely, nature, state, and development. The base of the pyramid points at society, as in a prism through which society might be examined.

Figure No. 1: The triad nature-state-development: A pyramid with three side faces

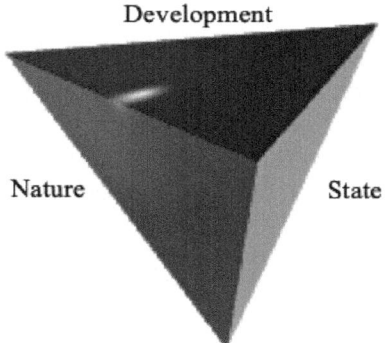

Source: Own diagram

As the discourse of "sow the oil" evolves into the study of the triad nature-state-development, it becomes a matter of contemporary development theories and thus entangled in a web of old and new disciplines such as (international) political economy, political science, sociology of development, development economics, and political ecology. These disciplines back the assessment of the role of the state in the development process in Latin America and its outcomes on society, and are highlighted through the observation of society through the three "side faces" of the triad nature-state-development.

First, the approach to the state's leading role in the development process opened the gates for a wider understanding of the social formation and social classes. Since local bourgeoisies were not considered able to overthrow the crumbling oligarchical state[37] of the first half of the twentieth century in Latin American social thought, the task was assumed by the classic *desarrollista* state. The leitmotiv of taking control of the economy was driven by the intention of transfer rents from oligarchical sectors linked to natural resources exports to the industrial sector (Cueva 2013, 162). State's support of industrialization was anchored in the creation of an internal market; therefore, the project of the Latin American classic *desarrollista* state is regarded as an endeavor to consolidate the capitalist mode of production. The assessment of the Latin American *desarrollista* state at the head of a coalition of social classes, mainly represented by "industrialists[38], [urban] middle classes, urban working classes" (Kay 1989, 19), in transit to a new capitalist economic and sociopolitical structure has been traditionally backed by political science and sociology of development.

Second, the study of the historical relationship between Latin America and the rest of the world opened the gates to approach the "external constraints" (Amin 1990, 5) imposed on the developmental endeavors of national states by the capitalist world-system. Baran (1968, 101) argued that capitalism steered natural resources-dependent economies to concentrate on their most competitive raw product for the external market. As a consequence of capitalist-led specialization, the fate of natural resources-rich countries was chained to the gambles of the world market and its international price policy (Baran 1968, 101). Such a neo-Marxist view of the North-South relations nourished the "resource curse" thesis and highlighted the shortcomings of the traditional outward-oriented natural resources-based development model in Latin America. Despite the different theoretical background, Baran's (1968) argument coincides with the mainstream of rentier theory in the economic diversification cul-de-sac in natural resources-rich countries. The critique of the "resource curse" thesis stems, as

---

37 Cueva (2013, 133) argued that hegemonic crisis within the oligarchical state set off when local bourgeoisies struggled with monopolistic capital to predominate within the oligarchical coalition.

38 Segments of the bourgeoisie that began to differentiate from the *latifundista* oligarchy due to its "modern entrepreneurial capacity, i.e. the ability to set in force a rational-capitalist mode of production" (Cardoso 1971, 76) were supported by Latin American governments in order to become the new industrialist class.

well, from diverse theoretical backgrounds; though it has been carried out with support of the (international) political economy. A widespread theoretical position advocates the prevalence of the study of domestic circumstances and points out the necessity of examining country's "social institutions, class structures and government policies" (Saad-Filho and Weeks 2013, 8) instead of considering natural resources' abundance as a curse *per se*. Whilst, a more empirical branch presents the evidence that international high commodity prices actually benefited the social and economic spheres in natural resources-dependent states.

Third, the theoretical approach to the relationship between nature and the state presented novel categories (such as Latin American neo-extractivism) that invite to revisit the state's ways of intervention in the national development process and the concept of development itself. As national states espoused an environmental discourse that backs the natural resources-based development model, widespread environmental awareness increasingly steers the discussions on the role of natural resources in development. During boom periods, when high international commodities' prices translated into transient socioeconomic improvements, Latin American states accumulated arguments in favor of a further reliance on the prevalent development model. Though, antagonist environmental discourses arose from different social factions and exposed the fissures in the apparent consensus on the pros of natural resources-dependence. Alternative meanings of nature, related to natural heritage and to ancient peoples' habitat and means of existence, are in the center of an alternative environmental discourse that dissents from the view of nature as mere natural resources available for commodification. These positions on nature are currently defended by different social actors and became a fundamental argument in the critique of development (Alarcón, Rocha, and Di Pietro 2018, 66). The approach of the evolution of the meanings of nature and development has been supported by political ecology, as it analyzes the context and the social actors that generated and were generated by the antagonist environmental discourses.

The Challenges of Latin American Social Thought

Latin American social thought has developed theoretical inputs powerful enough not only to dismantle pre-established notions about the triad nature-state-development but also to reassess the concepts themselves. Key contributions of Latin American (under)development thinking have to do with the inclusion of the state as ubiquitous actor of the development process, and the role of natural resources within a generously gifted region. Hence, classic debates have orbited around 1) the role of the state in national modernization and 2) national states' agency to face cycles within the capitalist world-economy. A more recent focus of research, which stems from Coronil's (1997) pathbreaking *The Magical State: Nature, Money and Modernity in Venezuela*, refers to the role of the state in the configuration of the relationship between society and nature. Coronil's work posits the centrality of oil to the Venezuelan state formation during the twentieth century, and attributes "magical properties" to the state in order to give rise to development and other illusions of modernity.

The triad nature-state-development aims to integrate these contemporary theoretical debates of Latin American social thought in one corpus. Latin American (under)development thinking has been approaching the triad in a separate way, with an emphasis on the relationships between pairs of "side faces" of the triad: 1) state-development, 2) development-nature, and 3) nature-state. *First*, the study of the relationship between state and development has been traditionally shaped by the state as the actor *who* is in charge of "sow the oil". Local bourgeoisies, which have been assigned central tasks in the development process in other theoretical perspectives, have been approached in Latin American social thought mainly from two standpoints: 1) their proximity to the traditional oligarchy, i.e. the Latin American economic and sociopolitical order which is dominated by domestic agro-exporters and landowners (*latifundistas*) linked to transnational capital[39], and 2) their rentier behavior, which releases them from the pressure of reinvesting their revenues (rent) on productive activities in order to remain competitive (Wilcock et al. 2016, 12). Thus, Latin American bourgeoisies have been wide and large blamed for their lack of Schumpeterian "will and action" (Schumpeter 1911, 284), and for mimicking the old oligarchy[40]. In Latin American development thinking, hence,

---

39 Latin American bourgeoisies were sometimes called "lumpenbourgeoisies" because of its dependence on (rather than its connection with) transnational capital (Frank 1972).

40 Elsenhans (1977, 38) characterized the bourgeoisie through its members, who compete in markets as owners of the means of production; in order to remain members of the class, they have to remain competitive by innovating the way in which they appropriate their corresponding part of the surplus. Hence, the bourgeoisie is chained to the profitability of its investments. In this book, the term bourgeoisie refers to a privileged class that allegedly detached from the Latin American traditional oligarchy.

local bourgeoisies are pictured as oedipal, not because of killing the agro-exporter father, but because of marrying the landowner mother.

Second, while the approach to the relationship between the state and development focuses on domestic circumstances within national states, the study of the relationship between development and nature concentrates in the regions' relations with the rest of the world, i.e. in the "external constraints" (Amin 1990, 5). Latin American development thinking traditionally exposed the region's developmental endeavors as attempts to depart from the natural resources-based development model, hence, to climb up the international division of labor. Indeed, Galeano (2014), in his 1971 groundbreaking *Open Veins of Latin America*, traced the path of natural resources extractivism since the *Conquista*; the way *how* Latin America was absorbed into the capitalist world-system prevails as the region's landmark and has decisively contributed to the creation of a social imaginary of the development-nature relationship. Pessimistic visions linked to natural resources abundance and backwardness converged in the resource curse thesis. A lesser explored field is the construction of the social imaginary that links natural resources abundance with a blessing; it is argued that this might be observed during boom periods.

Third, the relationship between nature and the state is the youngest field of research within the triad nature-state-development. A prevalent topic in this regard is the approach to the political economy of the environment; Johnston (1996), for instance, explains the state's possibilities to enforce measures to protect the environment within a framework provided by the capitalist world economy. Latin American contributions have mainly dealt with the role of natural resources 1) in the state's formation, and 2) in the relationship between state and society. On the one hand, the approach to the state's formation has been dominated by the rentier theory since the last decades of the twentieth century[41]. In her classic *The Paradox of Plenty: Oil Booms and Petro-States*, Karl (1997, 16) argued that the political (not economically prioritized) allocation of rent among society is a central characteristic of the rentier state. In a further contribution to the rentier state paradigm, Ross (2001, 357) connected oil extraction with authoritarian

---

41 Peters (2019) assessed the (positive and negative) effects of natural resources rent dependence on Global South societies through the innovative concept of "*Rentengesellschaften*" (rentier societies).

regimes[42]. On the other hand, the approach to the relationship between state and society, which gained momentum with the rise of socio-environmental thinking, has focused on the study of local conflicts on natural resources involving mainly native communities and social movements[43]. Thereby, the role played by the state is rather dualistic, supporting the commercial extraction of natural resources undertaken by public or private enterprises while bidding different kinds of compensations for compromised peoples and territories. Hence, the study of socio-environmental conflicts in territories concentrates on the antagonist relationship between the state and local factions or coalitions. Despite overall environmental awareness, such approaches rarely exceed the local level. In order to transcend the local level and to deal with the problem of the relationship between state and society from a wider perspective, this book proposes the approach to the antagonist environmental discourses of the state and social movements.

---

42 Peters (2015, 159) argued that the connection between authoritarian regimes (dictatorships) and rentier states has not been sufficiently approached in Latin America, hence, he advocated for "democratic rentierism" as an option to study the phenomenon within the region.

43 In *Ciudades del Milenio: ¿Inclusión o exclusión en una nueva Amazonía?* (Millennial Cities: Inclusion or exclusion in a new Amazonia), Vallejo et al. (2016) provide an example of the centrality of oil in the relationship between the state and society in a local context in Ecuador. During the twenty-first century commodities boom, the Ecuadorian government used oil rents to build so-called "Millennial Cities" and bring the illusion of modernity to native communities of the oil fields in the Amazonia. Though, local inhabitants mostly refused government's offer of moving into new houses and abandoning their ancestral way of life.

Chapter 3: Nature, State, and Development: A Dissection in Three Acts

"[...] the landlords, like all other men, love to reap
where they never sowed, and demand a rent even
for its natural produce" (Smith 2007 [1776], 43).

*Act I. The State and Development: Modernization and the Rise of Middle
Classes*

The compendium of ideas generated in Latin America from the post-Second World War period to the late 1970s not only influenced development thinking worldwide, but also shaped development policymaking across the region. As mentioned before, a central contribution was the inclusion of national states as ubiquitous actors of the development process within the natural resources-rich region. Besides, Latin American theoretical schools of (under)development placed a paradigm that linked successful development with industrialization: ISI (import-substitution industrialization). The original proposal of ISI was the kernel of Latin American *estructuralismo*, which arose from ECLA (now ECLAC, the Economic Commission for Latin America and the Caribbean)[44]. ECLAC's theoretical contributions to neoclassical economics attributed the region's underdevelopment to the lack of penetration of capitalist production techniques (Rodríguez 1977, 211). Hence, *estructuralismo* prescribed the enforcement of ISI in order to catch up with developed economies by "diversifying and homogenizing" the region's productive structure[45] (Rodríguez 1977, 206). Since the enforcement of the industrialization project was unconceivable without a

---

44 *Comisión Económica para América Latina y el Caribe* (CEPAL).
45 According to Rodríguez (1977, 206), the economic structure of a country entails 1) the productive structure (all sectors that produce goods), 2) the physical infrastructure, and 3) the services sector. The author argued that the productive structure of peripheral countries is specialized and heterogeneous. In Rodríguez' (1977, 206) view, "heterogeneity" is related to the prevalence of low productivity in most economic activities except those connected with the external market (i.e. raw products); on the contrary, productive structures of capitalist centers are "diversified and homogeneous". In a pathbreaking 1970 study, Aníbal Pinto con-

leading role of the state, ECLAC provided the rationalization for 1) state's protection of domestic industry, 2) state's investment in infrastructure and manufacturing, and 3) state's economic planning (Sunkel 1976, 8). In *estructuralismo*, envisioned state's participation in the industrialization project went further than creating the conditions to support the rise of domestic private industry. The proposal went one step beyond the enforcement of preferential credits, the reduction of taxes, and the regulation of import tariffs in order to protect domestic industry; ECLAC's writings emphasized the importance of the creation of public enterprises due to 1) their influence in decisive sectors of the economy, and 2) their ability to serve as agents of development policy (CEPAL 1971, 1). Besides the promotion of investments in import-substitution industrialization, the accomplishment of the whole strategy of *estructuralismo* (i.e. the enforcement of ISI as the masterpiece of the inward-oriented development model) required fostering private consumption in order to enhance the domestic market. ISI comprised a first stage in which locally manufactured intermediate and capital goods were destined for domestic demand, the so-called "easy phase of ISI" (Kay 2005, 1204), and an ultimate stage where industrialization's output was anticipated for the external market. The limited size of the internal market was a recurrent concern of *estructuralismo*'s classic authors (Furtado 1962, 239). The small[46] size of individual national markets was made responsible for the failure of the ultimate phase of ISI (Kay 2005, 1203). Consequently, *estructuralismo* supported regional integration.

Natural resources were promptly incorporated into the regional integrationist discourse. The Latin American Energy Organization[47] (OLADE) was established in November 1973 within a historical context where the "use and value of natural resources was in the arena of the public debate on development versus underdevelopment" (Oxilia 2013, 13). The Agree-

---

nected the region's "structural heterogeneity" with the prevalence of the "internal periphery", i.e. the "urban marginality" that results from the migration to more developed areas within a country. Pinto arrived to his conclusions by analyzing Brazil, Peru, and Ecuador (Pinto 1970, 91).

46 Small economy refers to an economy that has "negligible shares in world trade and in the global stock of assets" (de la Torre 1987, 8).

47 The Latin American Energy Organization (OLADE, *Organización Latinoamericana de Energía*) was established in 1973 by the Agreement of Lima (*Convenio de Lima*). Twenty-two heads of state signed the agreement: Argentina, Bolivia, Brazil, Colombia, Costa Rica, Cuba, Chile, Ecuador, El Salvador, Guatemala, Guyana, Honduras, Jamaica, Mexico, Nicaragua, Panama, Paraguay, Peru, Dominican Republic, Trinidad and Tobago, Uruguay and Venezuela.

ment of Lima, OLADE's foundation stone, emphasized the "right of the Latin American peoples" 1) to defend and utilize their natural resources "in the manner deemed by each as most appropriate for its interests", and 2) to "defend themselves individually or collectively from all kinds of pressures" or interests that oppose the sovereign rights of their peoples (Agreement of Lima, 1973). According to Oxilia (2013, 20), OLADE's main duty was to support the region's integration "aimed at using existing [natural] resources as an engine of social and productive development". As the nationalist discourse increasingly emphasized the imperative of defending natural resources against external interests, the anti-oligarchical vein of the Latin American *desarrollista* state might be linked with the state's intention to transfer surplus from rentier sectors of the economy to more productive sectors. Hence, in order to advance its economic diversification project, the classic Latin American *desarrollista* state was expected 1) to appropriate natural resources rents with acquiescence of foreign and domestic capitalist factions, and 2) to exert sovereign control over natural resources rents, i.e. to become an arbiter of rent allocation among society. State's control over natural resources rents was supported 1) on the claim on property of subsoil resources and 2) on the establishment of public-owned companies responsible of the extraction of natural resources. Whilst, rent allocation rested upon state bureaucracy and aimed at regulating the sociopolitical sphere.

Though, in such a model of the classic Latin American *desarrollista* state, a key social actor is missing: *whom* the state was supporting in order to forge the new industrialists class. According to Cardoso (1971, 76), segments of the bourgeoisie that began to differentiate from the traditional oligarchy due to its "modern entrepreneurial capacity, i.e. the ability to set in force a rational-capitalist mode of production", were historically foreseen to build a new industrialist class. Indeed, in line with Latin American populism, *desarrollismo* appealed to local bourgeois elites to integrate the anti-oligarchical coalition[48]. Though, this modern segment of the bourgeoisie was born into the core of the "traditional dominant classes" (Cardoso 1971, 119) and was nurtured by the natural resources-based develop-

---

48 In order to stress the importance of attaining an ample coalition, Chiasson-LeBel (2016, 891) argued that "the pursuit of an ISI development model interacts well with corporatism". According to the author, corporatism is understood as a form of state-society relationship characterized by "monopoly representation by sector-specific organizations, tolerated by business interest groups and protected by the state".

ment model and its original pact with foreign capital. Hence, the emerging modern capitalist bourgeoisie promptly (re)integrated the rentier classes with traditional agro-exporters and *latifundistas*, in a replica of the oligarchical coalition shaped by the possibilities of access to rent[49].

The kinship between modern bourgeoisie and traditional oligarchy, which linked them with natural resources rent, is central to the explanation of the rentier behavior of the Latin American bourgeoisies. Even modern capitalist segments of the bourgeoisie considered themselves released from the pressure of reinvesting their rents in productive sectors, or in large economic enterprises, like an industrialization project. According to Cardoso (1971, 119) the origins of the modern capitalist bourgeoisie determined its "opportunist" nature, which is the behavior of a faction that cannot aspire to hegemony and, therefore, builds alliances that respond to immediate interests. In this logic, Conaghan (1988, 15-16) argued that capitalists' opposition to or acceptance of developmental reformism can be regarded "as the product of complex and historically rooted calculations that encompass material interests, ideological predispositions, and speculations as to future outcomes and effects". The fact that state-supported local bourgeoisies were not able to take control of economic diversification in the long term nurtured the idea of the inability of the Latin American *desarrollista* state to crush the outward-oriented natural resources-based development model.

Though, the set of measures enforced by the Latin American *desarrollista* state since the end of the Second World War was central in tolling the knell of the crumbling oligarchical state and to the fall of the old oligarchy. Since "the concept of class is a relational concept" (Wright 1987, 21), the fall of the old oligarchy finds its counterpart in the rise of modern

---

49 Erik Olin Wright (1985, 124) argued that "the immediate class aspiration of people in contradictory locations is usually to enter the dominant exploiting class". In order to explain the mechanism of integration into the "dominant class", the author exposed two examples: 1) in feudalism, the rising bourgeoisie frequently used part of the surplus acquired through capitalist exploitation to buy land and feudal titles, i.e. to obtain feudal assets, 2) in capitalism, the exploitative transfers personally available to managers and professionals are often used to buy capital, property, stocks, etc., in order to obtain the unearned income from capital ownership. In the second example, the "unearned income from capital ownership" can be regarded as the access of the capitalists to rents. Following this logic, it can be argued that the mechanism of integration of the emerging modern capitalist bourgeoisie into the traditional oligarchy in Latin America followed through the acquisition (or inheritance) of land and participation in the agro-exporting business, i.e. through the access to natural resources rent.

urban middle classes. Hence, the state's developmental endeavor was reaped in the sociopolitical arena and not in the economic arena. During the years of prevalence of the ISI paradigm, "emergent middle classes" as the byproduct of the agency of the classic *desarrollista* state, were regarded as the social classes that would mostly contribute to economic development and political stability[50], i.e. as the carriers of modernization (O'Donnell 1978, 3). Middle classes played a triple role in the developmental endeavor of the Latin American *desarrollista* state: 1) as members of the anti-oligarchical coalition headed by state, 2) as potential members of the new industrialist class, and 3) as the objective base of an enhanced domestic market.

The Latin American *desarrollista* state dealt with the ISI requisite of increasing the size of the internal market by fostering the consumption of middle classes. Though, it did not fulfill the ultimate ISI requirement of bringing forth an enhanced internal market for *national* products. Instead, the Latin American *desarrollista* state decisively contributed to the integration of domestic middle classes into the capitalist world-economy by triggering its urban lifestyle and distinctive patterns of consumption based on *imported* manufactured goods. Hence, the Latin American *desarrollista* state endowed middle classes with "market capacities"[51] (Wright 1996, 694). A social class that is endowed with certain market capacities subscribes to the definition proposed by Wright (2009, 102-103): "class identifies those economically important attributes that shape people's opportunities and choices in a market economy, and thus their material conditions". According to the author, class is "a way of talking about the interconnections" between people's individual attributes and their material conditions of life. Hence, middle class "denotes people who have enough education and money to participate fully in some vaguely defined mainstream way of life

---

50 O'Donnell (1978, 3) explored the connection between middle classes and the emergence of the authoritarian state. The author argued that periods of political instability triggered by middle classes were solved by "more frequent authoritarian interventions". In this line, Amin (1990, 32) argued that emerging middle classes turned into the "objective base of authoritarian states".

51 According to Wright (1996, 694), Weberian and Marxist traditions identify the concept of class with the relationship between people and economically relevant assets or resources. Whereas the Marxist tradition places the "relations to the means of production" in the core of the definition of class, "market capacities" are the kernel of class characterization in the Weberian tradition. Furthermore, the Weberian tradition emphasizes the social relations of exchange in markets, which are defined by the nature of the assets that people bring to those exchange relations (Wright 2015, 94).

(which might include particular consumption patterns)". in this line, Amin (1990, 32) argued that the developmental endeavor headed by the state "strengthened the position of middle classes". The author also posited that "urbanization" was a main outcome of state-led economic diversification attempts (Amin 1990, 32).Hence, "modern urban middle classes" (Oleas 2013, 39) constitute a comprehensive epitome of the strengthened middle classes that emerged as a result of the Latin American *desarrollista* state's agency from the post-Second World War period until the 1970s.

Central to the consolidation of Latin American middle classes is the expansion of the state bureaucracy and the formation of a privileged state class or ruling class[52] of relative well paid public servants with guaranteed social safeguards, i.e. a "segment of the middle class in power", which is linked to structural conditions of countries in the Global South (Ouaissa 2014, 14). In this line, Elsenhans (1981, 121), argued that state classes (*Staatsklassen*) are situated at the top of the broad public sector and are composed by state officials, who enjoy a higher income than the average, as well as higher possibilities of political participation and prestige. State classes also play a prevalent role in decision-making on the allocation of natural resources rent (Elsenhans 1981, 121 in Peters 2019, 49). Since Latin American state classes emerged as a part of middle classes[53], there might be no conflict between them; middle classes are rather be regarded as a clientele (Ouaissa 2014, 14) of state classes regarding rent allocation. Conflict might arise among state classes when antagonist factions dispute different possibilities and hence different beneficiaries of rent distribution[54].

---

52 Elsenhans (1987, 77) argued that state classes (*Staatsklassen*) represent the modern version of centralized ruling classes in the Third World. According to the author, the centralization of ruling classes (in the state apparatus) was a consequence of the state's appropriation of rent (Elsenhans 1987, 77). In this book, *state* class and *ruling* class are rather used interchangeably in order to emphasize the leading role played by the state in the development process.

53 Ouaissa (2014, 13-14) recaps that Western middle classes are the result of intensified industrialization and consumer-oriented production; central to this economic origin of Western middle classes is the orientation toward profit. In contrast, the author suggests a political origin of Arab middle classes and, consequently, an orientation toward ensuring rent in natural resources-rich Arab countries. Similarities with Latin America are remarkable.

54 For the internal dispute within the Ecuadorian state class on the potential beneficiaries of industrialization policy between 2009 and 2013, see Andrade (2015).

Act II. Development and Nature: The Myth of Eldorado and the Legend of the Resource Curse

Just as art masterpieces, myths and legends prevail over time thanks to the significant portion of reality they reflect. The myth of Eldorado, which was originated in the sixteenth century during the conquest of the territories now called Latin America, pictures an unexpired modern representation of natural resources. The illusion of a city of gold and its quest promptly shaped the weltanschauung of the Western civilization. Not incidentally, in 1849, during the dawn of the Californian Gold Rush, Edgar Allan Poe published his poem *Eldorado*. The allegory persistently shows the connection between the domination of nature by some pioneers or *conquistadores* (conquerors) and long-term wealth thus neglecting "externalities" produced by the never peaceful subjugation of natural resources-rich territories and its peoples, the conquered. The worldview of the *conquistadores* became central to modernization theory and its premise of natural resources as a prerequisite for progress. On the other side of the coin (or on the other extreme of the world), Eldorado unveiled a hierarchical representation of the world-system based on what Coronil (1997, 29) calls the "international division of nature", i.e. the material foundation of the international division of labor. In the *Open Veins of Latin America*, Galeano (2014) maintained that the region's position in this particular world order was certainly not that of the *conquistadores*. Until present day, the fate of Global South natural resources-rich countries has been shaped by its proximity to the hallucinated city of gold due to its natural resources-richness and to the eagerness of the levels of consumption of the Global North.

Latin American social thought rationalized the hierarchical worldview of the international division of labor in its well-known center-periphery scheme, where peripheral countries occupy the niche of world's raw material suppliers by exporting their natural resources and importing intermediate and capital goods that are manufactured in capitalist metropolis. ECLAC scrutinized the outward-oriented development model through the lens of neoclassical economics, the Prebisch-Singer hypothesis showed that a long-term "deterioration of the terms of trade" takes place for natural resources-dependent economies since primary commodity prices tend to decline relative to the prices of imported manufactured goods[55] (Prebisch 1950, 10; Singer 1950, 477). ECLAC's assessment of the Latin American

---

55 According to UNCTAD (2017, 9), the main reason for the secular decline of primary commodity prices relative to the prices of manufactured goods is that the

economy concluded that reliance on the exploitation of comparative advantages (i.e. natural resources) did not contribute to internal accumulation in the long-term. Despite the early diagnosis of the resource curse[56], the compendium of ECLAC's writings never mentioned it explicitly. However, *estructuralismo* disapproved the region's specialization (on exports of natural resources) and denounced international free trade[57]. The ISI prescription for peripheral countries of embarking on the train of industrialization might then be regarded as *estructuralismo*'s vaccine against the symptoms of the resource curse in the economy.

Other representative theoretical school of (under)development, *dependentismo*, the Latin American school of dependency theory, argues that the historical development of capitalism is the fundamental cause of underdevelopment in the periphery. In his 1977 classic *El desarrollo del capitalismo en América Latina*[58], Cueva (2013, 219) forewarned that the advance of capitalism implies contradictions in time (a crisis-prone cyclical movement), and in space (growing contrasts between developed and backward countries as well as within individual countries). Hence, one essential tenet of *dependentismo* is to loosen up ties with the capitalist centers. At the same time, the postulate that development is not possible without breaking away from the capitalist world-system is a main source of criticism (Elsenhans 1987, 65). Kay (1989, 125) identified two main currents in *dependentismo*: The Reformist and the Marxist approaches to dependency. Whereas the imperative of detaching from the capitalist world-system might be re-

---

latter have a higher income elasticity of demand than primary goods. This means that with rising incomes, smaller shares of income are spent on primary goods.

56 A more recent version of the resource curse thesis affirms that commodity-based development models lead to modest average growth rates and hinder structural change, economic diversification and industrialization (Peters 2017a, 47).

57 The Economic Commission for Latin America and the Caribbean was established in 1948 within the United Nations System. Raúl Prebisch was appointed executive director of ECLAC in 1950. After serving for thirteen years in ECLAC, Mr. Prebisch became the first secretary-general of the United Nations Conference on Trade and Development (UNCTAD) and laid out an agenda of alternative policies for tackling the balance of payments constraints on economic development that the underdeveloped countries faced. Key points of Prebisch's agenda, which deeply influenced UNCTAD's normative principles in favor of "development-led globalization" (Bielschowsky and Silva 2016, 291), were 1) a general framework for international commodity agreements, and 2) a demand for temporary preferences for the industrial exports that underdeveloped countries exported to developed country markets (UNCTAD 2014, 30).

58 The development of capitalism in Latin America.

garded as a landmark for the Marxist stance[59], the Reformist branch might be identified with not so radical postures. For instance, Cardoso and Faletto (2002, 25) argued that societies might undergo radical transformations of their productive systems without becoming "completely autonomous" from the capitalist centers, within a so-called "dependent development" arrangement[60] (Cardoso 1973; Evans 1979 in Elsenhans 1987, 65)

Thus, the nationalist discourse in *dependentismo* is often understood as an invitation to seize the state in order to establish an "*autocentric* national economy" (Amin 1990, 11). Since natural resources epitomize the ultimate link between the periphery and the capitalist world-system, they carry a priori a negative charge in *dependentismo*. Therefore, to regain possession and control of natural resources became an imperative in *dependentismo*'s nationalist discourse. Natural resources turn into strategic resources when they are recovered for the sake of an "*autocentric*" national economy. With its critique of capitalism, *dependentismo* advocates a more complex and comprehensive analysis of development and opens the doors for a wider understanding of underdevelopment as a political matter. When André Gunder Frank (2006, 146) affirmed that "today's developed countries had never been *under*developed", the author stressed the need to draw attention to 1) international hierarchies, as the international division of labor, and 2) particular social and economic histories that caused underdeveloped countries or regions (Frank 2006, 145). In the same logic, Cardoso and Faletto (2002, 24), in their 1969 classic *Dependencia y desarrollo en América Latina: Ensayo de interpretación sociológica*[61], recapped that the notion of dependency alludes the relationships between the economic and the political system, not only in the domestic scenario, but also in the international arena.

The global commodity price collapse and the Latin American *década perdida* of the 1980s further contributed to cloud the optimistic vision of nat-

---

59 A late Prebisch (1984, 84) subscribed to this Marxist postulate of *dependentismo* when he asserted that "peripheral industrialization had been greatly delayed and took place during successive crises at the centers", i.e. when ties with the capitalist centers were loose. Alternatively, Cueva (2013, 96) recapped that peripheral industrialization was determined by the necessities of the capitalist centers and, thus, took place when the ties with the capitalist centers were tighter.

60 In this vein, Quijano (2014, 490) argued that despite of the important presence of nationalist factions in the *Gobierno Revolucionario de la Fuerza Armada* (Revolutionary Government of the Armed Forces), that ruled Peru between 1968 and 1975, the Peruvian state could only aspire to a "negotiated dependence".

61 Dependency and development in Latin America.

ural resources held in development economics. Despite its different theoretical origin, the resource curse thesis mostly coincides with the gloomy
vision of the Latin American theoretical schools of (under)development on
natural resources rent. Therefore, the resource curse gradually acquired the
characteristics of a *deus ex machina* to rationalize backwardness and economic underdevelopment in natural resources-rich peripheral countries.
Even during natural resources booms, when transitory improvements in
the barter terms of trade take place, the disconnection between natural resources and development in the periphery is highlighted through the
"Dutch disease" (Corden and Neary 1982), i.e. the symptoms of the resource curse in the national economy that tend to cause the shrinkage of
the manufacturing sector. The term disease was originally used to describe
the negative effects on the Dutch economy of oil discoveries in the North
Sea during the 1970s (Sinnott, Nash, and de la Torre 2010, 15). As Dutch
disease models[62] become the widespread measure of the resource curse in
natural resources-rich countries (even in the Global North), the term disease further contributes to link natural resources abundance with a curse.

Neoclassical economics traditionally imputed the impossibility of countries that rely on natural resources or other low value added sectors (e.g.
agriculture, raw material-, or labor intensive-manufacturing) to transit to
high value added sectors (e.g. technology-intensive manufactures) to its
low productivity, i.e. the output per unit of all inputs (Kuznets 1973, 248)
or the capacity to transform factors of production into manufactured products (Herrero 2019, 79). Kuznets (1973, 248) rationalized the phenomenon
under the umbrella of the "structural change of the economy"; for the author, major aspects of a structural transformation of the economy that add
to the shift away from agriculture to industry might include 1) the transit
from industry to services, and 2) a shift from personal enterprise to imper-
sonal organization of economic firms, with a corresponding change in the
occupational status of labor; in Domínguez' and Caria's (2016, 99) words,
the reallocation of production factors from the less productive sectors of

---

62 A common theme in the Dutch disease is that natural resources booms provoke
the reduction of the incentives to invest in manufacturing and generally make
the manufacturing sector uncompetitive. The mechanism of disincentive in the
models of the Dutch disease is the appreciation of the currency (Di John 2009,
location 1028). Exchange rate revaluations produced by a booming sector, such as
natural resources, make imports less expensive and increase the demand for other
sectors, such as services. Hence, a shift in production factors (capital and labor)
towards the natural resources sector and the services sector takes place at the expense of the manufacturing sector (Sachs and Warner 1995, 6).

the economy to more productive ones. As the concept of productivity turned particularly relevant to expose the failure of structural change initiatives in Latin America, scholars delve into 1) the total factor productivity (TFP), often understood as a measure of the pace of innovation and technological change[63] (Gordon 2017, 537), and 2) the labor productivity. Ferreira, Pessoa, and Veloso (2013, 18-20) argued that between 1960 and the late 1970s Latin American countries had high productivity levels relative to the United States; on average, TFP corresponded to 82 percent of the U.S. During that period, TFP in Latin America was close to that of Western Europe and 25 percent higher than East Asian TFP. However, the authors brought to light a collapse in the TFP annual growth rate after 1980, which resulted in a decline of relative productivity. By 2007, the mean TFP in Latin America reached only 54 percent of U.S. TFP, as Western Europe and East Asia surpassed the region's productivity by more than 50 percent. In this vein, Hofman et al. (2017, 259) argued that the negative contribution of TFP affected the region's economic growth during the last 20 years. Herrero (2019, 80-87) posited that the region's TFP plummeted during the *década perdida* and reached its historical minimum between 1996 and 2002; despite a slight recovery of the TFP during the twenty-first century commodities boom, so the author, the achievements were "not significant".

In a study conducted in Latin America during the period 1981-2010, Aravena and Fuentes (2013, 9) argued that labor productivity reduced by 0.3 percent in average. Table No. 4 depicts the growing gap between the labor productivity in Latin America (measured as GDP per working hour) and that of the United States, with the exception of Chile. Labor productivity in Latin America continued declining during the last decade and, in average, reached only one third of the U.S. in 2016. This deterioration contrasts with the growing productivity of South Korea and, more recently, of

---

63 Aravena and Fuentes (2013, 21) dissent from such vision. The authors posit that expansions and contractions of total factor productivity during boom and bust periods speak rather for a link between variation of TFP and financial constraints. In a strict definition, total factor productivity is "the portion of output not explained by the amount of inputs used in production", such as labor and capital. Hence, TFP is indeed a measure of "how efficiently and intensely" the inputs are utilized in production (Comin 2010, 260). This definition stems from Solow's (1957) groundbreaking *Technical Change and the Aggregate Production Function*, where the author sought to segregate "variations in output per head due to technical change from those due to changes in the availability of capital per head" (Solow 1957, 312).

China, and even with natural resources-exporter Australia (OCDE, CEPAL, and CAF 2016, 65).

Table No. 4: Labor productivity, measured as GDP per working hour, as percentage of the U.S., Latin America (selected countries) 1980-2010

	1980	1990	2000	2010
Argentina	36	28	31	27
Bolivia	21	13	7	7
Brazil	30	22	19	18
Chile	37	30	39	41
Colombia	23	21	17	17
Ecuador	29	22	15	16
Mexico	38	29	27	26
Peru	40	23	16	19
Uruguay	40	30	38	28
Venezuela	61	46	34	27

Source: Aravena and Fuentes (2013, 12)

Among other contributions of neoclassical economics to explore the bottlenecks of the transit from economies that rely on natural resources rent to economies based on high value added sectors number 1) the "middle-income trap" (Gill and Kharas 2007), sometimes called the "glass ceiling " (Wade 2018), which alludes to the enduring deceleration in growth of countries that attained middle income levels per capita due to their inability to complete the productive transformation (Domínguez and Caria 2016, 89; OCDE, CEPAL, and CAF 2016, 70), and 2) the "empty box", which refers to the fact that no Latin American country attained simultaneously "growth and equality" (Fajnzylber 1992, 23). Whereas, the phenomenon of the middle-income trap affects most countries of Latin America[64], the Middle East, and even some East Asian countries (Gill and Kharas 2007, 17),

---

64 About 75 percent of the world's population lives nowadays in middle-income countries (Domínguez and Caria 2016, 91). According to OCDE, CEPAL, and CAF (2016, 71), Latin America, with the exceptions of Chile and Uruguay, has been unable to escape the middle-income trap for the last seven decades. Only 13 out of 101 countries worldwide identified as 'middle-income' reached 'high-income' from the mid-twentieth century until the beginning of the twenty-first century (World Bank 2013 in Wade 2018, 523).

the "syndrome" of the empty box is exclusively Latin American (Fajnzylber 1992, 23). Domínguez and Caria (2014, 3) pointed out that countries facing currently the middle-income trap might have attained growth based on accumulation of the production factors, mainly natural resources and unskilled labor. This might converge upon what Fajnzylber (1992, 24) called "spurious competitiveness". According to the author, contrasting with "authentic international industrial competitiveness", which could lead to growth and equality, "spurious competitiveness" is based on a "geographical rent or natural resources" and might be attained through lower wages. Further, competitiveness is "spurious and ephemeral" when the income generated this way is not invested in technological progress but channeled through consumption (Fajnzylber 1992, 24). Among the most effective widgets to disarm the middle-income trap count the development of technological capacity (OCDE, CEPAL, and CAF 2016, 70) and the development of economies of scale (Gill and Kharas 2017, 18). Otherwise, in order to prevent the syndrome of the empty box, Fajnzylber (1992, 25) prescribes a productive transformation aiming at 1) sustaining "authentic international industrial competitiveness" on the basis of the incorporation of technological progress, 2) improving the productivity and the qualification of the workforce, and 3) expanding the Latin American industrial basis through effective cooperation between government and industrialists.

A key point of convergence between the visions of the middle-income trap and the empty box is Latin America's "enormous technological backwardness" (Ocampo 2015b, 100). Table No. 5 depicts the regions technological backwardness compared with other regions of the world on the basis of three indicators of the presence of technology in the productive structure, namely, 1) the relative contribution of engineering-intensive industries to industrial GDP, 2) investments in research and development as percentage of GDP, and 3) the number of patents per million inhabitants. According to Ocampo (2015b, 100) the differences with other regions are "considerable" regarding the first two indicators, and "dramatic" regarding patents.

Table No. 5: Indicators of the presence of technology in the productive structure, selected regions 1996-2007

	Relative[65] contribution of engineering industries to industrial GDP	Investments in research and development (as percentage of GDP)	Patents (accumulated per million inhabitants)
Latin America	0.23	0.40	0.5
Developed economies with 40 percent or more of exports based on natural resources	0.72	1.89	65.4
Emergent Asian NICs	0.99	1.21	30.5
Mature economies (USA, France, Italy, Japan, UK, and Sweden)	0.97	2.43	132.6

Source: Ocampo (2015b, 100)

Approaches as the "middle-income trap" or the "empty box" remind of the orthodox vision of development economics in which every country might attain development by invoking the vital forces of capitalism. Karl (1997, 5) recalled the "inadequacy of economic explanations" that fail to capture the political and institutional processes underlying poor development results in rentier states. Adding to this critique, in the influential study on Venezuela, *From Windfall to Curse? Oil and Industrialization in Venezuela, 1920 to the Present*, Di John (2009) questioned the validity of Dutch disease models to assess the performance of the Venezuelan economy over time. Di John based his contention on "the little evidence" that oil booms were the primary cause of the contraction of the manufacturing sector. The author rather argued that the manufacturing sector expanded hand in hand with oil activity between the early 1920s (the beginning of the Venezuelan oil era) and the late 1960s, and advocated the study of the role of the state in the national development process (Di John 2009, location 1810).

Nonetheless, it was the notion of the "paradox of plenty" (Karl 1997) that definitely doomed natural resources abundance in the Global South to be treated as a curse in academic literature. When Terry Lynn Karl coined the concept in her pathbreaking *The Paradox of Plenty: Oil Booms and Petro-States* (Karl 1997), the author added a sociopolitical dimension to

---

65 Compared to the U.S. 2002-07.

the resource curse and strengthened the link between oil and the devil's excrement. Karl (1999) summarized the "paradox of plenty" in the incapacity of oil rich-countries to engage in policy-making and construction of political and administrative institutions leading to break with the natural resources-based development model; in the author's words, rentier states "rely on an unsustainable development trajectory fueled by an exhaustible resource, and the very rents produced by this resource form an implacable barrier to change" (Karl 1999, 31).

However, even most pessimistic approaches such as the paradox of plenty leave the door open for criticism. Karl (1999, 47) argued that "periods of low oil prices offer the best opportunity for constructing the political and administrative institutions capable of managing petroleum". Following this logic, Saad-Filho and Weeks (2013, 19) argued that the Dutch disease and the resource curse are avoidable, since they are "policy outcomes or consequences of misguided policy choices" and, thus, can be filtered out by "coordinated fiscal, monetary, financial, and exchange rate policies". Hence, Saad-Filho and Weeks (2013) advocated for a broad-spectrum political economy perspective to address the abundance of natural resources, which includes the analysis of "social institutions, class structures and government policies" (Saad-Filho and Weeks 2013, 8).

Act III. Nature and the State: A Handbook on the Imposition of a Natural Resources-Based Developmental Project

The imposition of a national development model on society might be regarded as a task of the authoritarian state. As mentioned before, Malloy (1977, 4) identified authoritarian state configurations with the intention of "imposing on the society a system of interest representation". Besides, Coronil (1997) shed light on the possibilities of the state's imposition of a development project on society (or on the chances of society's acceptance of a particular development project) when he assessed the state's leading role in the insertion of the Venezuelan society into modernity; therein, the author explained how the state used its "magical" powers, which emanated from oil revenues, to conjure up development and other illusions of modernity. From the theoretical perspective of mainstream rentier theory, Ross (2001) exposed the causal mechanisms that linked oil revenues with the authoritarian rule of the rentier state in his groundbreaking *Does Oil Hinder Democracy?* Particularly relevant to understand the connection between oil rent and authoritarian state rule are the "rentier effect" and the "repression effect" (Ross 2001, 332-335). Whereas the former relates to the state's use of oil rent to "relieve social pressures that might otherwise lead to demands for greater accountability", the latter takes place when oil wealth and authoritarianism manifest in repression. According to Ross (2001, 332-334), the "rentier effect" occurs in three ways: 1) the "taxation effect", i.e. a tax burden[66] reduction thanks to inflated oil rents at state's disposal; as a consequence of this relief, society might become "less likely to demand accountability from and representation in their government", 2) the "spending effect" that consists in a greater spending in patronage, "which in turn dampens latent pressures for democratization", and 3) the "group formation effect", i.e. the capacity of the wealthy rentier state to "prevent the formation of social groups that are independent from the state and hence that may be inclined to demand political rights".

Even though, Ross' (2012; 2001) research focused on the Middle East, his proposal became central to understand the connection between oil rent and authoritarian state rule in other natural resources-rich countries of the Global South. Peters (2019, 48) enhanced Ross' (2001) initially quantitative perspective and drew attention to 1) the high autonomy of rentier states from society, and 2) the "extraordinary stability" of authoritarian regimes. According to the author, these both variables stemmed from the states' dependence on natural resources rents (Peters 2019, 48). Regarding the "rentier effect", Peters (2019, 48) argued that its mechanisms entail hidden and unhidden forms of state-led rent allocation, which are central to understand the autonomy of the rentier state and the stability of authoritarian regimes[67]. Besides 1) the reduction of the tax burden and 2) the overvaluation of currency, the author identified other forms of rent distribution, mainly related to 3) the expansion of the public sector, i.e. the increase of the state bureaucratic apparatus, 4) subventions (in the form of

---

66 Ross (2001, 332) and Peters (2019, 48) recalled the importance of the "fiscal contract" to the formation of the Western state. Tilly (1985, 180) argued that "war, state apparatus, taxation, and external debt advanced in tight cadence" in Europe between the sixteenth and the eighteenth century. In absence of a fiscal contract (i.e. when the state relieves society of taxes), society might relax its demands for accountability and representation. Then, the state might follow its own interests (Ross 2001, 332, Peters 2019, 48), financed further by rent rather than by the fiscal obligations of businesses and general population.

67 Regarding "petro-states", Karl (1999, 34) argued that the initial bargaining between foreign oil companies and local petro-states' rulers left a legacy of "overly-centralized political power". Whereas oil companies were anxious to secure new sources of crude, local rulers were eager to cement their own bases of support (Karl 1999, 34).

preferential credits) and subsidies (principally import subsidies and consumption subsidies such as electricity, fuel and public transport[68] subsidies), and 5) patronage. By comparing rentier states in Latin America, Sub-Saharan Africa, and the Middle East, Peters (2019, 48) suggested that these forms of state-driven rent allocation might result in the de-politicization of society, which in turn might enhance the power base of the state and legitimize authoritarianism. Hence, the politically driven distribution of natural resources rents might be regarded as a tool to exert control over the sociopolitical system or, in Peters' (2019, 49) words, natural resources rent might be used by the state to 1) create and consolidate clientelistic networks, and 2) to co-opt selected political actors in order to tie them to the state. This particular form of relationship between state and society shares origins with corporatism. In the corporative scheme of political domination proposed by Collier and Collier (1979, 968), the state "encourages the formation of a limited number of officially recognized, non-competing, state-supervised groups". According to the authors, two mechanisms are central to the formation of such groups of interest representation. On the one hand, the state imposed "constraints" (not necessarily through outright repression) on organizations or groups on "demand-making, leadership, and internal governance" (Collier and Collier 1979, 968). On the other hand, when the state provided organizations or groups with "structuring[69] and subsidy help", the authors identified not only benefits for the organizations or groups, but also "inducements" to motivate them to cooperate with the state's goals and accept the state-imposed constraints (Collier and Collier 1979, 969). The chirurgical task of enforcing such corporative system on rentier societies of the Global South is a responsibility of state classes. The creation of clientelistic networks as well as the co-optation of selected political actors are essential factors in the increase of the size of the public sector and hence the prestige of the state classes. The enforcement of corporative mechanisms of political domination have contributed to the consolidation of middle classes, the clientele of state classes, and made

---

68 Whereas Latin American upper and middle classes benefit from fuel subsidies, lower classes benefit mainly from public transport subsidies. The unequal nature of fuel/transport subsidies in Latin America becomes evident when the gains of upper and middle classes depend on the number of private automobiles a family or a person possesses. On the other hand, lower classes "enjoy" low quality and meager comfort in public transportation.
69 "Structuring help" took place when the state provided organizations or groups with "official recognition, monopoly of representation, and compulsory membership" (Collier and Collier 1979, 969).

them highly dependent on governmental decisions. Besides, it might be argued that the creation of clientelistic networks with lower classes might be regarded as a long term generator of middle classes.

The corporatist mediation between the state (via state classes) and lower classes fits well with the building of coalitions of "emergent elites with the popular sectors", which is an essential characteristic of populist politics (de la Torre 2000, 140). Nevertheless, in rentier states, the question of ensuring population's political loyalty does not follow the dynamics of democratic participation, it is rather shifted to the arena of the promises of participation in wealth, which originates in the distribution of natural resources rents (Peters 2019, 49). The fact that rentier states sometimes overlook democratic participation[70], and instead favor rent distribution based on corporative criteria, unveil the "ambiguous relationship with democracy", which is another characteristic of populist politics in Latin America highlighted by de la Torre (2000, 140); besides, the politically driven allocation of natural resources rent becomes central to the social construction of a leader "as a symbol of redemption", the ultimate landmark of populist politics. Whereas in rentier state theory society regards the distribution of natural resources wealth as a duty the state must fulfil, in Latin American populism the access to a slice of benefits is sometimes considered as a gesture of the leader's largesse rather than an acquired right.

Peters (2019, 50; 2017a, 49) argued that when the carrot of rent distribution does not suffice, rentier states dip into the stick of repression. Whereas Ross (2001, 335) linked the agency of rentier petro-states with overt repression in order to demobilize society, Peters (2019, 50) recapped that besides outright repression, rentier states might resort to latent repression in order to enforce the First Law of *Petropolitics*. Friedman (2006, 31) named as the "First Law of *Petropolitics*" the hypothesis that connects high international oil prices with growing proclivity of petro-state leaders to show disrespect for "free speech, free press, free and fair elections, an independent judiciary, the rule of law, and independent political parties".

---

70 Collier and Collier (1979, 968) related democratic participation with a pattern of interest politics based on autonomous, competing groups. According to the authors, antipodal to such arrangement is the total suppression of groups. In this logic, mobilization is related to the appeal made by governments to win support for their policies or its imposition.

Postlude to Nature and the State: Towards the New Meanings of Development

The irruption of environmental thinking into development studies marked a watershed in the approaches to the natural resources rent-based relationship between the state and society. The assimilation of environmental thinking by social movements and the construction of an environmental discourse decisively contributed to erode the apparent hegemonic[71] stance on the centrality of natural resources extraction to the achievement of modernization goals. Hence, with the irruption of environmental thinking, the authoritarian state faced a new set of challenges to impose on society the natural resources-based development model. The position of the Latin American state towards environmental thinking transited through three stations since the end of the Second World War. The journey began with 1) the hegemonic discourse on the central role of natural resources in economic development, which in turn was considered essential to trigger the social and cultural changes of modernization (the modernization imperative). Once the hegemonic discourse was eroded, 2) the dominant[72] discourse was sustainable development that advocated environmental protection and natural resources management (the environmental imperative). After the end of the youngest commodities boom, 3) the disputed discourse, which the state aims to impose on society, rests on the central role of neo-extractivism in economic and social development (the "extractive imperative") (Arsel, Hogenboom, and Pellegrini 2016, 880). Alternatively, during the twenty-first century commodities boom, social movements departed from the official discourse and denounced the negative socioecological consequences of natural resources extraction (the ecological

---

71 The term "hegemony" is used in this book in a Gramscian sense, which refers to an idea that is deeply anchored to society and confirmed and ensured by the state (Becker 2008, 19); hence, it alludes to a type of centrality that places a concept in the center of the rationalization in a concrete social formation (Laclau and Mouffe 2001, 7). In this sense, it might be argued that the "sow the oil" discourse had the characteristics of a hegemonic discourse, since it represented a general consensus among social actors on the centrality of oil extraction to the achievement of modernization. The arguments of the resource curse thesis, which gradually charged up natural resources (particularly oil) with a negative load, eroded the apparent hegemonic discourse that rested on progress and opened the gates to a wider debate on the concept of development.

72 The term "dominant" is used in this book for the most widespread and influential discourse among different social actors. Different from the hegemonic discourse, the dominant discourse might permeate the state, but it might not be confirmed and ensured by society, or vice versa.

imperative). On the basis of a critique of modernity, social movements condemned development as the cause of the global environmental crisis and advocated for less utilitarian forms of relationship between nature and society, which became central to the quest for alternative meanings of development. Table No. 6 depicts the evolution of the environmental discourses of the Latin American state and society from the end of the Second World War until present day, regarding the three relevant epochs of the relationship between natural resources and development.

Table No. 6: Developmental and environmental discourses in Latin America: An evolution

	ISI consensus	**Washington Consensus**	**Commodities consensus**
State	Hegemonic discourse: Modernization imperative The role of natural resources in economic development	Dominant discourse: Environmental imperative Sustainable development (Environmental protection, natural resources management)	Disputed discourse: Extractive imperative Legitimation of neo-extractivism on the basis of economic and social development
Social movements	Hegemonic discourse: Modernization imperative The role of natural resources in economic development	Dominant discourse: Ecological imperative Environmental awareness of socioecological consequences of extractivism	Disputed discourse: Search-out imperative Quest for alternative meanings of development

Source: Alarcón (2020, 220)

Ecuador and Bolivia are certainly the Latin American countries that most accurately portray the evolution of developmental and environmental discourses across the region. though, both states embraced Latin American neo-extractivism as the preferred development strategy during the twenty-first century commodities boom despite of environmental discourses of the state and social movements. Besides, both states dipped principally into corporative mechanisms, but also into outright repression[73], in order to

---

73 Particularly for the case of Ecuador, the spearhead of the state's latent repression apparatus was government's co-optation of moral, cultural, human, material, social and organizational resources (Jima and Paradela 2019, 8-15). Overt repression

deal with diverse forms of social resistance against the imposition of the natural resources-based development model.

Despite the defense of the natural resources-based development model (sometimes even explicitly) undertaken by many Latin American states, the discussion on the actual possibilities of "sowing the oil" is far from being exhausted. A significant arena, where debates took place during the twenty-first century commodities boom, was inside governments. State classes disputed the role of nature or natural resources in economic planning and even the revival of the classic ISI paradigm. As globalization emphasized the unbreakable link between economic diversification and technology, positions within governments were challenged to revisit the paradigm of the comparative advantages in many ways. Thereby, different meanings of nature became central to the construction of the concept of development in the twenty-first century.

---

strategies enforced by the Ecuadorian government during the second oil boom included 1) deployment of the armed forces repression apparatus, 2) criminalization of environmental protest and 3) imprisonment of activists by a government-controlled judiciary (Tibán, 2018; Pérez and Solíz 2014, 153).

Chapter 4: Ecuador 1972-2017: Case Study and Methodological Approach

> "Reality is always related to the state and
> the [international] division of labor"
> (Poulantzas 1978, 36).

Deep Diving into the Triad Nature-State-Development: Focus on Ecuador

Ecuador has traditionally been a natural resources-dependent economy, and since 1972 an oil rent-dependent state. It provides three remarkable conditions for scholars to approach the triad nature-state-development. *First*, Ecuadorian recent economic history mirrors Latin America's successive (re)insertions into the capitalist world-system based on natural resources. Three "consensuses" steered the region's development policymaking since the end of the Second World War and imprinted the domestic circumstance in Ecuador: 1) a consensus around the idea of import-substitution industrialization (ISI) as a way to depart from the natural resources-based development model, which historically linked the region with the rest of the world, 2) the Washington Consensus, which regarded natural resources as Latin America's key to neoliberal globalization (comparative advantages), and 3) the *consenso de los* commodities (Svampa 2013), which displayed an apparent general agreement among society around the centrality of natural resources in the development process and highlighted neo-extractivism as the prevalent development strategy across the region. *Second*, during the last half-century, the country underwent two oil booms: 1) The 1972-1980 oil boom, which coincided with the two global oil shocks and marked the beginning of the Ecuadorian oil era, and 2) the 2003-2014 oil boom that overlapped the twenty-first century commodities boom. During periods shaped by high international oil prices, state's agency, i.e. its capacity to intervene in the national development process, was significantly boosted. As the Ecuadorian state ruled over the economic sphere, governments declared the intention to prepare the leap beyond dependence on oil rent by promoting other economic sectors. In other words, governments at the head of the Ecuadorian developmental state intended to "sow the oil" with specific nuances during oil boom periods and expected to harvest economic diversification. With hindsight, the Ecuadorian state reaped a meager harvest in the economic sphere in the long term; transient achievements in economic diversification contrast with the prevalence of the traditional natural resources-based development model, which signalizes an unmistakable position within the international division of labor. *Third*, throughout the last half-century, Ecuador accurately exemplified Latin America's sociopolitical processes. Though, domestic sociopolitical processes connected with the three aforementioned "consensuses" might not completely be understood through the approach to the state's intervention in the national development process. Other social actors successively integrated and played essential roles in shaping the domestic circumstance. The gradual inclusion of environmental thinking and social environmental awareness epitomizes the irruption of new social actors into the discussion on the national development process.

In Ecuador, oil euphoria incubated since 1968, when Texaco announced the construction of the Trans-Ecuadorian pipeline. The dream of Eldorado "that lured both the Incas and the Conquistadores" (Maidenberg 1971) promptly began to shape the domestic sociopolitical sphere. By 1968, José María Velasco Ibarra, the "last *caudillo* of the oligarchy" (Cuvi 1977), was elected for the fifth time for the post of president of Ecuador. In the middle of growing oil euphoria, President Velasco Ibarra declared himself dictator in June 1970 and suppressed the election of his successor, which was planned for June 1972. According to Báez (1984, 93), in order to win support for his dictatorship, Velasco Ibarra offered the armed forces 50 percent of the expected oil royalties[74]. Optimism did overflow the national borders. By July 1971, a feature on Ecuador was headlined in The New York Times: "Oil Companies Find Ecuador's Long-Sought Eldorado" (Maidenberg 1971). The good news hinged on the hope that Ecuadorian oil was to be managed by private companies already in place, unlike in Venezuela (one of the world's main suppliers at that time[75]), where the government was "preparing to place the foreign oil operators under state control".

---

74 The actual portion of oil revenues received by the armed forces during the first Ecuadorian oil boom is shown in Table No. 8. Oil revenues nurtured the budget of the armed forces until the year 2000. From 2001 on, the budget of the military is centralized under the umbrella of the state's budget.

75 Remarkably, the feared specter of state's intervention in Venezuelan oil activity appeared nearly fifty years after the beginning of the Venezuelan oil era.

However, the oil bonanza was not to be left in hands of the civilian dictator nor his potential successor. According to Conaghan (1988, 79), as the possibility of massive oil exportation approached, "military's fears were focused on the specter of civilian politicians pillaging [oil] windfall revenues pouring into the state". Ecuador followed the course set by the majority of Latin American countries during the 1970s; with few exceptions (e.g. Costa Rica, Venezuela), authoritarian regimes, mostly in the form of military dictatorships, ruled over the region. General Guillermo Rodríguez Lara led a military coup that overthrew Velasco Ibarra short before the dawning of the oil era and installed the self-styled "revolutionary nationalist" government in February 1972. The *desarrollista* coalition summoned by the military dictatorship tolled the knell for the oligarchical state: the Ecuadorian oligarchical period ended in 1972 (Cueva 2013, 145). Though, indigenous peoples were excluded from the tacit anti-oligarchical pact; in September 1972, General Rodríguez Lara asserted that "there is no more *Indian* problem, we all become white when we accept the goals of national culture" (Stutzman 1981, 45). The negation of indígenas in the national modernization project converged with the widespread dualistic current of thought that linked indigenous peoples with backwardness and archaic societies (Stavenhagen 1979, 23).

Following the nationalist trend that prevailed in Latin America at that time, the "revolutionary nationalist" dictatorship claimed state's ownership over subsoil natural resources, and declared that rent was meant to serve the national development project. The industrialization bet of General Rodríguez Lara's dictatorship is sometimes known as "ISI *tardío*" or late ISI (Larrea 1987, 37), since a precursor attempt inspired on the ISI paradigm[76] was steered by the military junta (*Junta Militar*) which ruled over Ecuador between 1963 and 1966. The "revolutionary nationalist" dictatorship shared with the junta the faith in economic planning as a sort of alchemy that would transform the country's productive structure. Also, "late ISI" alludes to the early industrialization bets of different Latin American countries during the first half of the twentieth century, especially in the South Cone, Brazil, Mexico, and Colombia.

By 1979, the first oil boom reached an end, and Ecuador elected a new government that inaugurated a series of democratic regimes across the re-

---

76 Fernando Velasco (1981, 206), an economist educated in the tradition of Latin American *dependentismo*, put the "historical moment when ties with the [capitalist] metropolises were more tight" in the center of his explanation of the failure of the junta's ISI endeavor.

gion, thus bringing an end to the era of the Latin American military dictatorships. Nevertheless, during the 1980s, elected governments faced payback time for the "sow the oil" attempt of the previous decade. Ecuador and other natural resources exporting countries underwent the *década perdida* with low international commodity prices. During the 1990s, as international oil prices reached historical minimums, six Ecuadorian presidents served in office in a decade[77]. The Ecuadorian state, as other Latin American states, was accused of inefficiency and corruption. The enforcement of Washington Consensus-inspired neoliberal policies pursuing state's shrinkage appeared unviable or unable[78] to cope with the serious economic and social crisis that provoked the massive emigration of Ecuadorian citizens to North America and Europe. According to Acosta, López and Villamar (2004, 261), during the most critical years of the crisis, which reached its climax by 1999, circa one million persons, or one fifth of the total labor force, added to the emigration wave. Indigenous peoples, which were doomed to invisibility in the previous decades, irrupted into the Ecuadorian sociopolitical arena with a series of insurrections against neoliberal policies that began in 1990 with the *Inti Raymi* uprising. Together with worker's unions of public companies, the indigenous movement turned into the spearhead of protests during the crisis of the end of the twentieth century. Into the twenty-first century, the indigenous movement became "one of the most important political actors in Ecuador" (Jima and Paradela 2019, 4).

During the neoliberal crisis, Ecuador adopted the international environmental discourse of sustainable development and added to the wave of establishments of national environmental ministries and promulgations of environmental and biodiversity laws and regulations across the region. As the official environmental discourse was outlined, environmental awareness increased among the Ecuadorian society and encouraged the public denunciation of the disastrous consequences of ongoing oil extraction in the Ecuadorian Amazon Region (EAR). Despite of the environmental discourse, the Ecuadorian state implemented a set of economic measures to raise the attractiveness for foreign investments in oil extraction. Though,

---

77 Rodrigo Borja (1988-1992), Sixto Durán Ballén (1992-1996), Abdalá Bucaram (1996-1997), Rosalía Arteaga (1997), Fabián Alarcón Rivera (1997-1998), Jamil Mahuad (1998-2000).

78 The study of the devastating consequences of the enforcement of neoliberal policies in the economic and sociopolitical spheres is one of the drivers of current academic debate about the comeback of the *desarrollista* state to Latin America or its "renaissance" (Peters 2017b; Peters and Burchardt 2015, 7).

contrary to what was expected, the enforcement of neoliberal policies paved the way for the return of the state. Whilst, increased environmental awareness among society decisively contributed to catalyze a renewed claim on state's ownership of subsoil natural resources.

Short after the beginning of the new century, international oil prices skyrocketed again: The second Ecuadorian oil boom concurred with the global twenty-first century commodities boom. In 2006, a coalition of so-cial forces that adhered to the democratic "left turn" of a significant por-tion[79] of the Latin American region won the presidential election in Ecuador. The new government of the PAIS Movement (*Movimiento Patria Altiva i Soberana*, now *Alianza País*), which labelled itself as 'Citizens' Rev-olution', converged upon the nationalist trend of the 'pink tide' and re-claimed state's ownership of oil as a masterpiece to arbitrate in the nation-al development process. The first executive order signed by President Rafael Correa, who served in office from 2007 to 2017, convened a con-stituent assembly to draft a new constitution (Executive Order No. 2, pub-lished in the Official Gazette No. 8, January 25, 2007) in order to correct the "deficits of representative institutions" (de la Torre 2010, 157) left by state's withdrawal during the crisis of the previous decades. In the 2008 Constitution, nature or *pachamama* (mother nature) was accorded rights[80], and the extraction of natural resources was restricted to state's responsibili-ty. The codification of the rights of nature and the responsibilities of the state in the new constitution was in line with the adoption of the alterna-tive-to-development discourse of *buen vivir*. The indigenous worldview of *sumak kawsay* (good living) not only inspired *buen vivir*, but also official state documents relating development (e.g. development plans), and even impregnated the text of the 2008 Constitution. This blatantly contrasted with the invisibility of indigenous peoples previous to the 1990s' uprisings.

Buen vivir entailed an influential socioecological dimension inspired by the quest for a harmonious relationship between nature and society[81]. Par-ticularly relevant for this purpose was article 407 of the new constitution, which prohibited "activities for the extraction of non-renewable natural re-sources [...] in protected areas and in areas declared intangible assets"

---

79 According to Levitsky and Roberts (2011, 1), the "wave" began in 1998 when Hugo Chávez was elected president of Venezuela.
80 According to article 71 of the 2008 Constitution, "the right to integral respect for its existence and for the maintenance and regeneration of its life cycles" (Asam-blea Constituyente 2008a).
81 Other relevant dimensions of *buen vivir* are harmonious relationships between persons and between communities (León and Domínguez 2017, 116).

(Asamblea Constituyente 2008a). Domínguez, Caria, and León (2017, 138) referred to the stream of *buen vivir* that underscores an ecological approach as "utopian *buen vivir*". However, this dimension of *buen vivir* was meant to materialize in the Yasuní-ITT initiative, a plan to leave oil in the ground in the Yasuní National Park (YNP) in the Ecuadorian Amazonia. In exchange for saving the YNP from oil drilling, the Ecuadorian state applied for an international compensation of at least US$ 3,600 million. Though, concurring with its inclusion in the constitution and other official documents, the concept of *buen vivir* was despoiled of its "critic and transformer potential" (Peters 2014, 140) and gradually faded away by suggesting rather development alternatives (instead of alternatives to development) such as sustainable development (Alarcón and Mantilla 2017, 101) and human development (Cortez 2014, 338), i.e. "a quite traditional understanding" of the concept of development (Caria and Domínguez 2016, 18). In August 2013, Correa petitioned the National Assembly for authorization to drill for oil in the YNP in order to use oil rent to fight poverty. The National Assembly, with majority of *Alianza País*, approved the petition straightaway during the first days of October and declared that oil rent was central to achieve *buen vivir* (Resolution of the National Assembly, October 3, 2013). The unilateral termination of the Yasuní-ITT initiative had many consequences. While *buen vivir* turned into a "vague and polyphonic concept" (Alarcón and Mantilla 2017, 99), the approbatory resolution sent a strong signal that the Ecuadorian state succumbed to Latin American neo-extractivism.

Nevertheless, the discussion on "sow the oil", or the updated "leave oil in the ground", contributed to place environmental concerns at the top of the state's developmental agenda. However, Eisenstadt and Jones West (2017, 231) maintained on the basis of a wide-ranging survey conducted in Ecuador after the end of the second oil boom, that when environmental concerns occur, they "may be mitigated by the expectation of economic benefits". Just as the first oil boom, during the second oil boom, the active intervention of the Ecuadorian state in the national development process lasted until the aftermath of the dramatic drop of oil prices of 2014. Lenín Moreno, Correa's vice president between 2007 and 2013, won the presidential election in 2016 and assumed office in 2017 with limited room for maneuver. With a hefty debt burden and lower international oil prices, Moreno began his administration dismantling the ministries that were created by Correa. During the decade-lasting Correa's government, the faith in economic planning translated into the establishment of new ministries, which were regarded as the spearhead of the transformation of the country's productive structure. At the end of the twenty-first century commodities boom, concurring with a widespread withdrawal of 'pink tide' governments, the Ecuadorian state, as other Latin American states, was once again (or still) blamed for inefficiency and corruption.

The Case Study: Contemporary Approaches

Research on the (dis)connection between natural resources-abundance and development in Ecuador has been undertaken from different academic perspectives. This reinforces the idea of the need of an interdisciplinary approach; hence, this book aims to integrate the observations of half-century Ecuadorian recent economic history under the prism of nature-state-development. The approach to the sphere of the economy during both oil boom periods serves as a point of entry to expose state's management of oil rent, which was intended to achieve the common goal of economic diversification. Since state's agency had an impact also outside the sphere of the economy (i.e. on the sociopolitical sphere), an approach from the perspective of orthodox development economics would appear rather short-sighted. Therefore, this book lays a greater stress on the political economy, the sociology of development, and the political science in order to approach the impacts of either oil booms on Ecuadorian society.

Since no integrated research on *both* Ecuadorian oil booms has been undertaken at present, the approach proposed in this book is nurtured by separated studies (from diverse academic perspectives and disciplines) of the domestic circumstance and the external constraints during bonanza periods. Whereas specific assessments of the first Ecuadorian oil boom are available in academic literature, research on the period of the second boom is rather shaped by its closeness to the period of Correa's government. Research on the first Ecuadorian oil boom, published in the succeeding decade of the bonanza, focuses separately on the economic and the sociopolitical spheres. Bocco (1987) and North (1985) examined Ecuador during the 1970s from a political economy perspective in *Auge petrolero, modernización y subdesarrollo: el Ecuador de los años setenta*[82], and *Implementación de la política económica y la estructura del poder político en el Ecuador*[83], whereas Conaghan (1988), in her groundbreaking *Restructuring Domination: Industrialists and the State in Ecuador*, incorporated a political

---

82 Oil Boom, Modernization and Underdevelopment: Ecuador During the 1970s.
83 Enforcement of Economic Policy and Political Power in Ecuador.

science perspective focusing on the relationship between the state and local bourgeoisies. Other scholars studied the effects of the first Ecuadorian oil boom on particular fields, such as the political system (Martz 1987), and the economy[84] (Báez 1984; de la Torre 1987; Moncada 1989; Báez 1989). Besides, two specific country reports ordered by multilateral organizations (ECLAC and the World Bank) assessed the country's assimilation of the positive external economic conditions shaped by high international oil prices during the first oil boom: 1) *Ecuador: desafíos y logros de la política económica en la fase de expansión petrolera*[85] (CEPAL 1979), and 2) *Ecuador: problemas y perspectivas de desarrollo*[86] (World Bank 1980).

Otherwise, since the end of the second Ecuadorian oil boom is contemporary with the change of government in Ecuador in 2017, current academic literature is rather biased towards assessments of the outgoing administration, e.g. *Balance crítico del gobierno de Rafael Correa*[87], edited by Muñoz (2014), *Sumak kawsay o buen vivir como alternativa al desarrollo en Ecuador. Aplicación y resultados en el gobierno de Rafael Correa (2007-2014)*[88] (García 2016), and *Ecuador: Balance de una década. Crisis socioambiental, extractivismo, política e integración*[89], edited by Montúfar (2019). Indeed, Ecuadorian academic literature lacks in integrated analyses of the impact of the positive international conditions of the second oil boom on the country's political economy. Available academic research, which focuses on separated fields, mostly concentrates on *first* the "authoritarian direction" taken by Correa's government (Montúfar 2019; Conaghan 2016; Svampa 2016), *second* local socioecological conflicts on natural resources extraction (Solíz 2019; Vallejo et al. 2016), *third* investments and provision of infrastructure in energy and mining projects under the shadow of China's loans[90] (Villavicencio 2019; Zapata, Castro, and Benzi 2018), and

---

84 From a mainstream economics perspective, de la Torre (1987) applied the mathematical model of the "Dutch disease" to the Ecuadorian reality of the 1970s. For an explanation of the "Dutch disease" and its criticism, see the section *Act II. Development and Nature: The Myth of Eldorado and the Legend of the Resource Curse*.

85 Ecuador: Achievements and Challenges of Economic Policy During the Oil Boom Period.

86 Ecuador: Problems and Perspectives of Development.

87 Critical Assessment of Rafael Correa's Government.

88 *Sumak Kawsay* or *Buen Vivir* as an Alternative to Development in Ecuador. Enforcement and Outcomes During Rafael Correa's Government (2007-2014).

89 Ecuador: Assessment of a Decade. Socio-Environmental Crisis, Extractivism, Politics, and Integration.

90 Many of the loans taken out by Correa's government demand payment in barrels of oil.

fourth corruption[91] (Orozco 2019, 14-15; Villavicencio 2017). Hence, an additional methodological challenge was to focus on the political economy of the second Ecuadorian oil boom by surpassing the approach to the juncture.

Research Categories and Methodological Approach

The theoretical section of this book (chapters 1 to 3) is dedicated to outline a comprehensive academic approach to the triad nature-state-development. Consequently, the present section (chapter 4) aims to present the research categories that stem from the components of the triad, i.e. from the relationships between 1) the state and development, 2) development and nature, and 3) nature and the state. In order to examine the research categories under the lens of the triad nature-state-development throughout half-century of recent Ecuadorian economic history, this book entails two main methodological approaches: 1) a historical-structural approach that aims to transcend the phenomenological perspective of domestic dynamics by emphasizing the relationships within the world-system, and 2) a diachronic comparative approach, which seeks to identify processes of continuity and change by focusing on state's agency during both oil boom periods. The historical-structural approach a) highlights the peripheral position of natural resources-rich countries (like Ecuador) in the "international division of nature", i.e. the "material foundation" of the international division of labor (Coronil 1997, 29), and b) provides an important antidote to the deductive theorizing inherent in mainstream economics, in which historical facts are routinely ignored or distorted in an effort to validate abstract models (Thurbon and Weiss 2016, 638). By focusing on domestic circumstances as well as on external constraints (the historical-structural approach), this book aims to connect to the methodological tradition of the Latin American theoretical schools of (under)development. Also, by carrying out a diachronic comparative approach of the oil booms, the book presents a unique at this time contribution to the study of Ecuadorian recent economic history. In order to introduce the research categories (Table

---

91 In December 2017, Jorge Glas, Correa's vice president between 2013 and 2017 and close ally was sentenced to six years in prison after a court found him guilty of pocketing US$ 13.5 million from the Brazilian construction company Odebrecht in return for handing it contracts (Dell and McDevitt 2018, 108).

No. 7) in correspondence with the triad nature-state-development, three subtitles follow.

Research Categories: The State and Development

This book argues that the industrialization endeavor undertaken by the Ecuadorian state during both oil booms mirrored less in the sphere of the economy than in the domestic sociopolitical sphere. Hence, attempts of the state to "sow the oil" were not reaped as economic diversification, but as the fruits of modernization. During the first Ecuadorian oil boom, oil rent endowed the landlord-arbiter state with relative autonomy from social classes, which the state used to impose a developmental project on society. Such a capitalist project did not respond to the politics of any dominant faction, but to "the politics of the political elites or the politics of the bureaucracy" (Poulantzas 1978, 122). This cocktail of relative autonomy from social classes endowed by natural resources rent and the imposition of a state's capitalist developmental project is referred to in this book as the "Poulantzas' reformulation" of the developmental state theory.

In the pursuit of its developmental project, the Ecuadorian state poured oil rent into society through diverse mechanisms (e.g. reduction of the tax burden, preferential credits, wage increment, subsidies), which asymmetrically benefited all social classes. As a result, the state boosted the internal market. The enhancement of household final consumption expenditure speaks for an overall improvement in the consumption levels of the private sector. Though, the other side of the coin was shaped by the country's increasing external debt[92] and its dependence on imports of manufactured goods. The consolidation and strengthening of Ecuadorian modern urban middle classes, due to the developmental endeavor of the state, is considered as the prevailing legacy of the first Ecuadorian oil boom. The given definition of middle classes (Wright 2009, 102-103; Wright 1996, 694; Wright 1987, 21), which is exposed in the section *Act I. The State and Development: Modernization and the Rise of Middle Classes* requires 1) an individual attribute and 2) a way to identify or describe life conditions and consumption patterns that people share in this stratum. The individual at-

---

92 Increasing external debt has been also related to other factors, particularly to the expansion of infrastructure projects. A discussion on the destination of external debt is beyond the scope of this book.

tribute used is education[93], concretely enrollment in tertiary education, which increased during the analyzed period. Whilst, figures of household final consumption expenditure and imports of consumer goods aim to describe material life conditions and consumption patterns. The boost of the internal market that the state provoked was not necessarily functional to the establishment of an ISI strategy, since import-substitution industrialization required an enhanced market for *domestic* products, not for *imported* products. This might speak for the failure of the enforcement of the state's developmental policies in the economic arena. Though, the rise of Ecuadorian middle classes, as an outcome of the state's developmental endeavor in the sociopolitical arena, might be regarded as an argument against the robustness of the resource curse thesis.

The improvement in the figures of enrollment in tertiary education during the first Ecuadorian oil boom might be regarded as a modernizing outcome of the developmental endeavor of the Ecuadorian *desarrollista* state. Urbanization, which increased hand in hand with enrollment in tertiary education and increasing employment opportunities in the public sector might be regarded as another milestone of modernization during the first Ecuadorian oil boom, and as an ultimate descriptor of modern urban middle classes. Since class is a relational concept (Wright 1987, 21), this book argues that the developmental effort of the Ecuadorian *desarrollista* state, which resulted in the rise of middle classes, was mainly at the cost of the Ecuadorian *latifundista* upper class, particularly the *hacendados* of the highlands.

Research Categories: Development and Nature

The commitment of the *desarrollista* state to industrialization became central not only to the quest for a more advantageous integration into the world-economy, but also as an antidote to exorcise the resource curse from the domestic economy. For the Ecuadorian state, industrialization traditionally represented the materialization of successful economic develop-

---

93 Wright (2009, 103) argued that education is "the key individual attribute in economically developed societies". Since an ultimate goal of the developmental endeavor of the Latin American *desarrollista* state was to catch up with developed countries, education fits well as an individual attribute to describe Ecuadorian modern urban middle classes. According to the World Bank (2019g), tertiary education requires, as a minimum condition of admission, the successful completion of education at the secondary level.

ment. Though, as other peripheral states, Ecuador can grasp at few options to import capital, manufactured goods, and technology, i.e. to undertake an industrialization effort; a real alternative to the foreign exchange produced by their natural resources exports is external debt. The euphoria that characterized both Ecuadorian bonanza periods left no space to link oil with the devil's excrement, nor to attempt a social rationalization of the disconnection between the abundance of natural resources and economic development. Only a context of severe crisis, such as the one that began with the *década perdida* in the 1980s and ended with the beginning of the twenty-first century, blatantly evidenced the country's further reliance on the natural resources-based development model and its shortcomings.

Since the beginning of the Ecuadorian oil era in 1972, crude oil has been a permanent guest in the top of the mix of Ecuadorian exports. During both oil booms, the state channeled oil revenues into the manufacturing sector through a set of measures to support (new) industrialists. Though, the amount of incentives received by industrialists during the first oil boom is unparalleled in the oil era. State's support to industrialists during the first oil boom translated into an expansion of the manufacturing sector in the composition of Ecuador's non-oil GDP, which might challenge the applicability of the resource curse thesis (particularly its economic component, i.e. the Dutch disease) to the Global South. During the height of neoliberal globalization, as oil ceased to be the champion of Ecuadorian exports, other natural resources proved to be a reliable source of foreign exchange. The country presumed on a more "diversified" portfolio of export products composed, besides crude oil, by traditional natural resources (mainly banana, coffee, and cocoa) and non-traditional natural resources (mainly natural flowers, canned sea food and mining products). Despite a further expansion of the share of the manufacturing sector in Ecuador's non-oil GDP, economic diversification meant by far not industrialization. With the exemption of Mexico and other countries in Central America (Peters 2019, 158), the twenty-first century commodities boom underlined the trend of re-primarization of the economies across the Latin American region (CEPAL 2017, 40; CEPAL 2014, 61). For Ecuador, the temporary expansion of the manufacturing sector did not represent any deviation from the re-primarization trend, which is understood as the growing weight of natural resources or raw material in the total volume of the country's exports.

Research Categories: Nature and the State

During the severe crisis of the last decades of the twentieth century, as external debt continued growing and debt service significantly improved, natural resources rent (from traditional and non-traditional export products) brought the country from the brink of bankruptcy and remittances of emigrants prevented the total wipe-out of the improved living standards reached during the first oil boom. The concept of the environment emerged in such a context of domestic turmoil and the environmental discourse of sustainable development was embraced. It goes without saying that during the first Ecuadorian oil boom the concept of the environment was non-existent, nor other "theories that considered the importance of the environmental factor in their world views" (Romano, Kelly, and Lavornia 2020, 107); therefore, it is argued that if there is an epitome of nature during the first oil boom it was certainly that of *natural resources*, which was meant to play a central role in economic development. Since this book aims at putting forward the thesis that different meanings of nature were capable to shape the relationship between the state and society during oil boom periods, it proposes land reform as a proxy (see the section *Nature and the State: The Political Economy of Oil-Rentierism*).

Previous to the beginning of the second Ecuadorian oil boom, as the state embraced the environmental discourse of sustainable development, a social environmental discourse emerged, which was built on increased awareness of the negative socioecological consequences of the natural resources-based development model. Positions of social movements, which were rooted on the cultural critique of modern society, gradually permeated through the Ecuadorian state. As a result, after embracing the environmental discourse of sustainable development, the Ecuadorian state adopted the alternative-to-development position of *buen vivir* during the very years of the second Ecuadorian oil boom. Hence, the country study presented in this book shows a brief convergence of the antagonist environmental discourses defended by the state and by social movements in *buen vivir*. The transit from a vision of development that rests on the concept of natural resources to a development alternative founded on the quest for a harmonic relation between society and nature is epitomized in the Yasuní-ITT initiative, the case study within the country study. The end of the initiative in 2013, short before the end of the second Ecuadorian oil boom, marked a watershed that returned the environmental discourses of the state and society to their habitual divergent streams and unveiled a potential conflictual relationship between the state and society based on the construction of a meaning of development for the aftermath of the second oil boom. Central to the construction of different meanings of development during the twenty-first century are 1) the agency of the *desarrollista* state, which reappears with an official environmental discourse with a specific meaning of nature, and 2) the commitment of other (new) social actors (indigenous movement, urban activists, ecologists, scholars), who defended an opposed environmental discourse, with alternative meanings of nature, on the basis of the legacy of circa thirty years of Ecuadorian environmental thinking.

Table No. 7 presents the research categories as a synthesis of this section. The research categories proposed in this book stem from the approach to the components of the triad nature-state-development, i.e. the relationships between 1) the state and development, 2) development and nature, and 3) nature and the state. The next paragraphs of this section aim to describe the methodological strategies used to deal with the research categories.

Table No. 7: Research categories

The triad nature-state-development		
state-development	**development-nature**	**nature-state**
Modernization	Economic development	State-society relationship
The landlord-arbiter state	Economic diversification	Environmental discourses
Rent distribution among society	Portfolio of export products	Meanings of development

Source: Own diagram

The critical review of specialized academic literature that deals with the political economy of Ecuador of the last half-century by including specific assessments of the 1970s oil boom and evaluations of Correa's government is part of a flexible methodological strategy that aims to analyze and discuss processes of continuity and change between both oil booms. Executive orders issued by the president's office and supreme orders signed by dictators, as well as laws issued by the National Congress (or the National Assembly) and other official documents (such as national development plans), provide a perspective of the state dynamics during oil boom periods. Whereas quantitative macro data of national entities, mainly the Central Bank of Ecuador (*Banco Central del Ecuador*, BCE), as well statistics of multilateral organizations (mainly United Nations, World Bank, and the

Economic Commission for Latin America and the Caribbean), open the discussion on the consequences of internal decisions in the economic and social spheres. Key informant interviews[94] complete the set of primary sources. Semi-structured interviews with academics, former government officials, representatives of commerce and industry chambers, retired professionals, representatives of environmental organizations, and activists aim to support the observation of both oil booms through the prism of the triad nature-state-development. Statements of retired professionals are central to 1) the exposition of the air of optimism that preceded the beginning of the Ecuadorian oil era and 2) the consolidation of modern urban middle classes during the first oil boom. Whilst, interviews with academics, representatives of commerce and industry chambers, representatives of environmental organizations and activists support the discussion on the meanings of development during the twenty-first century. The interviews were recorded and, subsequently, relevant statements for the approach to the research categories were selectively transcribed.

A complex methodological challenge was the approach to *buen vivir* due to the divorce between discourse and practice. Though, the quest to find elements of *buen vivir* that imprinted social relations ended with the inclusion of the Yasuní-ITT initiative into the research. This book argues that the Ecuadorian project epitomized *buen vivir* as it configured quotidian reality and established a specific social order (Foucault 2002). The Yasuní-ITT initiative was launched by Correa's government in 2007 as a state policy; until its unilateral cancellation in 2013, the initiative strongly imprinted governmental action. Even beyond its period of validity, the Yasuní-ITT initiative, that illustrates the somber fate of *buen vivir*, configured the relationship between state and society. The approach to the discourse of *buen vivir* and the Yasuní-ITT initiative is based mainly on the author's previous works (Alarcón and Mantilla 2017; Alarcón, Rocha, and Di Pietro 2018).

---

94 Interviews with key informants were conducted by the author between February 2015 and February 2019. Dr. Stefan Peters conducted the interviews during August-September 2015 and September 2016.

Chapter 5: "Sow the Oil": The Ecuadorian Classic *Desarrollista* State

"It is true that history does not repeat to the letter. Though, it does not mean that there is not to find a certain number of structural symmetries, repetitions, which are the expression of the laws that govern the formation, operation, and development of any particular mode of production" (Cueva 2013 [1977], 65).

Overture: Amazonian Oil and the Ecuadorian National Construction

Despite oil extractivism can be traced back since the early twentieth century in the Ecuadorian Pacific coast, the historical milestone that paved the way for the beginning of the Ecuadorian oil era was the integration of the Amazon region (*el Oriente*) into the world-system. Multinational oil corporations not only discovered the Ecuadorian Amazon Region (EAR) for the world-economy, but also shaped the social imaginary of the *Oriente* (Alarcón, Rocha and Di Pietro 2018, 57). After nearly fifteen years of oil exploration in a concession area of 2.5 million ha., the Leonard Exploration Company[95] stepped aside in 1937 adducing "undetermined results" (Acosta 2001, 325). Next was the turn of the Royal Dutch Shell Co.; the corporation got a 10 million ha. concession, and established the township of *Shell*-Mera in the Pastaza province. When Shell announced its negative to start business in Ecuador in 1949, President Galo Plaza (1948-1952) pronounced his well-known catchphrase "the *Oriente* is a myth". Lago Agrio, the current capital of the Sucumbíos province, was named after the first oil field drilled by the Texaco Petroleum Company in Texas: Sour Lake. The consortium Texaco-Gulf received a first concession of 1.4 million ha. in 1964. With the drill of well Lago Agrio One, in 1968, the multinational

---

95 According to Galarza (1983, 14), the Leonard Exploration Company was the Rockefeller's Standard Oil Company in disguise. For comparison, Ecuador's present area is 28.3 million ha. In 1941, Ecuador lost 20 million ha in the war against Peru (*Guerra del 41*). Galarza (1983, 16) argued that the war was triggered by the conflicting interests of Royal Dutch Shell Co. and Standard Oil Co. in both countries.

joint venture granted the country a certain capability to meet specific demands of the ongoing stage of capitalism. A requisite for Ecuador's renewed integration into the world-economy as raw material provider was the placement of Amazonian oil in international markets. Thus, the consortium Texaco-Gulf started the construction of a 500 km pipeline to cross the Andes range, from the Amazonia to the Esmeraldas seaport in the Pacific coast.

Ecuador's rush in the international oil circuit as a marginal exporter[96] started with the inauguration of the Lago Agrio-Esmeraldas Trans-Ecuadorian pipeline (*Sistema Oleoducto Trans-Ecuatoriano*, SOTE) in 1972. During the inauguration ceremony, former dictator General Guillermo Rodríguez Lara, the head of the self-styled "revolutionary nationalist" government (1972-1976), outlined a modernization project *à la* Ecuadorian where Amazonian oil played a central role:

> [Oil] will help us [...] to resolve the problems that afflict the fatherland and particularly the Ecuadorian people [...], the marginalized, the dispossessed portion that still [...] struggles within misery, ignorance, dump, in lack of health services (General Guillermo Rodríguez Lara, presidential address, July 26, 1972).

The speech closed with the fill of symbolic oil barrels to be delivered to each of the regions (*provincias*) of Ecuador. The day after, the first barrel of oil marched epically through the streets of Quito at the top of a military parade from the city center to the Military School, where it occupied a central place in the Temple of the Heroes (Bustamante 2007, 9). The new champion of Ecuadorian raw material exports was responsible for the upsurge in the real share of exports in GDP; from an average of 15 percent during the 1966-1971 period to 34 percent by 1973, whilst the share of oil exports in the total volume of exports of goods reached 67 percent (de la Torre 1987, 38). Due to oil rent, the state's budget nearly doubled within only two years (from 1972 to 1974) and increased steadily during the 1970s (Báez 1984, 47). Oil revenues were also central to the 9 percent average growth of the Ecuadorian economy during the 1970s decade, which outstripped the "respectable" 5.5 percent of the second half of the 1960s (World Bank 1980, vi). Furthermore, a few years into the oil bonanza, Ecuador was removed from the list of low-income countries and placed among the middle income (de la Torre 1987, 2).

---

96 By the beginning of Amazonian oil extraction, the export capacity of Ecuador was barely two percent of that of Saudi Arabia (Philip 1979, 1).

The modernizing vision of the dictatorship was articulated in the *Philosophy and Action Plan of the Revolutionary Nationalist Ecuadorian Government* (*Filosofía y plan de acción del gobierno revolucionario y nacionalista del Ecuador*) (Gobierno Revolucionario y Nacionalista del Ecuador 1972). The document avowed the purpose of "providing the state with the capacity to manage [oil] wealth with the aim to identify and act on issues as poverty, [domestic] regional inequality and dependency" (Moncayo 2017, 156). One of the pillars of the action plan was the promotion of the industrial sector, which was expected to become the "most dynamic area of the economy, in such a fashion as to pull the whole system toward the generation of growth of per capita income that will be self-sustaining in the long-term". Domestic intermediate and capital goods were projected to substitute imports and "iron and cement industry as well as oil refining and other minerals" were declared "basic industries" to be developed with direct participation of the Ecuadorian state (Gobierno Revolucionario y Nacionalista del Ecuador 1972, 23). In order to achieve these goals, the "revolutionary nationalist" dictatorship relied on economic planning and entrusted the National Board of Planning and Economic Coordination (*Junta Nacional de Planificación y Coordinación Económica*, JUNAPLA) with the task of drafting the *Integral Plan of Transformation and Development 1973-1977* (*Plan Integral de Transformación y Desarrollo*) (JUNAPLA 1972).

JUNAPLA was first established in 1954 during Velasco Ibarra's third administration (1952-1956), but its task found the "most favorable circumstance thanks to the invigorating effect of oil in the economy, and the [revolutionary nationalist] military dictatorship". As mentioned before, the "revolutionary nationalist" government (1972-1976) shared with the *Junta Militar* (1963-1966) the belief in the reformist potential of economic planning; though, the inspiration of JUNAPLA was different during both military dictatorships. Whereas the Alliance for Progress (*Alianza para el Progreso*), a cooperation platform launched President John F. Kennedy in 1961 in response to the influence of the Cuban Revolution in Latin America, was the a priori motivation for economic planning during the junta (Pérez Sáinz 1984, 20), the inspiration of JUNAPLA during Rodríguez Lara's dictatorship can be traced back in the ECLAC mission[97] that visited Ecuador in 1949. However, during the first oil boom the board acted as a "technocratic-military agency" in charge of planning the allocation of oil rent (Moncayo 2017, 156).

---

97 As a main outcome of the mission, in 1954 ECLAC published the country's assessment with the title "*El desarrollo económico del Ecuador*" (CEPAL 1954).

The state-led industrialization proposal of the "revolutionary national-ist" dictatorship was meant to collide against the natural resources-based development model that benefited the traditional oligarchy, i.e. agro-ex-porters from the coastal region, landlords from the highlands, and their al-lies within the banking and financial oligarchy. Hence, the dictatorship styled its administration with an anti-feudal discourse linked to the offer to enforce land reform[98] in order to eradicate "unjust land ownership" and to "hinder that privileged families take advantage of national resources and efforts that should benefit popular masses" (Gobierno Revolucionario y Nacionalista del Ecuador 1972, 4). Nonetheless, General Rodríguez Lara's anti-oligarchical coalition sheltered dominant-class groups besides middle-class technocrats, urban working classes, and, of course, groups of the mili-tary (Conaghan 1988, 80). The presence of local elites in the state-led anti-oligarchical coalition was linked to the creation of an industrialist class. According to Bocco (1987, 29), the intention of the dictatorship was to lead the state to support a "not so influential faction of the bourgeoisie and relieve it of most conservative economic interests of traditional groups" in order to turn it into the spearhead of domestic industrialists.

Since the oil boom transformed the structure of the state's income from a basis on taxation on private agro-export activity to dependence on sur-plus produced by the sale of national oil overseas, the transfer of oil rent to the industrial sector was essential for the realization of the state's develop-mental project. The process of appropriation of oil rent, and hence the di-rection of the booming oil sector, was entrusted to Naval Captain Gustavo Jarrín Ampudia, one of the "most progressive" members of the cabinet (Martz 1987, 100), whom the dictator appointed minister of natural re-sources. According to Philip (1979, 8), Jarrín Ampudia "had always aimed at long-term nationalization". The "revolutionary nationalist" dictatorship implemented three principal mechanisms of state's appropriation of oil rent: 1) the enforcement of contractual systems instead of concession sys-tems for oil activity, 2) the creation of a state oil company, and 3) Ecuador's membership in the Organization of Petroleum Exporting Coun-tries (OPEC). As responsible of this set of measures, Jarrín Ampudia ap-peared as the one who was going to bell the cat (Augusto Tandazo, inter-view, September 18, 2015), as the kingpin of the dispute with the most powerful multinational oil corporations (Galarza 1978, 12; Báez 1989, 146) for a larger portion of oil rent. By that time, the consortium Texaco-Gulf,

---

98 The effects of the enforcement of land reform are discussed in the section *Nature and the State: The Political Economy of Oil-Rentierism*.

the owner of the Trans-Ecuadorian pipeline, controlled 99 percent of Amazonian oil extraction.

The main idea behind the switch from concession systems[99] to contractual systems was the pursuit of a "compensation via a share in profits, rather than solely royalty payments" (Martz 1987, 104). Whereas in concession systems, foreign companies own oil extraction and its outcomes and the state participates in the generation of rent with royalties and taxes, in contractual systems companies receive payment in kind or cash as counterpart for undertaking oil extraction (instead of possessing oil extraction or its outcomes). The legal framework for this *first* nationalist measure was provided by the Hydrocarbons Law (*Ley de Hidrocarburos*), which was issued during Velasco Ibarra's fifth presidency (1968-1972) (Supreme Order No. 1459, published in the Official Gazette No. 322, October 1, 1971), and set in force by Rodriguez Lara's dictatorship (Supreme Order No. 430, June 6, 1972). Main dispositions of the law 1) established the obligation of concessionaires to return areas held in excessive quantity, 2) required the payment of surface rights from October 1971 forward, and 3) obliged concessionaires to subscribe new contracts with the state (Martz 1987, 103). The enforcement of the law resulted in the state's recovery of 80 percent of the granted area to foreign companies (Báez 1984, 51), and the limitation of existing concessions to maximum 20 years (Marshall 1988, 56). Besides, the new legal framework legitimized a "complex scheme of taxes and royalties" that enabled the state to raise revenues from oil extraction activities (de la Torre 1987, 39), thus, allowed the state to appropriate a larger portion of oil rent.

The creation of the national oil company *Corporación Estatal Petrolera Ecuatoriana* (CEPE) in June 1972 (Supreme Order No. 522, published in the Official Gazette No. 88, June 26, 1972), just one month before the inauguration of the Trans-Ecuadorian pipeline, was the *second* nationalist measure that ensured the state a gradual access to domestic oil activity. By 1973, a new contract was signed with Texaco-Gulf, which allowed the Ecuadorian state to purchase shares of the multinational consortium (Marshall 1988, 57). After purchasing a 25 percent share of Texaco-Gulf, CEPE started oil exploitation in the Ecuadorian Amazon Region (EAR) in 1974 as a shareholder. In 1977, as Gulf Oil Corporation retired, the Ecuadorian government acquired its share, and CEPE arose as the principal sharehold-

---

99 Galarza's (1972) *The Oil Feast* (*El festín del petróleo*), the "first best-seller in Ecuadorian history" (Philip 1979, 7), was a precursor of public censure against concession systems.

er of the novel CEPE-Texaco consortium with 62.5 percent participation. Besides, CEPE acquired 50 percent of the Trans-Ecuadorian pipeline and its facilities. The *third* nationalist keystone of the state's struggle for the appropriation of a larger portion of oil rent was Ecuador's admission as a member of the Organization of Petroleum Exporting Countries (OPEC) in 1973. As mentioned before, the cartel exerted pressure on importing countries to recognize a higher value of oil rent for exporting countries; its agency derived in two global oil shocks (1973-1974 and 1979-1980) that caused a tenfold increase in the international price of oil in less than a decade. Besides the membership in OPEC, the integration of the Latin American Energy Organization (OLADE) in the same year[100] epitomized the regional nationalist "effervescence" during the 1970s (Augusto Tandazo, interview, September 18, 2015).

The set of measures enforced by the "revolutionary nationalist" dictatorship to ensure state's control of a larger portion of national oil rent was fruitful. The Ecuadorian state arose as 1) the ultimate owner of national subsoil deposits, and 2) the major owner of the surplus generated by the extraction of Amazonian oil, with a 62.5 percent share. The state's share of oil rent fluctuated between 63 percent and 92 percent during the 1974-1980 period[101] (CONADE 1982 in de la Torre 1987, 39). The Ecuadorian Navy (*Armada del Ecuador*) was granted a permanent position in the oil sector with the creation of the national oil tanker fleet (*Flota Petrolera Ecuatoriana*, FLOPEC). The fleet was initially established in September 1972 as a joint venture between the state-owned shipping company[102] (*Transportes Navieros Ecuatorianos*, TRANSNAVE) and a Japanese corporation (Supreme Order No. 1048, published in the Official Gazette No. 145, September 15, 1972), "the idea was to prevent that the consortium Texaco-Gulf, which already owned the pipeline, took control over the transport of

---

100 The establishment of OLADE's permanent headquarters in Quito mirrored the commitment of General Rodriguez Lara's "revolutionary nationalist" dictatorship with the creation of the organization.

101 Oil nationalizations worldwide had its golden years in the 1960s and 1970s (Ross 2012, 39). For comparison, expropriations raised the states' share of oil profits from 50 percent in the early 1960s to 98 percent in 1974 (Mommer 2002 in Ross 2012, 39). Forerunners of oil nationalization in Latin America were Argentina in 1910, Bolivia in 1937 (by nationalizing Standard Oil), and Mexico in 1938 (Ross 2012, 37; Haslam and Heidrich 2016, 3).

102 The state-owned shipping company TRANSNAVE was established during Velasco Ibarra's fifth presidency (1968-1972) through Supreme Order No. 1447-C (published in the Official Gazette No. 325, October 6, 1971). The company engaged in transporting cargo by sea to national and international ports.

national oil by sea" (Augusto Tandazo, interview, September 18, 2015)[103]. By 1978, FLOPEC was declared property of the Ecuadorian Navy (Supreme Order No. 2450, published in the Official Gazette No. 579, May 4, 1978; Supreme Order No. 2625, published in the Official Gazette No. 624, July 7, 1978).

Conaghan (1988, 47) argued that "with oil revenues at its disposal, the state occupied an unprecedented dominant position in the economy". Hence, the Ecuadorian state emerged in the role of "effective landlord" (Coronil 1997, 65), since it was able to exert control over the rent produced by the extraction of its national oil. When the Ecuadorian state determined the beneficiaries of rent allocation, then it turned into the "arbiter of the new oil wealth" (Conaghan 1988, 78). With ups and downs, the landlord-arbiter state configuration prevailed through the 1970s and became the landmark of oil-*desarrollismo à la* Ecuadorian[104]. Though, already by 1975 discontent among local elites, multinational oil corporations (particularly the Texaco-Gulf consortium), and more conservative factions of the armed forces was ripe enough to challenge the *desarrollista* proposal of the "revolutionary nationalist" dictatorship, which was accused of leftist by its opponents. On September 1st, a military revolt failed to overthrow General Rodríguez Lara[105]. One of the few high-ranking officers involved in the coup, General González Alvear, the armed forces Chief of Staff, after applying for political asylum in the Chilean embassy "announced in a radio communiqué that he had moved his troops [...] because of alleged mismanagement of the country's rich oil resources" (United Press International 1975). The failed coup was the prelude of General Rodríguez Lara's replacement by a more conservative military triumvirate, the *Consejo Supremo de Gobierno*, which ruled over Ecuador between 1976 and 1979. Despite its declared intention of accomplishing with the objectives of the Integral Plan of Transformation and Development 1973-1977, the triumvirate was expected to reform the state's participation in oil activity in order to favor private actors (Báez 1984, 109).

---

103 Though, the first tankers of the fleet were bought from Gulf Oil Co. (Augusto Tandazo, interview, September 18, 2015).

104 The imposition of a developmental project as the politics of the political elites and the relative autonomy from social classes gained through oil rent remind of the "Poulantzas' reformulation" of the developmental state theory.

105 Since the dictator General Rodríguez Lara prohibited any public allusion to the incidents of September 1st, the Ecuadorian press referred to the episode as the "coup of the 32nd of August" (*Golpe del 32 de agosto*) (Ana Cevallos, interview, September 19, 2017).

However, the mechanism of oil rent allocation created by the "revolutionary nationalist" dictatorship outlived the coup d'état. The National Development Fund[106] (*Fondo Nacional de Desarrollo*, FONADE) was established in 1973 (Supreme Order No. 1393, December 14, 1973) with the purpose of "providing a productive use to [oil] surplus" (Moncayo 2017, 211), i.e. to bankroll development projects prioritized in the Integral Plan of Transformation and Development 1973-1977. Besides, in order to promote domestic industrial development, a key duty of FONADE was to "provide funding to public financial entities to be channeled to the private initiative" (Oleas 2013, 46). In an assessment of the economic policy[107] enforced during the first Ecuadorian oil boom, ECLAC estimated that in 1976 FONADE received about one third of total oil income and became the public entity that most gathered oil revenues (CEPAL 1979, 13). Besides FONADE, by 1976, the Ecuadorian central government held 27.8 percent of total oil income, the armed forces 11.0 percent, the National Electrification Institute (*Instituto Nacional de Electrificación*, INECEL) 10.4 percent, and CEPE 6.1 percent (CEPAL 1979, 13). The National Electrification Institute (INECEL) was founded in 1961 during Velasco Ibarra's fourth administration (1960-1961) in order to manage the country's electricity sector, i.e. generation, transmission, and distribution of electricity. During the "revolutionary nationalist" dictatorship, INECEL received a significant boost. Table No. 8 shows the beneficiaries of oil revenues as of 1972, 1974, and 1976.

Table No. 8: Distribution of oil income among public entities (percent), Ecuador 1972, 1974, and 1976

Public entity	1972	1974	1976
National Development Fund (FONADE)	n.a.	31.6	33.3
Central government	46.1	30.9	27.8
Armed forces	13.3	10.5	11.0

---

106 In 1979, FONADE became the Development Bank of Ecuador (*Banco de Desarrollo del Ecuador*).

107 The set of measures enforced by the Ecuadorian state in order to promote industrial development and its outcomes are examined in the section *Development and nature: A demystification of the resource curse*. Concrete measures included preferential credits, the reduction of taxes, the regulation of import tariffs, and the issuance of laws and regulations (Fernández 1989, 194). It is argued that the enforcement of the industrial policy translated into an effective way to channel oil rent to the industrialists.

Public entity	1972	1974	1976
National Electrification Institute (INECEL)	13.2	10.0	10.4
State oil company (CEPE)	n.a.	n.a.	6.1
Ministry of Labor and Social Welfare	2.4	2.7	2.5
Ecuadorian Housing Bank (BEV)[108]	2.4	2.7	2.5
Local governments	n.a.	n.a.	2.3
Public universities	3.3	2.7	1.7
Ministry of Public Health	1.2	1.4	1.3
Province of Esmeraldas	0.8	0.6	0.7
Others: Mainly private universities and Central Bank (BCE)	n.a.	n.a.	0.4

Source: Philip (1979, 12); CEPAL (1979, 13)

This scheme of allocation of oil surplus resulted in a boost to physical infrastructure, which the government regarded as a prerequisite for the state's industrialization project or as a "mythological carrier" of progress (Cueva 2013, 112). Table No. 9 depicts the overall boost in infrastructure. Especially relevant was the construction of roads, which was comparable with the total amount of investments in social infrastructure. The domestic energy sector highly benefited of the provision of infrastructure. The construction of the nowadays biggest hydropower complex of Paute began in 1976 (with the 1,075 MW-plant of Molino). The plant started operations in 1983 and largely surpassed the hydropower plant of Pisayambo (73 MW), which was inaugurated in 1977 as the largest of the country. The *Refinería Estatal de Esmeraldas*, at the present time Ecuador's biggest oil processing plant[109], was inaugurated in 1977 after two years of construction with funds of FONADE and CEPE (Martz 1987, 115).

---

108 *Banco Ecuatoriano de la Vivienda* (BEV).

109 The output of the three refineries that operate in Ecuador has never been sufficient to meet the domestic demand of oil products. The difference between the domestic consumption of oil products and the domestic supply has been historically covered by imports. This became the paradox of the Ecuadorian oil era: An oil exporting country that imports oil products. Data of imports of oil products is shown in Figure No. 9.

Table No. 9: *Sectorial composition of public investment (percent), Ecuador 1973-80*

	1973	1974	1975	1976	1977	1978	1979	1980
Production sectors	**7.2**	**7.9**	**8.4**	**9.0**	**10.2**	**7.4**	**1.5**	**4.6**
Agriculture	7.2	7.9	8.0	8.8	10.0	7.1	1.3	4.4
Other	n.a.	n.a.	0.4	0.2	0.2	0.3	0.2	0.2
Natural resources	**20.3**	**21.7**	**12.2**	**20.3**	**22.0**	**24.7**	**34.2**	**34.7**
Petroleum	2.3	9.7	2.8	7.0	8.6	9.2	12.2	11.3
Electricity	18.0	12.0	9.2	13.0	12.9	15.4	21.9	23.1
Other	n.a.	n.a.	0.2	0.3	0.5	0.1	0.1	0.3
Physical infrastructure	**39.4**	**42.5**	**48.4**	**39.5**	**37.7**	**38.5**	**40.4**	**34.1**
Roads	39.4	42.5	38.0	31.3	27.0	24.1	20.7	21.8
Other transport	n.a.	n.a.	4.2	3.8	5.9	6.5	11.3	6.3
Hydraulic	n.a.	n.a.	4.3	3.0	3.4	4.0	3.7	2.3
Other	n.a.	n.a.	1.9	1.4	1.4	3.9	4.7	3.7
Social infrastructure	**16.7**	**10.2**	**28.3**	**28.6**	**28.2**	**27.6**	**22.2**	**23.9**
Water supply	n.a.	n.a.	10.6	7.0	4.5	4.2	5.6	4.5
Sewage	n.a.	n.a.	1.6	3.3	2.7	2.2	1.8	2.9
Urban equipment	n.a.	n.a.	5.7	4.9	5.9	6.5	5.0	5.6
Health	4.2	2.0	5.2	6.7	7.6	8.3	5.5	3.9
Education	12.5	8.2	5.0	6.4	5.8	6.4	4.3	6.3
Other	n.a.	n.a.	0.2	0.3	1.7	n.a.	n.a.	0.7
Other investments	n.a.	n.a.	**2.7**	**2.6**	**1.9**	**1.8**	**1.7**	**2.7**

Source: Gelb and Marshall (1988, 184)

The State and Development: Modernization and Pouring Oil Rent Into Society

The destiny of oil surplus during the first Ecuadorian oil boom raised attention among multilateral organizations. In 1979, ECLAC dedicated a full report to assess the "challenges and achievements of economic policy during the oil growth phase" (CEPAL 1979) and, one year later, the World Bank (1980) published a special report on Ecuador and its "problems and perspectives of development". Both studies asserted that "middle- and lower-middle classes" most benefited of the change of the income structure experienced between 1968 and 1975 (CEPAL 1979, 104; World Bank 1980,

18). According to the World Bank (1980, 18), middle- and lower-middle classes accounted for 55 percent of the total population. Such social sectors, benefited from the average reduction of the income of more privileged groups (20 percent of the population) and even of the decline in income of the less privileged strata (25 percent of the population). Table No. 10 depicts the share in total income by population strata. The positive difference between the years 1975 and 1968 speaks for an improvement of the middle stratum. Since class is a relational concept (Wright 1987, 21), the positive increase in the income of middle classes mirrors in a declining income of the upper and the lower strata. Despite the decrease in the participation of the upper stratum in the total income, a "top 0.5 percent" of upper classes benefited also from the first Ecuadorian oil boom.

Table No. 10: *Share in total income by population strata (percent), Ecuador 1968 and 1975*

Population strata	Share in total income (percent)		Difference (percent)
	1968	**1975**	
Poorest 20 percent	3.4	3.0	- 0.4
Lower middle 30 percent	12.6	16.0	+ 1.4
Middle 25 percent	20.7	23.5	+ 2.8
Upper middle 15 percent	23.0	23.3	+ 0.3
Higher 5 percent	12.7	10.7	- 2.0
Upper 5 percent	27.6	23.5	- 4.1
(Top 0.5 percent)	(4.6)	(4.9)	(+ 0.3)

Source: Chiriboga (1985, 94); CEPAL (1978, 973)

Both multilateral organizations highlighted the importance of the expansion of the public sector to the overall growth of the economy and its role in the consolidation of urban middle classes. Increasing employment opportunities in the public administration was central to the booming of urban centers (World Bank 1980, 6) and the rise of middle classes, which "practically did not exist a couple of decades earlier" (CEPAL 1979, 105). In this line, Conaghan (1988, 48) argued that an "immediate use" of oil revenues was to expand the state apparatus itself, especially in the education, labor, social welfare, and health sectors. Public sector employment alone accounted for about 36 percent of all urban jobs created in the period 1974-82 (de la Torre 1987, 213). Between 1972 and 1980 the number of state bureaucrats increased in more than 140,000, from approximately 97,000 to nearly 238,000 (Moncada 1989, 14), as upward adjustments in their remunerations took place (de la Torre 1987, 47). Infrastructure built during the 1970s also benefited urban middle classes as "social projects were undeniably directed less to rural areas than to the big urban centers" (World Bank 1980, iv). ECLAC's 1979-study reiterated that the first Ecuadorian oil boom was "especially evident" in main cities[110] (CEPAL 1979, 26) as rising state bureaucracy constituted an effective mechanism of transference of oil surplus to urban middle classes[111] and new oil wealth mirrored in their enhanced consumption possibilities. By 1982, 50 percent of the Ecuadorian population lived in urban areas, compared to 36 percent in 1962 (de la Torre 1987, 213). Another effective way in which oil wealth overflowed to urban middle classes was through the Ecuadorian Housing Bank (*Banco Ecuatoriano de la Vivienda*, BEV) and the Social Security Institute (*Instituto Ecuatoriano de Seguridad Social*, IESS). The BEV received 2.5 percent of oil income in 1976 (Table No. 8), in order to enforce a policy of preferential credit to facilitate access to housing. Parallel, the IESS provided housing loans to households. The BEV was established in 1961 during Velasco Ibarra's fourth administration (1960-1961) with the main objectives of 1) enforcing a preferential credit policy, and 2) building inexpensive solutions to face the deficit of middle- and low cost housing (Executive Order No. 23, published in the Official Gazette No. 223, May 26, 1961).

Appropriation of oil rent also allowed the Ecuadorian state to expand subsidy programs, which intended to benefit lower income groups (Gelb and Marshall 1988, 195). Public enterprises were central to subsidize goods and services provided by the state; the National Enterprise of Vital Products (*Empresa Nacional de Productos Vitales*, ENPROVIT) subsidized the consumption of basic food-stuffs and the National Enterprise of Storage and Commercialization (*Empresa Nacional de Almacenamiento y Comercialización*, ENAC) intervened in markets for agricultural products in order to stabilize prices and to soften seasonal fluctuations (de la Torre 1987, 130).

---

110 "The city of Quito expanded to the north and to the south during the [first] oil boom. Families that lived traditionally in the city center moved to the north and to the south, to live in new neighborhoods, in recently-built city districts or in zones that began to be occupied during the 1950s or 1960s" (Javier Espín, interview, October 10, 2018).

111 Though, ECLAC's report warned that the rise of middle classes was accompanied by "the lack of [class] self-consciousness", which was commonplace in Latin America, and mirrored in the imitation of the "values of higher classes" (CEPAL 1979, 7).

In order to ensure compliance with the official pricing system, the Superintendence of Prices (*Superintendencia de Precios*) was created in 1973 (Supreme Order No. 162, published in the Official Gazette No. 253, February 23, 1973), and given broad regulatory powers to control the "largest single branch of Ecuadorian industry", i.e. food processing (Conaghan 1988, 87). Also subsidies on domestic electricity and oil products for domestic consumption were intended to benefit lower classes. Cheap electricity and the improvement in electricity supply indeed benefited lower classes with a bias toward urban areas; though, the regressive nature of these subsidies further sponsored private accumulation of middle classes. According to de la Torre (1987, 129), the maintenance of oil products for domestic consumption significantly below international prices gave rise to a subsidy equivalent to an average of 5 percent of GDP during the 1974-1980 period.

Middle classes further benefited from income tax deductions. De la Torre (1987, 128-129) argued that, between 1973 and 1976, tax legislation introduced significant changes in exemption allowances and deductions, which were the main cause behind the relaxation of direct taxation of household income. According to the author, during the first oil boom, household income taxes decreased from an average of 1.7 percent of GDP in 1970-72 to an average of 1.0 percent of GDP in the 1974-79 period. The number of households paying income taxes dropped from 105,050 in 1972 to 98,802 in 1976[112]. Only as a result of measures enforced by the military triumvirate to curb tax evasion and to reduce exemptions and allowances, the number of tax-payers began to raise again after the replacement of the "revolutionary nationalist" dictatorship. All in all, tax revenues amounted to about 40 percent in average of total fiscal revenues for the period 1973-79, compared to over three-quarters of total fiscal revenues by 1971, before the oil boom (BCE 2017, 152).

As oil revenues pouring into society asymmetrically benefited the majority of the population, the minimum wage steadily increased during the 1970s decade[113] (BCE 2017, 178) together with the remunerations of public servants. These mirrored in an increment in the household final con-

---

112 This fact has to do with the breakage of the fiscal contract mentioned in the section *Act III. Nature and the State: A Handbook on the Imposition of a Natural Resources-Based Development Model*. Tax revenues are detailed in Table No. 18.

113 The minimum wage doubled in real terms from 1979 to 1980, reaching US$ 144, a level which was only equaled in 2003 (BCE 2017, 178) at the beginning of the twenty-first century commodities boom.

sumption expenditure that grew at an annual average of 8 percent between 1973 and 1980, and peaked at the historical record of 15 percent in 1974 (World Bank 2019b). Enrollment in tertiary education also increased unprecedentedly. According to the World Bank (2019g), the gross enrollment ratio in tertiary education, i.e. the "ratio of total enrollment, regardless of age, to the population of the age group that officially corresponds to the tertiary level of education", more than tripled between 1972 (7.5 percent) and 1976 (24.5 percent), and peaked at 34.1 percent in 1981, which means that about one out of three persons of the age group that officially corresponds to the tertiary level was actually enrolled in that year. Though, despite the improvement in material life conditions and consumption patterns, the Ecuadorian *desarrollista* state failed in its attempt to create a market for domestic products. In other words, when the *desarrollista* state endowed all social classes (and particularly middle classes) with "market capacities" (Wright 1996, 694), it indeed succeeded in creating a market, but for *imported* products, not for *domestic* products. Hence, the *desarrollista* state accomplished the capitalist requisite of the enhancement of the internal market, but broke the ultimate commandment of ISI. The other side of the coin was growing dependence on 1) imports[114] of consumer goods, which rose fivefold (in thousands of US$) between 1972 and 1980 (BCE 2017, 119), and on 2) internationally borrowed funds, which were facilitated by oil windfalls. Total debt increased tenfold between 1972 and 1979 (BCE 2017, 128-129), as external debt grew from 17.1 percent to 33.7 percent of gross national income (GNI) (World Bank 2019a).

Development and Nature: A Demystification of the Resource Curse

The simile of a sailing ship has properly described Ecuador's natural resources-led development model across time, in the metaphor proposed by Salgado (1978, 26), natural resources exports are like the sails, which unfurl thanks to the world's winds. In order to steer the ship, Salgado (1978, 27) advocated for a) the creation of a significant internal market, and b)

---

114 "I remember my father; he was born in 1910. Imported liquors were not common in gatherings or family get-togethers. My father *incorporated* whisky into a family celebration during the [first] oil boom. It was rare. Two things must have happened: whisky was available in the neighborhood store, and my father had the money in his pockets to buy it" (Ana Cevallos, interview, September 19, 2017).

the diversification of exports. The metaphor highlights the country's null influence to face world's winds (like commodity international prices) but overlooks the fact that they are also capable of unfolding an air of euphoria among the ship's crew. Even though Amazonian oil was expected to play a key role in the "revolutionary nationalist" developmental project, the government seemed aware not to rely exclusively on one natural resource: "[Oil] is a fundamental resource, not the only one, it is an indispensable source, not unique, it is a real basic resource, never, never[115], the ultimate" (General Guillermo Rodríguez Lara, presidential address, 26 July 1972).

General Rodríguez Lara's dictatorship understood the "sow the oil" discourse as the necessity of state-led broad-based economic diversification to go beyond dependence on oil rent. Domestic industrialization was envisioned as the masterpiece of the construction of an inward-oriented development model. State's agency made the difference from previous natural resources booms, in general, and, in particular, from the cacao and banana booms of the twentieth century, where the economy was dominated by the private sector and economic growth was governed by a "rigid relationship between the external sector of the economy and the evolution of agriculture" (Bocco 1987, 41). Since the "narrowness" of the internal market (JUNAPLA 1972, 233) was a persistent concern of the General Rodríguez Lara's administration, a prioritized objective of the "revolutionary nationalist" dictatorship was trading within the Andean Pact (now *Comunidad Andina*, CAN), integrated by Bolivia, Colombia, Ecuador, and Peru[116]. Hence, the initial boost to industrialization was directed to support domestic industries, which production was destined for the Andean countries. In Fernández' (1989, 193) words, Ecuador sought to first integrate the "intraregional" division of labor.

In order to transfer oil revenues to the industrial sector, the "revolutionary nationalist" dictatorship enforced a set of measures to support and protect industrialists. Not only economic mechanisms accounted for the incentives for industrialists, but also wage freeze and suppression of the right to strike of workers (Báez 1984, 97). Among the principal economic incentives were preferential credits, state's participation in private enterprises, and exemptions and reductions of import tariffs and taxes. To these measures added subsidies on industrial electricity and oil products and subsidies on industrial supplies such as fertilizers and pesticides (CEPAL 1979,

---

115 Repeated in the original version.
116 The Andean Pact was established in 1969 with the aim of trade liberalization between member countries. Chile integrated the organization until 1976.

89). The state's banking and financial system, through the Central Bank (BCE), the National Development Bank (*Banco Nacional de Fomento*, BNF), and the National Financial Corporation[117] (*Corporación Financiera Nacional*, CFN), played a key role in the expansion of the flow of state's resources to industrialists. The system of the Financial Funds (*Fondos Financieros*) was created within the Central Bank not only to channel state's resources towards the industrial sector by expanding and directing credit selectively at low, subsidized interest rates (Supreme Order No. 374, April 5, 1973), but also to stimulate private banks and financial institutions to expand credit to priority sectors using their own resources (de la Torre 1987, 48). According to de la Torre (1987, 136), the annual volume of real credit disbursed by the Ecuadorian banking system (i.e. BCE, BNF, CFN, as well as the private banks) nearly doubled during the period 1972-1980. Table No. 11 depicts the distribution of credit disbursed by the national banking and financial system by sector of economic activity during the period 1964-82. Therein it might be argued that the increasing trend of credit disbursed to all sectors (particularly manufacturing) was at the cost of the commercial sector.

Table No. 11: Sectorial distribution of credit disbursed by the national banking and financial system (percent), Ecuador 1964-82

Economic sector	1964	1970	1974	1976	1978	1980	1982
Agriculture	8.1	14.8	19.0	19.3	18.9	17.3	16.4
Manufacturing	15.4	20.8	17.5	21.8	27.1	30.1	33.0
Commerce	67.3	52.5	48.0	45.7	39.4	38.4	33.4
Other (mainly fishing)	9.2	11.9	15.5	13.2	14.6	14.2	17.1

Source: De la Torre (1987, 151)

Regarding tariff protection, the Ecuadorian state generated an asymmetric tariff structure (Fernández 1989, 197) based on 1) the imposition of high tariffs on imported manufactured goods that could be produced locally,

---

117 The emphasis of the National Development Bank (BNF), which started operations in 1944, was to provide credit to the agricultural sector. Though, it became a principal lender of small industry, craftsmanship, fisheries, and tourism. During the first Ecuadorian oil boom, the BNF was capitalized by oil revenues through FONADE. The National Financial Corporation (CFN) was established in 1964 with the main objective of providing long-term credit to large scale manufacturing industries (de la Torre 1987, 134).

and 2) the exemption (partial or total) of tariffs on imported intermediate and capital goods needed by the Ecuadorian industry. The Industrial Promotion Law of 1973 (*Ley de Fomento Industrial*) enabled enhanced fiscal incentives and tax exemptions for industries that were declared priority by the government in an annual selection process. Incentives of the Industrial Promotion Law of 1973 included 1) exonerations of import duties on new machinery, accessories, and spare parts, 2) exonerations of import duties on raw materials not produced in the country, 3) exonerations of taxes and duties on the formation of companies, 4) income tax deductions from the re-investment of profits and from investments on fixed capital (Supreme Order No. 1248, published in the Official Gazette No. 431, November 13, 1973).

With the enforcement of this set of measures, Ecuador became one of the countries in Latin America with the most "generous" incentives to the industrial sector (World Bank 1980, 253 in Fernández 1989, 197). In de la Torre's (1987, 126) words, the generosity of the incentives granted by the Industrial Promotion Law of was "striking". The idea behind the measures was indeed not new; according to Pérez Sáinz (1984, 20), the Industrial Promotion Law of 1962 was the spearhead of the industrialization project of the *Junta Militar* (1963-1966). Though, the amount of incentives for industrialists during the first Ecuadorian oil boom was unparalleled. De la Torre (1987, 127) estimated that the revenue sacrifice due to exemptions from tariff and import duties, tax benefits, and subsidies as production incentives amounted to 4 percent of GDP annually during the years of oil bonanza. Table No. 12 depicts the composition of Ecuador's non-oil GDP. The table aims to mirror the outcomes by sector of the enforcement of the measures to support and protect industrialists during the first Ecuadorian oil boom. A counterpart to the decline of the share of agriculture, a predominant sector before the oil boom, might be found in the increases of the tertiary sector[118] and the manufacturing sector.

---

118 The expansion of the tertiary sector of the economy might be related to enhanced private consumption possibilities facilitated by the first Ecuadorian oil boom. A discussion on such a correlation is beyond the scope of this book.

Table No. 12: Real non-oil value added by sector (percent), Ecuador 1965-80

Economic sector	Value added (percent)			Annual change (percent)	
	1965	1972	1980	1965-72	1972-80
Agriculture (includes livestock, fishing, and forestry)	27.0	24.9	16.8	4.0	2.7
Non-petroleum mining	0.3	0.3	0.4	5.7	11.0
Manufacturing	16.0	18.0	21.3	7.0	10.1
Construction	6.8	6.4	5.5	4.2	5.8
Utilities	0.6	0.9	0.9	10.4	8.2
Tertiary sector (includes commerce, government services, transport, other services)	49.4	49.6	55.2	5.2	9.3
Total real non-oil value added	100.0	100.0	100.0	5.2	7.8

Source: De la Torre (1987, 208)

Since the manufacturing sector expanded and the total factor productivity (TFP) followed the Latin American trend, which neared productivity levels of the United States and other industrialized countries[119] (Ferreira, Pessoa, and Veloso 2013, 20), it might be argued that the economic component of the resource curse thesis, i.e. the Dutch disease, is indeed a legend. This argument adds to the "little evidence" that Di John (2009) found to connect oil booms with the contraction of the manufacturing sector. As mentioned before, the author rather found that the Venezuelan manufacturing sector expanded hand in hand with oil activity between the early 1920s and the late 1960s. Hence, the economic component of the resource curse thesis might apply exclusively for countries in the Global North with a consolidated industrial structure that experience a natural resources boom.

Despite the enforcement of the set of measures to support and protect industrialists during the first Ecuadorian oil boom, and even despite the relative high productivity, the country's industrialization profile did not change (Fernández 1989, 201). In Larrea's (2013, 11) words, "industrializa-

---

119 TFP and labor productivity, with few exceptions in Latin America, followed a decreasing trend that began only after 1980 (Ferreira, Pessoa, and Veloso 2013, 18; Aravena and Fuentes 2013, 9).

tion was mostly a short lived effect of demand expansion in protected sectors of the economy between 1972 and 1982". In absence of a significant qualitative change, Table No. 13 aims to depict the slight quantitative change in the structure of the manufacturing sector during the first Ecuadorian oil boom.

Table No. 13: Manufacturing output by sub-sectors (percent), Ecuador 1965-82

	1965	1972	1977	1982
Food, beverages, and tobacco	58.1	46.3	42.8	41.6
Textiles and clothing	16.2	22.1	23.6	22.1
Wood and wood products	6.2	6.0	5.9	5.3
Paper and printing	7.4	7.1	6.0	6.3
Chemical products (includes plastics)	4.8	5.7	6.5	6.1
Non-metallic minerals and basic metals	5.4	9.1	10.0	12.4
Metal products and machinery	2.0	3.6	5.3	3.1
Other	0.0	0.0	0.0	2.9

Source: Larrea (2013, 12)

Hence, the increase of the share of the manufacturing sector in non-oil GDP might be understood as an upsurge in already dominant segments (i.e. small- and medium-sized industries of finished consumer goods, such as food processing and textiles and clothing) in a context of domestic demand expansion[120]. Though, a principal shortcoming of the manufacturing sector was its dependence on imports of industrial inputs, mainly intermediate and capital goods (Vos 1987, 21); in this line, Oleas (2017, 216)

---

120 The decrease of the sub-sector food, beverages, and tobacco in the share of the manufacturing sector (Table No. 13) might be related to the escalation of imports to satisfy increasing domestic demand. "My father-in-law used to smoke national tobacco from *Fábrica El Progreso*. During the late 1970s, imported tobacco appeared in the market just at the same price as domestic tobacco. My father-in-law switched straight to imported tobacco, which allegedly tasted better. *El Progreso* outlived until the 1990s" (Javier Espín, interview, November 14, 2018). Cheap imports (due to appreciated currency) and the contraction of the domestic tobacco industry might unveil the symptoms of the Dutch disease pinpointed in the sub-sector. Though, an analysis of the reasons of the decrease of the sub-sector food, beverages, and tobacco in the share of the manufacturing sector during the first Ecuadorian oil boom is beyond the scope of this book.

argued that by 1978, about 50 percent of intermediate industrial input was imported. Other flaws in the character of the Ecuadorian manufacturing sector, which remained practically unchanged during the first oil boom, have to do with 1) the low domestic linkages (Vos 1987, 53-72 in Larrea 2013, 11), and 2) the reduced employment generation (Larrea 2013, 11).

Regarding Ecuadorian export products, it might be argued that whereas traditional exports (mainly banana, coffee, and cacao) benefited from favorable commodity prices (Larrea 2013, 12), non-traditional exports experienced a setback during the first oil boom. On the one hand, measures aimed at supporting non-traditional exports enabled traditional exporters to shift production from unprocessed to slightly processed agricultural goods (de la Torre 1987, 205); on the other hand, the protection of larger-scale manufacturing was achieved at the expense of non-traditional exports, actual and potential (de la Torre 1987, 219). A significant example of the type of larger-scale manufacturing established during the first Ecuadorian oil boom is automobile assembly. Today's Ecuadorian largest assembly plant, ranked within the largest companies in Ecuador by total revenue, was established in 1975 during the height of protectionism. Though, the company, in particular, and the segment of automobile assembly, in general, is well-known for import-dependent manufacturing and for insufficient inter-industrial domestic linkages; "as the name implies, *assembly* might not be called manufacturing or industry *sensu stricto*, almost all component parts of the automobile are imported. The actual share of accessories manufactured locally has hovered around 15 percent of the total component parts of the vehicles, which are fitted together locally". By 1981, General Motors Company bought an important share of the local automobile assembly industry, and the company began to assemble exclusively General Motor's brands. In the early 1990s, the multinational became the major shareholder of the local automobile assembly industry; "in order to protect this so-called domestic *industry*, the tax burden on imported used cars is extreme in Ecuador" (Fabián Alarcón, interview, September 19, 2017).

The modest growth of the manufacturing sector during the first oil boom (even at the expense of non-traditional exports) did definitely not mean the take-off of Ecuadorian industry. The increase of the share of manufacturing in non-oil GDP did not translate into a modification of the country's productive structure, nor mirrored in a significant diversification of foreign exchange resources. Both features, 1) scarce modification of the productive structure and 2) insufficient diversification of foreign exchange sources blatantly antagonized with the envisioned inward-oriented development model. The meteoric upsurge in oil output shown in Figure No. 2 aims to depict the country's increasing reliance on oil as a main source of foreign exchange even after the years of the oil bonanza, as more than two thirds of the Amazonian oil extracted was destined to exportation (Gelb and Marshall 1988, 176).

Figure No. 2: Oil output, number of barrels exported, Ecuador 1972-2016

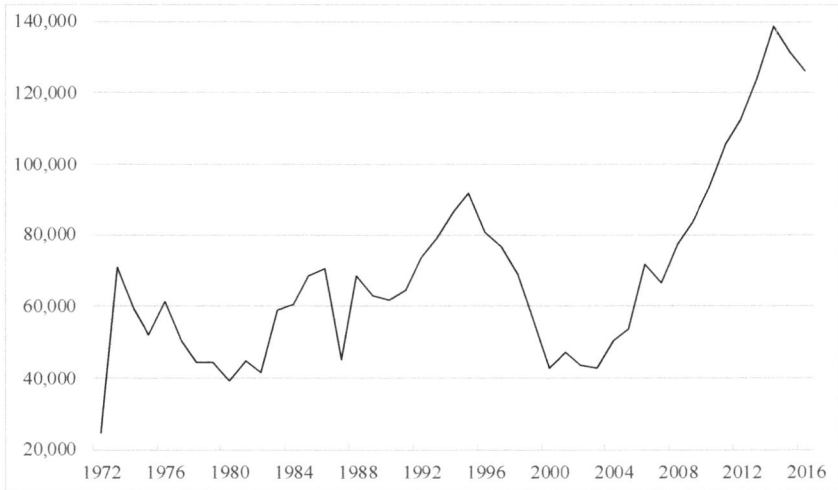

Source: Own diagram based on BCE (2017, 193)

Beyond the first Ecuadorian oil boom, and for the rest of the twentieth century, further reliance on natural resources exports unveiled the failure of intended broad-based economic diversification and thus the impossibility of establishing an inward-oriented development model. Hence, the transfer of oil rent to industrialists mirrored at the most in pseudo-industrialization. Table No. 14 shows the "diversification" of the Ecuadorian export portfolio from the first oil boom until the turn of the century. Whereas the negligible share of manufactured goods in Ecuadorian exports appears under non-traditional products, oil, bananas, and sea products accounted for about 80 percent, in average, of Ecuadorian exports during the last four decades (Larrea 2013, 12).

Table No. 14: Average share of export products (percent), Ecuador 1973-2001

Export product	1973-81	1982-91	1992-2001
Oil products (mainly crude oil)	58.9	54.8	36.4
Traditional products (banana and plantain, coffee and coffee products, shrimp, cocoa and cocoa products, tuna and fish)	28.8	38.5	42.1
Non-traditional products (mainly natural flowers, canned sea food and mining products)	12.3	6.7	21.5

Source: BCE (2017, 111)

Coinciding with a decreasing trend in the net barter terms of trade, which began in the 1980s and lasted until the end of the twentieth century (Table No. 2), and with the deterioration of international oil prices, oil lost weight in the share of Ecuadorian export products (Table No. 14). During the 1980s, fish and farmed shrimp exports accounted for the biggest contribution to the expansion in exports of traditional products. Whilst, non-traditional exports experienced a setback, mainly as an outcome of the enforcement of the aforementioned incentives that resulted in support of traditional exports. During the 1990s, traditional export products proved to be a reliable source of foreign exchange during the continued deterioration of international oil prices, as non-traditional exports, mainly fresh flowers and canned sea food, contributed to the diversification of the natural resources export portfolio. According to Larrea (2013, 12), fresh flowers have been the "only new significant addition" to Ecuador's export basket since the 1990s. Nevertheless, the total volume of Ecuadorian exports quadrupled between 1980 and 1999 (Larrea 2006b, 1). Though, the improved export performance did not mirror in economic growth (see Figure No. 4; Table No. 19).

Nature and the State: The Political Economy of Oil-Rentierism

The prevailing reliance on natural resources exports of the Ecuadorian economy speaks for a state's failure in the creation of a new industrialist class out of the old oligarchy. A plausible explanation to the deafness shown by potential new industrialists to the appeal of the *desarrollista* state during the first oil boom might be found 1) in the origins of the Ecuadorian bourgeoisie, and 2) in its heterogeneous structure and strategies. Regarding the origins of the Ecuadorian bourgeoisie, Cueva (2013, 85) underlined the close linkages with the landowning (*latifundista*) aristocracy, which was most representative within the dominant coalition of the Ecuadorian oligarchical state. When the *desarrollista* state challenged the oligarchical order, the leading position of the traditional landowning oligarchy was disputed by the ascending "intermediary [modern] bourgeoisie" and the transnational capital (Cueva 2013, 133). In this vein, Moncada (1989, 35) argued that the "birth and growth of the bourgeoisie, simultaneous with the overwhelming inflow of foreign capital" was central to the construction of a class stance that consisted in not opposing to and not antagonizing with foreign capital when it came to pursue a more autonomous development project. The behavior of this modern, intermediary bourgeoisie, attached to the landowning oligarchy and dependent on transnational capital, responded to "complex calculations linked to own interests, goals, and strategies" (Moncayo 2017, 188). Moncada (1989, 17) posited that due to the activities it controlled and its varied interests, the Ecuadorian bourgeoisie cultivated strong links with the state and even with government officials[121]. Due to the heterogeneous interests, goals, and strategies, Moncayo (2017, 187) argued that "the Ecuadorian bourgeoisie was not made up of segregated fractions, but of an amalgamation of interlinked, entangled groupings".

An alternative explanation to the Ecuadorian bourgeoisie's lack of commitment with economic diversification might be supported on rentier theory. Coronil (1997, 248), in his influential study about the Venezuelan petro-state, highlighted the rentier behavior of dominant-class groups:

> [rentier] capitalists not necessarily act akin to afford industrial investments to increase the productivity of labor, since expansion of circulating money during boom periods creates opportunities for profit (in sectors as real state, finance, commerce, and construction), which do not depend on productive investments or on efforts.

Among the sectors mentioned (real state, finance, commerce, and construction), in which boom periods create opportunities to profit without an effort, Coronil (1997, 248) forgot to mention the very manufacturing

---

121 This behavior of the Ecuadorian bourgeoisie reminds of Coronil's (2008, 20) characterization of rentier societies in opposition to capitalist societies: "if in capitalist nations based on the generation of value through human labor the business of politics is business, in oil exporting societies based on the extraction of rents through the capture of natural riches the business of business is politics".

sector. As mentioned before, during the first Ecuadorian oil boom, the state "generously" and "strikingly" protected domestic manufacturing. Oil rent was central to the availability of national and international credits that bankrolled a set of incentives for industrialists from 1973 until the end of the decade, which in turn nurtured their rentier behavior. Due to the "close and family-based" nature of local industry (Luna 1993, 66), proper-tied classes benefited from the enforcement of state's industrial promotion measures. Luna (1993, 65) argued that the "oligarchical familiar structure", which was a legacy of colonial social relationships based on the color of the skin and the nobility of the family name, persisted beyond the 1960s together with new social classes "under construction"; furthermore, this fact disturbed the professional and entrepreneurial management of indus-tries since the lack of a functional separation between owners and man-agers and staff members, due to kinship or adscription to a common elite, translated into low productivity and low quality of products manufactured locally. Hence, the "close and family-based" nature of local industry was central to the conformation of what Luna (1993, 60) called the "anti-en-trepreneurial spirit" of industrialists, i.e. a behavior, which was not cen-tered on the generation of value through human labor (Coronil 2008, 20), but on the exploitation of more "natural" conditions such as kinship, birthright, or adscription to a common elite. The rentier behavior of local industrialists was also fostered by prevailing pre-capitalist relations of pro-duction. Until the 1970s, the hacienda system[122], which epitomized pre-capitalist relations of production in the highlands, was well-known for its lack of entrepreneurship that mirrored in scarce initiatives to improve agri-cultural production and to incorporate technological advances into the productive process. This lack of entrepreneurship might be closely related to the availability of inexpensive labor force in the hacienda (Luna 1993, 64), and is central to understand the rentier behavior of *latifundistas*. Anal-ogously, benefits from oil revenues put at the industrialists' disposal, in the form of incentives for the manufacturing sector, become central to under-stand their rentier behavior.

With the "revolutionary nationalist" dictatorship pouring oil rent into the manufacturing sector, conflict with industrialists might had appeared

---

122 "Large haciendas not only monopolized more than three-quarters of the total area of the highlands, according to the 1954 census, they were also institutions that politically, ethnically, and economically dominated the rural indigenous population" (Zamosc 1994 in de la Torre 2000, 213).

unthinkable; though, the enforcement of land reform policies[123] unveiled the common foundation of industrialists and *latifundistas*, who unified positions with other local elites and more conservative factions of the armed forces, and forged an alliance to overthrow General Rodríguez Lara (Bocco 1987, 31). With the Land Reform Law of 1973, the government was entrusted with the power to expropriate any "inefficient" landholding where landlords failed to exploit economically at least 80 percent of the usable area by January 1976. The prevalence of precarious employment relationships in agriculture, i.e. pre-capitalist relations of production, was also penalized (Supreme Order No. 1172, published in the Official Gazette No. 410, October 15, 1973). Guillermo Maldonado Lince (1980, 49), General Rodríguez Lara's minister of agriculture[124] between December 1972 and March 1974, argued that such a progressive vein of the Land Reform Law of 1973 doomed it to be nicknamed the "Snatch Law" (*Ley del arranche*) by local elites. The *Consejo Supremo de Gobierno* (1976-1979), the military triumvirate that followed the "revolutionary nationalist" dictatorship, enacted a new legal framework under pressure of the *latifundistas* (North 1985, 441). The Agrarian Development Law of 1979 (*Ley de Fomento y Desarrollo Agropecuario*) (Supreme Order No. 3289, published in the Official Gazette No. 792, March 15, 1979) despoiled the Land Reform Law of 1973 of its "reformist" potential (North 1985, 441), as it abolished the criteria by which an estate was to be considered efficient, particularly the rule of the 80 percent (Barsky 1984, 248).

North (1985, 442) argued that an implicit objective of land reform enforced during the first Ecuadorian oil boom was industrial promotion. In the same vein, Bretón (2008, 586) posited that during the years of the import-substitution industrialization (ISI) consensus, "it was believed that the

---

123 Land reform was first enforced by the Junta Militar (1963-1966) through the Law of Land Reform and Settlement and the Law of Idle Lands and Settlement of 1964 (Gondard and Mazurek 2001, 16). The Ecuadorian Institute of Land Reform and Colonization (*Instituto Ecuatoriano de Reforma Agraria y Colonización*, IERAC) was first established in order to enforce land reform policies. At that time, redistribution of land ownership was not a national initiative, but a mandate of the Alliance for Progress (Luna 1993, 66). As mentioned before, the Alliance for Progress was a cooperation platform launched President John F. Kennedy in 1961 in order to avert the "perils" of the spread of the Cuban Revolution into the Latin American region. Local elites gave an apparent positive response to the enforcement of land reform since their fears were focused on potential uprisings and social unrest.

124 According to Martz (1987, 121), Mr. Maldonado Lince had an utmost nationalistic stance on land reform.

transformation of agrarian structures was a necessary condition for economic take-off"; hence, land reform was not itself an objective of the military dictatorships of the 1970s. The statement alone serves as a plausible explanation for the "asymmetric results" (Bretón 2008, 591) of the enforcement of land reform policies. Still, Maldonado Lince (1980, 46) argued that *latifundistas* systematically sabotaged the task of the Ecuadorian Institute of Land Reform and Colonization (IERAC) since its creation in 1964. As a result, in the early years of the bonanza, a weak IERAC was only able to show a humble budget implementation of 25 percent (Maldonado Lince 1980, 51). Table No. 15 depicts the evolution of the Ecuadorian agrarian structure for the period 1954-2000. By 1954, circa three-quarters of the landholdings (73.1 percent) were smaller than five hectares and accounted for only for 7.2 percent of all arable land. Whilst, only 2.1 percent of the estates, those larger that 100 hectares, accounted for far more than the half of all arable land (64.4 percent). Thirty years later, by 1984, the percentage of arable land comprised by farms smaller than 20 hectares increased substantially to 35.6 percent, while estates larger than 100 hectares did not account for more than 34 percent of the arable land[125]. Though, according to Bretón (2008, 591), "this apparently greater equity is more illusory than real".

Table No. 15: Evolution of the agrarian structure, Ecuador 1954-2000

Size of units	Number of units (percent)			Arable land (percent)			
	1954	1974	2000	1954	1974	1984	2000
Less than 5 ha	73.1	66.8	63.5	7.2	6.8		6.3
From 5 to 20 ha	16.7	18.6	21.0	9.4	11.8		13.8
Less than 20 ha						35.6	
From 20 to 100 ha	8.1	12.5	13.2	19.0	33.5		37.3
More than 100 ha	2.1	2.1	2.3	64.4	47.9	ca. 34.0	42.6

Source: Chiriboga (1985, 99); Bretón (2008, 592)

---

125 Figures of the year 2000 are included in Table No. 15 in order to show a rather sluggish trend in land redistribution. An explanation for the evident recoil in the redistribution of estates larger than 100 hectares is beyond the scope of this book.

Bretón (2008, 593) argued that the change in landholding patterns was mainly related to the expansion of arable land, "two million hectares in only twenty years". In the same vein, Barsky (1984, 305) argued that the agricultural frontier was pushed by colonization of land by workers of the haciendas fostered by IERAC. Colonization had, in turn, two main outcomes. On the one hand, it indeed accelerated the breakup of estates that had difficulties adapting to the efficiency requirements imposed by law. On the other hand, colonization guaranteed the rationalization of "the best lands and those susceptible to be turned into capitalized units of production oriented towards the domestic urban market or export trade" (Bretón 2008, 592). The figures exposed in Table No. 16 show the relative importance of colonization to the redistribution of land for the period 1964-83. Table No. 16 aims also to depict the comparative effectiveness of land redistribution during the period ruled by the Land Reform Law of 1973 or the "revolutionary nationalist" dictatorship's re-launching of land reform first enforced by the *Junta Militar*. Though, Bretón (2008, 592) posited that often only the worst estate lands (those unsuitable for cultivation) were redistributed. Further, the author argued that land reform severed peasants from mechanized (i.e. efficient) haciendas. Hence, the only possibility of access to land for peasants was through the fragmentation of the holdings distributed by IERAC, which throughout the years became smaller and smaller, or through a further expansion of the agricultural frontier.

Table No. 16: Redistribution through land reform and colonization, Ecuador 1964-83

	Land reform (hectares)	Colonization (hectares)	Total
1964-66	85,602.8	207,612.1	293,214.9
1967-70	74,034.5	253,710.7	327,745.2
1971-79	482,420.9	1,069,592.7	1,552,013.7
1980-83	166,663.7	654,632.2	821,295.9

Source: Barsky (1984, 304-313)

However, land reform is central not only to understand the processes of migration from rural to urban areas (i.e. urbanization), and migration abroad (particularly during the 1990s), but also to elucidate the decay of the traditional oligarchy with its rural base, the hacienda. Gondard and Mazurek (2001, 36) argued that a drastic reduction of the annual rural population growth rates in the coast and the highlands took place during the 1970s, as a sign of massive rural migration. Table No. 17 shows national rural population growth rates; compared to country's total population growth rates, rural figures are remarkably smaller for the period 1974-90.

Table No. 17: Annual rural population growth rate, Ecuador 1962-90

	Ecuador total (percent)	Ecuador rural (percent)	Highlands rural (percent)	Coast rural (percent)
1962-74	3.30	2.54	2.12	2.61
1974-82	2.77	0.81	0.89	0.26
1982-90	2.77	0.63	0.26	0.49

Source: Gondard and Mazurek (2001, 36)

Then, in might be argued that land reform did not solve the inequalities in land owning and neither other problems of wealth distribution in rural areas, but decisively impacted on oligarchical social classes, which had to compete with more modern segments of the bourgeoisie represented by a "modern commercial agricultural economy" (CEPAL 1977, 25). Such groups, which were characterized by their more capitalistic relations of production, indeed emerged from old *latifundistas*, but were able to make better use than any other group of the state's allocation of oil rent in the form of infrastructure projects and credit disbursed by the national banking and financial system (Table No. 11). However, land reform did definitely not mean the take-off of the Ecuadorian economy. Regarding middle classes, land reform had an ambiguous impact. Urbanization, the other side of the coin of land reform, not only nurtured middle classes, but also was related to a looming crisis for the next generation, with migrants who often ended as "[informal] construction laborers and street vendors" (Conaghan 1988, 48), thereby increasing informal employment (World Bank 1980, iv). Therefore, North (1985, 452) argued that the "illusion of [urban] prosperity veiled the underlying contradictions of the [natural resources-based] development model", as social peace was "temporary purchased through *asistencialismo* instead of [wealth] redistribution and structural change".

Postlude to Nature and the State: The Political Economy of the End of the First Ecuadorian Oil Boom

Whereas last section focused on Ecuador's domestic circumstance, the present section explores central external conditions that linked the country with the next stage of capitalism. By the time when the "revolutionary nationalist" dictatorship confronted with the opposition of the traditional oligarchy to the enforcement of land reform, foreign oil companies also raised their voice against allegedly deprivations caused by the enforcement of nationalist oil policies tending towards the appropriation of a larger portion of oil rent. Texaco-Gulf "actively engaged" in promoting the removal of the Minister of Natural Resources Jarrín Ampudia; a press campaign was mounted, while the consortium threatened a possible withdrawal from Ecuador if the minister remained (Martz 1987, 134). Jarrín Ampudia's reputation reached a highpoint in 1974 when he was appointed president of OPEC's conference to be held in Quito. The minister was regarded as the personification of oil nationalism thanks to his reiterated demands for raised taxes and royalties, and the observation of OPEC's directives on managing oil supply, which often contradicted the business plans of foreign oil companies. The precipitating factor for his removal was a proposed new negotiation with Texaco-Gulf launched in September 1974, where the minister sought to secure majority shareholding for CEPE by purchasing an additional 26 percent of the consortium (Martz 987, 125). Jarrín Ampudia's proposal was "quietly dropped" when he resigned at the beginning of October (Philip 1979, 18). His departure revealed the real measure of the multinationals' counteroffensive. By November, Texaco-Gulf announced that the Trans-Ecuadorian pipeline was being shut down and oil exports had halted (Martz 1987, 127). This measures added to other sabotage actions such as cancellation of contracts with subcontractors, cessation of purchase orders, and interruption of exports (Martz 1987, 132). Concessions made by the dictatorship, which included tax reduction and noncompliance with OPEC's resolution of an increase in oil price (Marshall 1988, 58), resulted in a diminution of the state's share of oil rent.

Conditions created by foreign oil companies added to weakening international oil prices. Such a cocktail mirrored in the meager oil output of 1975 (Figure No. 2). Besides, the U.S. Foreign Trade Law of 1975 excluded all member states of OPEC[126] from preferential tariffs in their commerce

---

126 Philip (1979, 14) recapped that since the beginning of 1974, the United States launched a diplomatic offensive against OPEC.

with the United States (Martz 1987, 133), as a retaliation for the oil embargo of 1973-1974, which caused the first global oil shock. According to Marshall (1988, xvii), only the joined action of the Andean Pact could end the restriction for country members Ecuador and Venezuela. External conditions aggravated the internal circumstance, which turned explosive in 1975. Due to declining exports of (yet cheaper) Amazonian oil, the regime imposed import restrictions on a number of luxury goods, in order to tackle with the worsening balance of payments position (Báez 1984, 104; Philip 1979, 24). According to Philip (1979, 23), this measure accelerated the process of replacement of the "revolutionary nationalist" dictatorship by the triumvirate of the *Consejo Supremo de Gobierno*, which assumed office by the beginning of 1976.

The principal undertaking of the *Consejo Supremo de Gobierno* was the installation of the scenario for the return of democratic regimes. Therefore, the triumvirate appointed a commission with the duty of drafting a new political constitution (Supreme Order No. 995, published in the Official Gazette No. 239, November 23, 1976). Despite the scenario of national decision-making was shifted to the arena of the civilians, the armed forces kept close control on policy making (Freidenberg and Pachano 2016, 21). The resulting 1978 Constitution was meant to enter into force with the debut of the next elected government (Supreme Order No. 2400, published in the Official Gazette No. 564, April 12, 1978). The text of the new constitution was ratified in a national referendum in January 1978, and the dictatorship called for general elections in July of the same year. In the second ballot, held on April 1979, Jaime Roldós was elected president and assumed office in August for a five-year period. The new government, which was supposed to deal with the return of democracy to the domestic arena[127], and its successors faced indeed a greater challenge, i.e. to cope with the end of the first Ecuadorian oil boom. After peaking in 1980, international oil prices dropped steadily until a decade's minimum in 1986, and a historical minimum in 1998 (MWV 2018), when the income of Ecuadorian banana exports surpassed oil revenues (Acosta 2001, 341; BCE 2017, 111) for the first time since the beginning of the oil era.

The share of oil rent in the gross domestic product (GDP) steadily declined during the two last decades of the century (Table No. 32), with a historical minimum in 1998 (World Bank 2019d). Household final consumption expenditure followed the decreasing trend to an average of two

---

127 Jaime Roldós died in a plane crash in 1981 and Osvaldo Hurtado, his vice-president, succeeded him as president until the end of the term in 1984.

percent growth for the period 1982-2001, which markedly fell behind the annual average of eight percent growth for the period 1973-80 (World Bank 2019b). Even the gross enrollment ratio in tertiary education declined after peaking in 1981. At the end of the century, the ratio reached levels comparable with those of the mid-1970s (World Bank 2019g). Whilst, the minimum wage reduced progressively in real terms after peaking in 1980 (BCE 2017, 178). Nevertheless, debt service improved from an average of 3.5 percent of GNI for the period 1972-81 to 7.8 percent for the rest of the century and peaked at the historical record of 13.2 percent of GNI in 1999 (World Bank 2019e) for increasing external debt stocks that surpassed the barrier of 40 percent of GNI in 1982 and kept over 70 percent during the 1990s, with a historical peak of 104.5 percent of the GNI in 1999 (World Bank 2019a). in this line, Oleas (2017, 216) argued that by 1980, Ecuador disbursed an equivalent to 78 percent of its exports for external debt service.

The worldwide triumph of international financial capital, which mirrored in the Latin American debt crisis, was also palpable in Ecuador during the last decades of the twentieth century. Democratically-elected governments responded to the new external conditions with the enforcement of neoliberal policies inspired by the Washington Consensus (WC). The pursuit of overall market prevalence began to erode the landlord-arbiter state configuration, which predominated during the last stage of capitalism. A concrete response to decreasing international oil prices was openness to foreign capital, i.e. the pursuit of enhanced participation of multinational oil corporations in exploration and exploitation activities. By 1992, Ecuador abandoned OPEC in a bet to counteract decreasing income with increased oil exports without any quota restriction[128].

The prevalence of the private initiative was confirmed as the new status quo in 1993 when the Ecuadorian Congress issued the Law of Modernization of the State, Privatizations, and Delegation of Public Services to the Private Initiative (*Ley de Modernización del Estado, Privatizaciones y Prestación de Servicios Públicos por Parte de la Iniciativa Privada*), which followed the regional trend of limiting national states' active role in the economy in benefit of free market rules. Article 8 of the law established the National Council of Modernization of the State (*Consejo Nacional de Modernización del Estado*, CONAM) in charge of enforcing the legal reform, i.e. releasing the state of key responsibilities regarding the national development

---

128 Ecuador resumed in 2007 within the renewed nationalist trend inspired by the 'pink tide'.

process (Congreso Nacional 1993). Despite the existence of the National Council of Development (*Consejo Nacional de Desarrollo*, CONADE)[129], the CONAM, since its creation, was regarded as the official entity in charge of economic planning (former official of CONADE, interview, January 9, 2017). One of the main duties of CONAM, the barbarian[130], was the privatization of state companies. Non-profitable state companies were doomed to extinction; this was the fate of the National Enterprise of Storage and Commercialization (ENAC) (Executive Order No. 967, published in the Official Gazette No. 223, December 26, 1997) and the National Enterprise of Vital Products (ENPROVIT) (Executive Order No. 197, published in the Official Gazette No. 47, October 15, 1998). Though, the destiny of the jewels in the crown, the national oil company (CEPE) and the National Electrification Institute (INECEL), remained unforeseen.

By 1989, the *Empresa Estatal Petróleos del Ecuador* (Petroecuador) replaced CEPE[131]. The renewed state-owned oil company was meant to assume Texaco's duties (including the operation of the Trans-Ecuadorian pipeline) by the time when the multinational had left the country in 1990. Since its creation, Petroecuador was intended to comply with the privatization dictates of the WC; hence it operated as a holding with three main subsidiaries, 1) *Petroproducción*, in charge of undertaking extractivist activities, 2) *Petroindustrial*, mainly in charge of operating the Esmeraldas refinery, and 3) *Petrocomercial*, which controlled the local distribution of oil products. Meanwhile, the 1996 Law of the Electric Sector (*Ley de Régimen del Sector Eléctrico*) tolled the knell for INECEL. The idea behind INECEL's dissolution was to split the country's electricity sector, i.e. generation, transmission, and distribution of electricity, into several business units to be privatized (Congreso Nacional 1996). With the benefit of hindsight, it might be argued that a main reason for the state's failure to comply with the privatization mandate was the resistance of workers' unions. In an ap-

---

129 CONADE was created by the 1978 Constitution to replace JUNAPLA, and was extinguished by the 1998 Constitution. According to Moncayo (1987, 153), the main difference between JUNAPLA and CONADE was the composition of the latter; CONADE's directory incorporated "representatives of universities, workers, and industrialists".

130 During the 1990s decade, street paintings with the motto "Stop CONAM the barbarian!" appeared in Quito as a symptom of opposition to privatization of state companies (Ximena Estévez, interview, October 10, 2018). The motto alluded to the 1982 film "Conan the barbarian", directed by John Milius.

131 The Law of Creation of Petroecuador (*Ley Especial No. 45*) was published in the Official Gazette No. 283 of September 26, 1989 (Congreso Nacional 1989).

parent paradox, article 31 of the 1978 Constitution, which was drafted during the military dictatorship of the *Consejo Supremo de Gobierno*, granted unionization and the right of workers to strike (Primera Comisión de Reestructuración Jurídica del Estado 1979). Hence, during the 1980s, organized workers became the key social actor that faced the end of state's distributive policies and the embracement of neoliberal policies. According to Marega (2015, 33), the National Federation of State Petroleum Workers of CEPE (*Federación Nacional de Trabajadores Petroleros Estatales de* CEPE, FE-TRACEPE) was established in December 1980 with a strong commitment to "defense of strategic resources". This sense of commitment comprised a vision of the state company as "an expression of national sovereignty and work source". During the 1990s, the union switched name to National Federation of Workers of the State Petroleum Company (*Federación Nacional de Trabajadores de la Empresa Estatal Petróleos del Ecuador*, FE-TRAPEC) and significantly grew in members and in political organization (Marega 2015, 33) and turned into the spearhead of the defense of against private capital. The struggle entailed a reminiscence of the nationalist vein of the 1970s oil-*desarrollismo*. The growing role of unions against the enforcement of neoliberal policies was only to be surpassed by that of the indigenous movement during the 1990s. As a result, the intended denationalization of principal state companies did not succeed.

Though, the outcomes of the participation of foreign capital in the oil sector became tangible in 2003, when multinational corporations overtook the national company in Amazonian oil output[132] (BCE 2017, 192; Larrea 2006a, 67). Besides, private companies that started extractivist activities in the *Oriente* during the second half of the 1980s (Ortiz 2011, 12), inaugurated the new heavy crude oil[133] pipeline (*Oleoducto de Crudos Pesados*, OCP) after two years of construction. The private OCP pipeline is meant to be transferred to the Ecuadorian state in 2023 after twenty years of private operation. Privatization of state companies would have signified a giant leap to address one of the main concerns of neoliberalism: the size of the state apparatus.

No other strategy to assure the prevalence of market rules had a stronger impact on middle- and lower-middle classes than the reduction of employ-

---

132 Incidentally (or not), in 2003 began an upward trend in international oil prices, which was the dawn of the twenty-first century commodities boom.

133 A heavy crude oil is a denser, more viscous oil. The American Petroleum Institute gravity (API gravity) measures how heavy or light a crude oil is compared to water. A heavy crude oil has an API gravity of less than 20 degrees API.

ment opportunities in the public administration. Since no labor-intensive alternative to public service was available to absorb the workforce of modern urban middle classes, the strategy to cope with neoliberal marginalization was found overseas: Personal remittances increased from US$ 1 million in 1989 to US$ 1,421 million in 2001 (World Bank 2019f), as the number of Ecuadorian migrants to the Global North skyrocketed. Along with massive migration, during the crisis of the end of the twentieth century, people who benefited from the first Ecuadorian oil boom "were clearly declassed" (Vera 2013, 137), not only because of the disappearance of their social status, but also because of the "loss of the elections in which their class identity was based", i.e. reduction in the household final consumption expenditure, limited access to tertiary education, and decreasing employment opportunities in the public sector. Though, remittances threw a lifeline to urban modern middle classes and hence avoided the total wipeout of the development gains of the first Ecuadorian oil boom.

Chapter 6: "Sow the Oil" Revisited: Nature and the Ecuadorian Neo-*Desarrollista* State

"Hegel remarks somewhere that all great world-historic facts
and personages appear, so to speak, twice. He forgot to add:
the first time as tragedy, the second time as farce"
(Marx 1869, 1).

Prelude: Dollarization and the Ecuadorian National De-Construction

In absence of a strong external sector with diversified foreign exchange sources, monetary policy was the preferred tool to cope with the financial crisis of the end of the twentieth century. During the 1980s, the Central Bank of Ecuador, with allegedly apolitical technocrats (Oleas 2017, 219), undertook the remaining tasks of economic planning, and became the "ideal interlocutor" (Oleas 2017, 236) of international financial institutions (IFI), such as the International Monetary Fund (IMF). The new actors of national economic policymaking feared most the specter of inflation and thought highly of the capacity of devaluation to tame macroeconomic indicators. By 1994, the National Congress passed the General Law of Institutions of the Financial System (*Ley General de Instituciones del Sistema Financiero*) in the pursuit of private initiative's prevalence over state's agency. The legislation followed the canons of liberalization of financial markets dictated by the Washington Consensus; a key financial regulation introduced by the law was the liberalization of interest rates. Besides, bankers were allowed to undertake other economic activities in the private sector (Congreso Nacional 1994). Vera (2013, 79) argued that the new legislation significantly reduced state's control on private banks and financial institutions, and relaxed surveillance of their investments. Further, so the author, the new law left the doors open to bank bailout (*salvataje bancario*).

Already by 1997, four banks and seven financial institutions failed (Vera 2013, 66). The insolvency of the country's largest bank, *Filanbanco*, added to the list of failures of banks and financial institutions that topped the agenda of the newly-elected President Jamil Mahuad (1998-200). By the beginning of 1999, escalating financial uncertainty led to massive withdrawals. In order to prevent bank run, on March 8, the government announced a bank holiday (*feriado bancario*), which lasted for five days. During the *feriado bancario* the president decreed a bank account freeze (*congelamiento de cuentas*[134]) in which deposits of minimum 2,000,000 sucres (the equivalent to twenty minimum wages in 1999) would be frozen for one year (Executive Order No. 685, published in the Official Gazette No. 149, March 16, 1999). Neither the bank holiday nor the bank account freeze prevented the failure of the *Banco del Progreso*. Vera (2013, 79) argued that the reason behind the domino effect, which manifested in the failure of seventeen banks and financial institutions between 1998 and 2000, was high-risk loans provided to shareholders and connected enterprises[135]. In this vein, Bustamante (2001, 67) recapped the "close and family-based" nature of Ecuadorian socio-economical elites that act as a "family corporation" or as a "conglomerate of *patresfamilias*", who exert a certain influence on national politics. The bank bailout, which rounded out the case of local crony capitalism, amounted circa eight billion dollars[136] (US$ 8,072 million until 2007) and was largely regarded as a transference of state's resources to already privileged social sectors (i.e. socio-economical elites).

Loans provided among cronies, and the bank bailout orchestrated by government unveiled the conjunction of state elites with economic elites and, thus, the loss of state's relative autonomy from social classes. Hence, the "Poulantzas' reformulation" of the developmental state theory, which was presented earlier in this book, might not be valid for Ecuador during the crisis of the end of the twentieth century. The "Poulantzas' reformulation" of the developmental state theory is related to the state's option of carrying out a national developmental project as "the politics of the political elites or the politics of the bureaucracy" on the basis of relative autonomy from social classes gained through oil rent. Such a reformulation of the developmental state theory is proposed in the core of the landlord-arbiter state configuration, which in turn is central to understand the Latin American *desarrollista* state.

---

134 Bank account freeze was also enforced in Argentina during the crisis of 2001 under the name of "*corralito*" (small enclosure or pen).

135 A significant example was *Banco del Progreso*. Since the General Law of Institutions of the Financial System was issued in 1994, the bank provided loans for 1.7 billion sucres to 86 connected enterprises; 24 of these borrowers provided no loan guarantee at all. Among the beneficiaries were companies owned by Fernando Aspiazu, the principal shareholder of the bank (Vera 2013, 79).

136 By 1999, the state owned circa 57 percent of the assets of the private banking system (Vera 2013, 9).

Escalating inflation (Figure No. 3) was a close companion of the banking crisis (*crisis bancaria*). By 1999, inflation reached the historical record of 96.1 percent for the period between 1970 and 2018 (World Bank 2019j) and helped setting in the financial apocalypse of the end of the century.

Figure No. 3: Annual inflation (percent), consumer prices, Ecuador 1970-2018

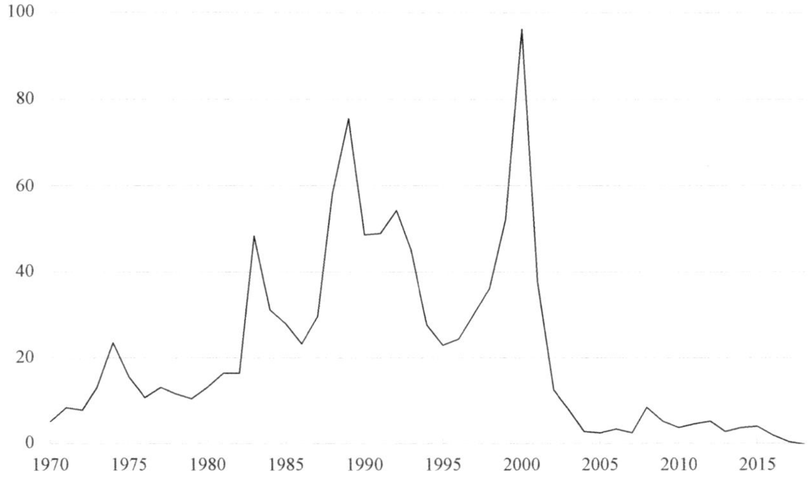

Source: Own diagram based on World Bank (2019j)

Figure No. 4 aims to depict the financial crisis juncture of the year 1999 through the variation in the annual GDP growth; the negative peak indicates the worst financial crisis in Ecuadorian economic history[137] for the period 1970-2018. Acosta and Schuldt (2000, 31) argued that central to the

---

137   The graph of the annual GDP growth (Figure No. 4) might also be used in an exercise to recognize several events in Ecuadorian economic history. The inauguration of the first Ecuadorian oil boom, and hence the beginning of the oil era, is identifiable in the positive peak by 1973. Negative peaks by 1983 and 1987 are signals for the particularly destructive occurrence of the ocean-atmosphere phenomenon of El Niño and the earthquake that severely damaged the Trans-Ecuadorian pipeline, respectively. The influence of external conditions is detectable in the negative peak by 2015, when international oil prices dramatically dropped.

origination of hyperinflation is the accelerated substitution of national currency by other assets that do not devaluate, e.g. foreign exchange[138].

Figure No. 4: Annual GDP growth (percent), 2010 U.S. dollars, Ecuador 1970-2018

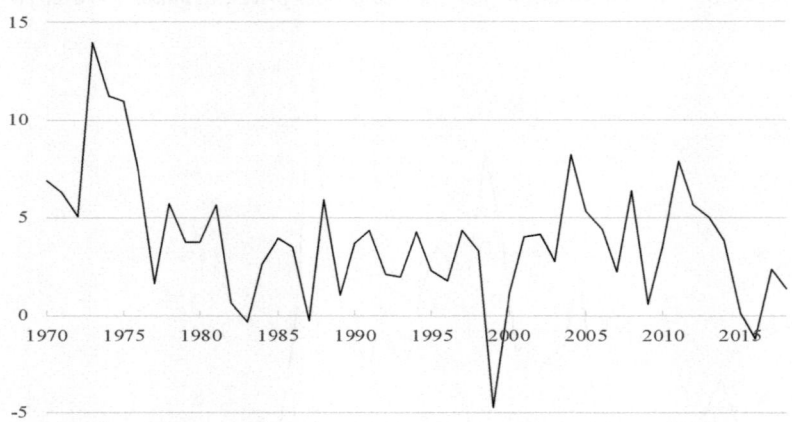

Source: Own diagram based on World Bank (2019h)

Notwithstanding growing inflation (Figure No. 3), and the severe financial crisis (Figure No. 4), Acosta and Schuldt (2000, 26) maintained that Ecuador was not under threat of hyperinflation, and that fears were "unjustified" (Acosta 2004b, 54). Though, hyperinflation was indeed the justification given by national economic authorities for the adoption of the U.S. dollar as national currency on January 9, 2000. Despite the United States was Ecuador's principal business partner at that time, reasons for the "selection" of the U.S. dollar as national currency were rather political than economic; Larrea (2006b, 1) argued that "commercial liberalization and market friendly policies, as well as expectations for a continental-wide trade bloc [which finally did not succeed], led to an increasing influence of the U.S. dollar in Latin America".

---

138 Hyperinflation is understood as a process of "deteriorating trust in national currency resulting from skyrocketing prices and monetary collapse" (Acosta and Schuldt 2000, 30). "About one year before official dollarization, informal dollarization was commonplace, transactions were already in U.S. dollars. Prices of cars, apartments..., the whole real state sector was already dollarized" (Pepe Vásquez, interview, October 11, 2018).

Despite the removal from office of President Jamil Mahuad (1998-2000) only two weeks after the enforcement of dollarization, it might be argued that the loss of national currency added little fuel to the already big fire of social unrest that was originally sparked by the enforcement of neoliberal policies[139]. Living standards steadily deteriorated since the end of the first Ecuadorian oil boom. By 1980, when the minimum wage reached a peak at 4,000 sucres, it was worth US$ 144. Ten years later, in 1990, the minimum wage was 32,000 sucres, which corresponded to US$ 39. Close to the financial crisis of the end of the century, in July 1997, the minimum wage was fixed at 100,000 sucres, equivalent to US$ 25; already by 1999, it was worth only US$ 8. Short before dollarization, when the exchange rate was fixed at 25,000 sucres per dollar it corresponded to US$ 4 (BCE 2017, 178).

Indeed, the years previous to the enforcement of dollarization were characterized by above-average growth of poverty; in Matthes' (2019, 149) words, the "fastest impoverishment in Latin American history". National poverty went up from 56 percent in 1995 to 63 percent in 1998, and 69 percent in 2000 (Larrea 2006, 12); for comparison, poverty in Latin America followed a stabilizing trend around circa 44 percent during the same period (1995-2000) (CEPALSTAT 2019a). According to Larrea (2006, 12), "recovery" and "post-crisis [macroeconomic] stabilization" followed the enforcement of dollarization. By December 2001, national poverty receded to 53.5 percent and followed a decreasing trend that converged with the region's average in the second half of the 2000s decade (CEPALSTAT 2019a). Whilst, the minimum wage recovered levels of the 1970s and reached US$ 158.1 by 2003 (BCE 2017, 178). That same year, inflation reached one digit levels (Figure No. 3).

The country's disastrous financial situation did not hinder debt service (Figure No. 5). Figure No. 5 depicts the total external debt service (principal repayments and interest) as percentage of GNI for the period 1975-2017. By 1999, coinciding with financial apocalypse, debt service peaked at about 14 percent of GNI culminating an upward trend, which began in the second half of the 1990s decade. According to Matthes (2019, 49), between 1980 and 2000 Ecuador expended circa US$ 76 billion in its

---

139 Dollarization indeed precipitated the fall of Mahuad (1998-2000), but social and political unrest was commonsense during the last decades of the twentieth century and even into the twenty-first century. Only three years before President Mahuad's fall in 2000, President Abdalá Bucaram (1996-1997) was overthrew by Congress. In 2005 President Lucio Gutiérrez (2003-2005) was also removed from office.

external debt, which translated mainly into further credits provided by international financial institutions, i.e. into an increase in the country's debt burden. In order to provide more credits, international financial institutions such as the International Monetary Fund (IMF), demanded the compliance with the agenda of structural adjustment programs (SAP).

Figure No. 5: Total debt service (principal repayments and interests) as percentage of GNI, Ecuador 1975-2017

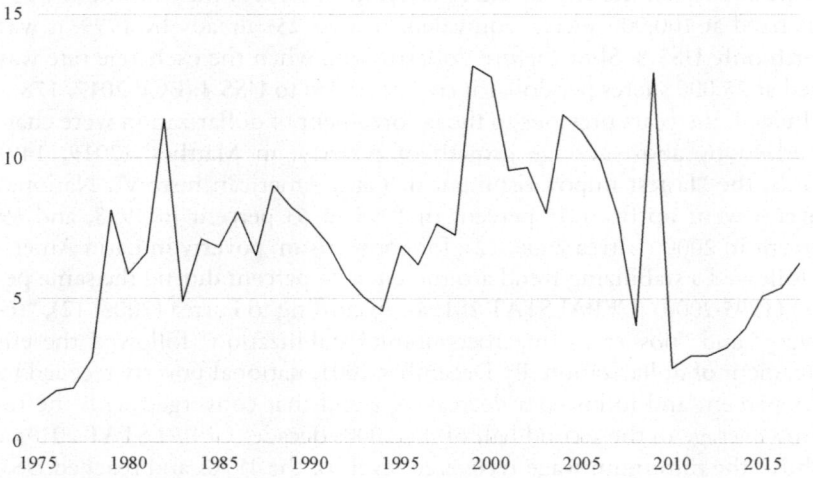

Source: Own diagram based on World Bank (2019e)

Within the context of the financial crisis of the end of the twentieth century, debt service might speak for a further loss of state's relative autonomy, at this point, from international financial institutions (IFI). Furthermore, meeting debt obligations with external creditors during the severe domestic crisis might be regarded as a strong signal of the ultimate dismantlement of the landlord-arbiter state configuration in which the state, as during the 1970s, allocates financial resources to serve the national development purposes.

Adding to the problem of declining state income due to the dropping international commodity prices, a relative relaxation of the tax burden took place during the 1980s (Table No. 18). Whereas Table No. 18 presents the average share of oil revenues and tax revenues in total state's income for the period 1971-2015, Figure No. 6 aims to depict both kinds of revenue as the principal components of total state's income since the beginning of the oil era. A relaxation of the tax burden is linked in this book with a breakage of the fiscal contract (see section *Act III. Nature and the State: A Handbook on the Imposition of a Natural Resources-Based Developmental Project*). Ross (2001, 332) argued that such a state relieve might be related to increasing oil revenues. Remarkably, the tax relaxation of the 1980s occurred when Ecuador underwent low international oil prices, thus adding another ingredient to the cocktail of the crisis of end of the twentieth century. During the 1990s, tax revenues recovered as a result of the enforcement of SAP dictates, which advocated a weightier tax burden on society[140].

Table No. 18: Average share of tax revenues and oil revenues in total state's income (percent), Ecuador 1971-2015

	Tax revenues (percent)	Oil revenues (percent)
1971-72	77.8	9.4
1973-80	42.2	34.0
1981-90	38.9	39.3
1991-2000	43.9	37.6
2001-10	55.5	29.2
2011-15	52.8	38.3

Source: BCE (2017, 150-155)

---

140 Besides a weightier tax burden, SAP recommended significant cutoffs of subsidies on oil products and electricity for domestic consumption.

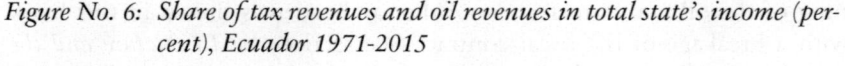

Figure No. 6: *Share of tax revenues and oil revenues in total state's income (percent), Ecuador 1971-2015*

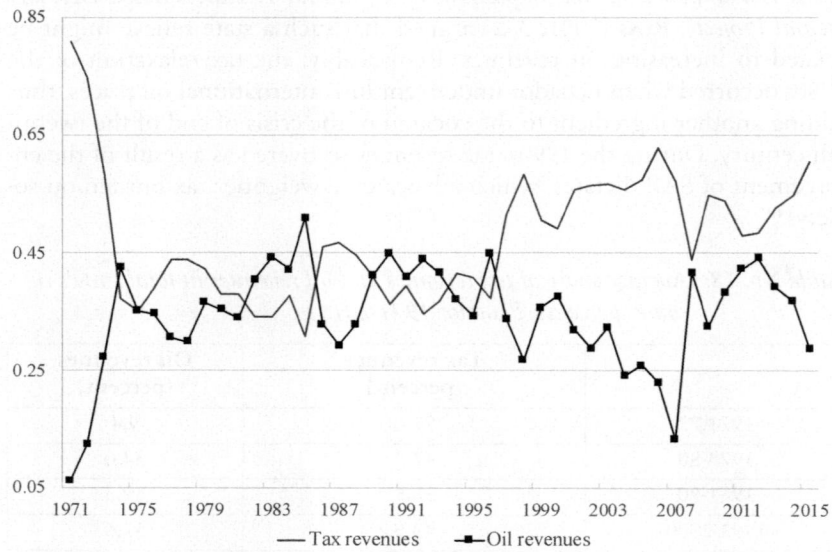

Source: Own diagram based on BCE (2017, 150-155)

The exodus of Ecuadorian nationals to the Global North, which constituted the most notorious human face of the crisis, contributed decisively to sustain the dollarization scheme. Remittances of emigrants[141] reached the historical peak of 8.1 percent of GDP by 2000 (Meireles and Martínez 2013, 90), and together with the improvement of international oil prices experienced from 2003 on (Figure No. 8), massively inoculated fresh petrodollars into the Ecuadorian economy. Thus, the U.S. dollar prevailed as the national currency, but neither as a result of economic planning nor as the outcome of a planned national development model. The Ecuadorian process that led to dollarization epitomized a short-term response to a severe financial crisis, which was enforced overnight by political elites in col-

---

141   It might be discussed if remittances of emigrants should be considered as a type of rent. For the families that stayed, remittances indeed comply with the definition of rent. Though, families in Ecuador received such benefit at the cost of its separation.

lusion with economic elites[142]. Consequences of dollarization on the construction of the Ecuadorian nation have not been sufficiently studied in academic literature. With the exception of Vera's (2013) groundbreaking study, dollarization has been mainly approached from the viewpoint of macroeconomics, which fails to expose the aftereffects of the loss of national currency on society. Within the context of social and political unrest that was prompted by the enforcement of neoliberal policies, during the first year of dollarization, artist collectives in representation of diverse social groups undertook numerous performances, which focused on the relation between the absence of the state and the enforcement of dollarization (Kingman 2012, 180). Figure No. 7 most accurately depicts the sense of state's abandonment left by the loss of national currency.

Figure No. 7: Dollarization and the loss of national currency, Ecuador 2000

Source: Left: Marshal Antonio José de Sucre, independence leader and Bolívar's close ally, on a 1987 five-sucre bill (Pedro Alarcón, personal archive). Right: Poster *"Hasta la vista*, baby" designed by Ana Fernandez (2000) (Trinidad Pérez, personal archive, in Batista 2013, 129)

---

142 For comparison, the planned process of introduction of the Euro as official currency of the European Union took three years from 1999 to 2002.

Overture to the Return of the State: The Recovery of the National Oil Sector

The crisis of the end of the twentieth century was the prelude to the return of the Ecuadorian state. External conditions for the state's comeback were shaped by an increasing trend in international oil prices that began in 2003 (Figure No. 8), i.e. by the beginning of the twenty-first century commodities boom. Figure No. 8 depicts the evolution of the price of the Ecuadorian oil basket[143], in U.S. dollars per oil barrel, for the period of the oil era. By 1972, at the dawn of the oil era, the price of Amazonian oil in international markets was US$ 2.50. Whereas the highest price during the first oil boom was US$ 34.73 in 1980, the peak during the second oil boom (and the historical record) was US$ 98.50 in 2012. Though, after the downfall of international prices that began in 2014, already by 2016 the price of Ecuadorian oil plummeted to US$ 35.25. On the contrary, the lowest prices are to be found during the crisis of the end of the twentieth century, US$ 9.91 in 1988 and US$ 9.14 in 1998 (BCE 2017, 193).

---

143 An oil basket is a weighted average of the prices of different crudes. The Ecuadorian oil basket is determined by a blend of *Crudo Oriente* and *Crudo Napo*. In this book, the blend of *Crudo Oriente* and *Crudo Napo*, both extracted from the Ecuadorian Amazon Region (EAR), is referred to as "Amazonian oil".

Figure No. 8: Prices of Amazonian oil, US$ per barrel, Ecuador 1972-2016

Source: Own diagram based on BCE (2017, 193)

Skyrocketing international oil prices and increasing export volumes due to the operation of the newly inaugurated private pipeline, the *Oleoducto de Crudos Pesados* (OCP), translated into growing state income. Orozco (2012, 44) argued that the extraction of oil jumped from 393,000 barrels per day in 2002 to 526,000 barrels per day in 2004 due to the operation of the OCP. Artola and Pazmiño (2007, 3) assessed the annual growth rate of state's oil revenues at an average of 38.1 percent between 2002 and 2006. The favorable circumstance triggered economic growth. Table No. 19 depicts the annual growth rates of per capita GDP for the period 1981-2017 in order to show the recovery of the Ecuadorian economy after the crisis of the last decades of the twentieth century. Also, Table No. 19 shows an above average growth of the country's per capita GDP (compared to the region's), which coincides with increasing international oil prices.

Table No. 19: Annual growth rates of per capita GDP (percent), Ecuador 1981-2017

	Ecuador	Latin America and the Caribbean
1981-90 at 1980 prices	-6.6	-8.9
1991-2000 at 1995 prices (at 2010 prices)	-0.4 (-0.1)	1.6 (1.4)
2001-10 at 2010 prices	2.4	1.9
2011-17 at 2010 prices	1.8	0.5

Source: CEPALSTAT (2019b); CEPAL (2002, 53); CEPAL (1993, 31)

Parallel to rising oil prices and increasing export volumes began the recovery of the control over the national oil sector, which was dominated by multinational oil corporations that overtook the national oil company in the amount of oil extracted in the Amazon Region since 2003 (Figure No. 12). During the government of President Alfredo Palacio (2005-2007), the National Congress passed the Law 42-2006, a Reformatory Law to the Hydrocarbons Law (Congreso Nacional 2006a). Under the regulations of the law, foreign oil companies were required to pay the Ecuadorian state a 50 percent share of the extraordinary profits or windfall gains, i.e. any revenue in excess due to the difference between the selling price and the price agreed on the contract (Executive Order No. 1583, published in the Supplement II of the Official Gazette No. 302, June 29, 2006; Executive Order No. 1672, published in the Supplement of the Official Gazette No. 312, July 13, 2006). Fresh revenues arising from the enforcement of the law were deposited in an account at the Central Bank (Table No. 20), which amounted US$ 235.1 million by the end of 2006 (Artola and Pazmiño 2007, 4).

On May 2006, Palacio's government cancelled the contract with U.S.-based Occidental Petroleum Corporation (OXY) to drill oil field 15 (Limoncocha, Edén Yuturi, Yanaquincha) after accusing the multinational of transferring 40 percent of its shares to Encana Corporation from Canada without state's authorization[144], thus violating the Hydrocarbons Law. By that time, OXY was Ecuador's largest investor (Reuters 2006) and extracted

---

144 The take-over converged upon the nationalist trend followed by pink tide governments. The contract revocation came short after the Venezuelan Congress passed a law that increased royalties for foreign oil companies and Bolivia's President Evo Morales ordered the military to occupy natural gas fields (Reuters

about one fifth of Ecuador's total oil supply (Orozco 2012, 45). Oil field 15 was taken over by Petroecuador, and the national company was then able to rival multinational corporations in oil extraction in the EAR (Figure No. 12) (BCE 2017, 192). The new state revenues were accumulated in the Energy and Hydrocarbon Investment Fund (*Fondo Ecuatoriano de Inversión en los Sectores Energético e Hidrocarburífero*, FEISEH), which was established by Law 57-2006 (Congreso Nacional 2006b). The fund was earmarked mainly for financing Petroecuador's new duties in field 15 and for energy infrastructure projects, such as hydropower plants and refining facilities[145] (Congreso Nacional 2006b).

As a stabilization fund, the FEISEH was linked to previous contingency mechanisms designed to ensure what neoclassical economists call "expenditure smoothing" in response to movements in commodity prices (Agénor 2004, 107). The Stabilization Fund for Social and Productive Investment and Reduction of Public Debt (*Fondo de Estabilización, Inversión Social y Productiva y Reducción del Endeudamiento Público*, FEIREP) was established in 2002 before the inauguration of the OCP private pipeline in order to accumulate state's revenues arising from the extraction of heavy crude oil undertaken by private companies (e.g. OXY) in the Ecuadorian Amazon Region. Until 2005, the resources of FEIREP were mainly destined to public debt buybacks; only 4 percent of the fund was channeled to social investment (Artola and Pazmiño 2007, 12). In this logic, Orozco (2012, 51) argued that the FEIREP was heavily criticized for being an indirect mechanism to serve external debt. By July 2005, Palacio's government

---

2006). Russia and Chad rounded up the nationalizations occurred in 2006 worldwide. The five countries thereby interrupted the trend of lack of expropriation acts during the period 1986-2005 and gave rise to renewed academic debates on resource nationalism (Arbatli 2018, 101; Pryke 2017; Haslam and Heidrich 2016; Wilson 2015). Though, Manzano and Monadi (2010, 452) argued that during oil booms, contract renegotiation is commonsense and might take many forms independently of the "ideological content of the government [...], as in fact it happened in many other countries, with different ideologies, around the world". In this line, Arbatli (2018, 104) argued that whereas resource nationalism was rooted on ideological and political reasons during the 1970s, pragmatism steered oil policy during the twenty-first century.

145   "The main idea behind the establishment of the fund is that oil revenues are not used to bankroll current spending, or low output spending. Oil revenues should be used to tide the country over the lean years, when oil is cheap (*el tiempo de las vacas flacas*) ... investing in energy infrastructure, big hydropower plants, a new refinery, that was our vision of *sow the oil*" (former adviser to President Alfredo Palacio, interview, September 18, 2015).

replaced the fund by the Special Account for Social and Productive Investment, Scientific Development and Fiscal Stabilization (*Cuenta Especial de Reactivación Productiva y Social, del Desarrollo Científico Tecnológico y de la Estabilización Fiscal*, CEREPS). The main idea was to exert more control over the resources of the fund and to increase social investment[146] (Orozco 2012, 51). Parallel to the creation of the special account, Palacio's government established a saving mechanism, the Savings and Contingency Fund (*Fondo de Ahorro y Contingencias*, FAC), which was nurtured by one fifth of CEREPS resources. The fund was only to be used when 1) actual oil revenue was below budgeted level, or 2) national emergency was declared (Sinnott, Nash, and de la Torre 2010, 74).

Contingency mechanisms (savings and stabilization funds) were outside the government's budget. The predetermined allocation of its resources left the central government little room for maneuver, particularly when the funds were steered by boards that were not akin to the administration. From 2003 (one year after the creation of FEIREP) to 2006, the central government's budget relatively declined vis-à-vis the weight of the contingency mechanisms. Table No. 20 shows that the central government, Petroecuador, and the contingency mechanisms, earmarked for specific purposes, were the main beneficiaries of oil revenues during the period 2003-06. By 2006, 43.4 percent of total oil revenues went to three main funds (FEIREP/ CEREPS, FEISEH, FEP) vis-à-vis 31.6 percent to the central government's budget and 10.8 percent to Petroecuador. The Oil Stabilization Fund (*Fondo de Estabilización Petrolera*, FEP) was established in 1999 in order to accumulate any oil revenues in excess of the budgeted amount. By 2003, resources of the FEP were earmarked as follows: 45 percent for FEIREP, 35 percent for construction and maintenance of roads in the EAR, 10 percent for local development of backward provinces, and 10 percent for the National Police (Almeida, Gallardo, and Tomaselli 2006, 27). Twenty-seven other state's entities shared a small part of oil revenues (row "other" in Table No. 20); among them, the ministries of health and labor, public universities, the Esmeraldas province, the Ecuadorian Housing Bank (BEV), the Central Bank, the State's Bank[147], and the Amazon Development Fund (*Fondo para el Ecodesarrollo Regional Amazónico*, ECORAE). ECORAE was

---

146 By 2006, about 20 percent of the resources of CEREPS was destined to social investment (Artola and Pazmiño 2007, 13).

147 The State's Bank (*Banco del Estado*) was the successor of the *Banco de Desarrollo del Ecuador*, which in turn succeeded FONADE.

first established in 1992 and accumulated US$ 0.10 per barrel of Amazonian oil to be invested in regional development (Congreso Nacional 1992).

Table No. 20: Distribution of oil income (percent), Ecuador 2003-06

	2003	2004	2005	2006
Central government	51.2	33.4	35.5	31.6
FEIREP/CEREPS	5.8	25.9	22.8	16.0
FEISEH	0.0	0.0	0.0	15.9
FEP	15.6	17.6	17.6	11.5
State oil company (PETROECUADOR)	22.4	18.4	14.6	10.8
Law 42-2006	0.0	0.0	0.0	5.2
Other	5.0	4.7	9.5	9.0

Source: Artola and Pazmiño (2007, 6-8)

By 2008, the Constituent Assembly, which summoned after President Correa assumed office in 2007, eliminated the contingency mechanisms (savings and stabilization funds) and almost all other oil-revenue earmarks through the Law of Recovery of State's Oil Resources and Restructuration of Debt Processes (*Ley Orgánica para la Recuperación del Uso de los Recursos Petroleros del Estado y Racionalización Administrativa de los Procesos de Endeudamiento*) (Asamblea Constituyente 2008b). Only ECORAE outlived the law. The fund was hitherto reformed and was granted US$ 1.00 per barrel of oil extracted in the EAR (Congreso Nacional 2008; Asamblea Constituyente 2008b). However, the enforcement of the law put fresh financial resources at the state's disposal and granted the government centralized control over oil income. Only the liquidation of the FEISEH provided the government with extra US$ 2 billion (US$ 1,991.8 million) in 2008 (Orozco 2012, 51). According to Pablo Lucio Paredes, "faith in technocracy" was central to the dismantlement of the stabilization mechanisms (Pablo Lucio Paredes, former member of the Asamblea Constituyente, lecturer at USFQ Ecuador, interview with Dr. Stefan Peters, September 21, 2016).

The journey back to the landlord state, i.e. a state that is able to exert control over the rents produced by the extraction of its national oil, began already during the first year of administration of the fresh-elected government. In November 2007, Ecuador resumed OPEC and sent a strong signal that the renewed struggle with foreign oil companies for a larger portion of oil rent was to be backed by the cartel's strengthened[148] bargaining position (Alarcón 2008, 25). Only a couple of weeks before, President Correa had reformed the regulation of Law 42-2006 in order to increase the state's share in the extraordinary profits of private oil companies from 50 percent to 99 percent (Executive Order No. 662, published in the Official Gazette No. 193, October 18, 2007). The measure remained just good intentions when only two months later, in December 2007, the Constituent Assembly passed the Reformatory Law of Fiscal Equity (*Ley Reformatoria para la Equidad Tributaria en el Ecuador*), which fixed the state's share at 70 percent (Asamblea Constituyente 2007). Though, the "99/1 remained in the peoples' mind due to its media coverage, and contributed to create a social imaginary of an oil-nationalist government" (former adviser to President Alfredo Palacio, interview, September 18, 2015).

Another meaningful measure taken by Correa's government, which reminded of the nationalist direction of the 1970s oil boom, was the involvement of the navy in the national oil sector. The president declared Petroecuador in emergency due to "inefficiency generated by the withdrawal of the state and the loss of its capacities" and ordered the minister of defense to authorize personnel of the navy to serve in the oil company (Executive Order No. 766, published in the Official Gazette No. 231, December 13, 2007). The Ecuadorian Navy participates in the national oil sector since 1972 as owner of the oil tanker fleet (FLOPEC); though from the end of 2007 until the beginning of 2010, the navy controlled all duties of Petroecuador through navy officers, who had been appointed managers or directors of the oil company[149]. In order to sustain the levels of oil extraction of former OXY field 15 (i.e. one fifth of total country's oil extraction), Correa's government established Petroamazonas as part of the Petroecuador holding in 2008 (Executive Order No. 1116, published in the Official Gazette No. 359, June 13, 2008). The main idea behind the creation of Petroamazonas was to ensure the resources needed by the state-owned

---

148 The strengthened bargaining position of OPEC was not only an outcome of skyrocketing oil prices, but also of geopolitical conditions. By 2007, OPEC member states supplied about fifty percent of the oil consumed worldwide and controlled circa three quarters of world's oil reserves (Alarcón 2008, 24-25).

149 By 2000, during the administration of President Gustavo Noboa (2000-2003), the National Congress passed a bill to wean the military from oil revenues (Rohter 2000). Instead, the armed forces were to be bankrolled by the state's budget. The alleged reason was the end of the longstanding border dispute with Peru and the definitive border demarcation of 1998.

company in order to operate as a "private enterprise"[150] (Wilson Pástor, former head of Petroamazonas, interview with Reuters, December 18, 2007). The restructuring of the oil sector (mainly the elimination of the contingency mechanisms) ensured the central government control of a larger portion of oil rent, as the participation of the navy contributed to cement the social imaginary of a nationalist government. Between 2008 and 2010, an average of 66 percent of total oil revenues was put at the central government's disposal (Orozco 2012, 84-85). Such share nearly doubled the average of the oil revenues controlled by the central government between 2003 and 2006 (Table No. 20). Whilst, Petroecuador passed from controlling 17 percent of oil revenues in average during the period 2003-06 (Table No. 20) to 28 percent in average between 2008 and 2010 (Orozco 2012, 84-85). In order to ensure further control over the oil sector, Correa's government reformed the statute of Petroecuador in April 2010. The holding, which was created in 1989, and whose entire shareholding belonged to the Ecuadorian state, was replaced by the public enterprise *Empresa Pública de Hidrocarburos del Ecuador* (EP Petroecuador) (Executive Order No. 315, published in the Official Gazette No. 171, April 14, 2010). Also, Petroamazonas, which was mainly in charge of field 15 since 2008, was renamed *Empresa Pública de Exploración y Explotación de Hidrocarburos* (Petroamazonas EP) (Executive Order No. 314, published in the Official Gazette No. 171, April 14, 2010). With the creation of EP Petroecuador, the navy concluded its service in the oil company.

That same year, the National Assembly passed a reformatory law to the Hydrocarbons Law that aimed at compelling private enterprises to switch from any previous contractual scheme[151] to service contracts exclusively. In service contracts, the total amount of oil is property of the Ecuadorian state, and the companies receive a fixed payment for their service, i.e. for

---

150 The statement of the former head of Petroamazonas and former Minister of Energy and Non-Renewable Natural Resources unveils a social imaginary that reigned during the crisis of the end of the twentieth century and even into the twenty-first century: The "inefficiency" of the state.

151 A preferred contractual scheme between the state and private companies during the previous decades was the participation contract, in which the state owned a fixed share or "participation" in the company's revenues due to the oil extraction. A principal shortcoming of such contract type was that any increase in international oil prices did not mirror in an increase in the state's participation. In existing contracts, since companies were providing the Ecuadorian state the "service" of oil extraction, they were exonerated from the payment of royalties (Bustamante and Zapata 2007, 107-111).

each barrel of oil extracted from the ground. In order to provide private companies with an incentive for switching to service contracts, the reformatory law included 1) the further exoneration from the payment of royalties, and 2) the reduction of companies' income tax from 44.4 percent to 25 percent. The Reformatory Law also established the Secretariat of Hydrocarbons (*Secretaría de Hidrocarburos*) with the duty of administering new contracts (Asamblea Nacional 2010). The reform of the Hydrocarbons Law, which was celebrated by the government as nationalist, was labeled as "clumsy and superficial" (Acosta 2011,97), and even as "contrary to national interests" (Llanes, 2011, 106). In this line, Rosales (2019, 78) argued that the renegotiation of contracts in the Correa administration continued to benefit foreign corporations, despite the nationalist sentiments that originated. Furthermore, as a consequence of the measures enforced by the government between 2007 and 2010 in the oil sector, five foreign companies took legal action against the Ecuadorian state and demanded compensations in the International Centre for Settlement of Investment Disputes (ICSID) (*Centro Internacional de Arreglo de Diferencias Relativas a Inversiones*, CIADI), a World Bank tribunal (Orozco 2012, 90); "this added further controversy to the effectiveness of the reforms undertaken in the oil sector, not to mention the investor's trust... legal processes are long-term, but one might ask how much they will cost the Ecuadorian state... take the OXY case as an example" (Augusto Tandazo, interview, September 18, 2015). In 2006, ICSID required Ecuador to pay OXY a compensation for seizing its assets; despite its nationalistic discourse, the government payed the company circa US$ 1 billion (980 million) in 2016 (Valencia 2016).

However, the stronger participation of the Ecuadorian state in the national oil sector mirrored in an enhanced collection of tax revenues. Table No. 21 aims to depict the increase in tax revenues generated by oil extraction, as percentage of GDP and as percentage of total tax revenues (compare with Figure No 6), for the period 2000-13. By 2011, tax revenues generated by oil extraction peaked at 16.3 percent of GDP (Gómez, Jiménez, and Morán 2015, 44); this performance located Ecuador in a group of Latin American countries, which is considered "highly dependent" on oil-generated fiscal income, with Bolivia, Venezuela and Trinidad and Tobago (Gómez, Jiménez, and Morán 2015, 45).

Table No. 21: Tax revenues generated by oil extraction, Ecuador 2000-13

	As percentage of GDP	As percentage of total tax revenues
2000-03	5.7	29.3
2005-08	8.7	35.3
2010-13	13.4	40.3

Source: Gómez, Jiménez, and Morán (2015, 45)

Alongside with enhanced tax collection, the state's share of oil rent grew to 69.3 percent for the period 2010-13[152]. Such a high participation in total oil surplus was used by the government to bankroll 30 percent or more of public social spending (Gómez, Jiménez, and Morán 2015, 45). According to CEPALSTAT (2019c), social expenditure is defined as the resources allocated to 1) environmental protection, 2) housing and community amenities, 3) health, 4) recreation, culture, and religion, 5) education, and 6) social protection. Table No. 22 aims to depict the increase in central government public social spending (as a percentage of GDP) parallel to the appropriation of a larger portion of oil rent for the period 1990-2016. It is to note that despite the state's larger participation in oil revenues, public social spending did not outstrip the region's average. Particularly during the 1990s, and during the aftermath of the crisis into the twenty-first century, public social spending in Ecuador was relatively low in comparison with Latin America (CEPAL 2016, 64).

Table No. 22: Central government public social spending as percentage of GDP (average), Ecuador 1990-2016

	Ecuador	Latin America
1990	2.7	n.a.
1991-95	2.8	n.a.
1996-2000	4.8	n.a.
2001-05	3.9	8.8
2006-10	6.7	9.7

---

152 For comparison, the state's share of oil rent in Venezuela amounted 36.2 percent, in Trinidad and Tobago 38.4 percent, in Mexico 67.7 percent, and in Bolivia 73.6 percent during the same period (Gómez, Jiménez, and Morán 2015, 45).

	Ecuador	Latin America
2011-15	8.7	10.7
2016	9.3	11.2

Source: CEPALSTAT (2019c); CEPAL (2019, 112)

Nonetheless, increasing allocation of oil rent to social expenditure might speak for state's enhanced relative autonomy from dominant social classes. This, in turn, recalls the "Poulantzas' reformulation" of the developmental state theory, which is related in this book to the state's option of carrying out a national developmental project as "the politics of the political elites or the politics of the bureaucracy". In absence of contingency or earmarking mechanisms, the larger portion of oil rent seized by the state was channeled to different socioeconomic sectors by the central government; such allocation scheme meant the ultimate return of the landlord-arbiter state configuration. In order to manage the new oil wealth, Correa's government undertook reforms of the executive function that resulted in the creation of 21 new state entities until 2009 (seven ministries of coordination, five sectorial ministries, two national secretariats, and seven state's or technical secretariats[153]). These new entities added to the already existing 16 sectorial ministries. By 2013, a further reform incorporated two national secretariats and eliminated two ministries of coordination and three technical secretariats (Freidenberg and Pachano 2016, 111)[154]. All in all, in ten years of administration, Correa's government created at least 50 new state entities (ministries of coordination, sectorial ministries, national secretariats, technical secretariats, public enterprises, agencies, councils, research institutes) (Hurtado 2017, 489; Tibán 2018).

A meaningful epitome of the return of the faith in centralized economic planning was the creation of the new National Secretariat of Planning and Development (*Secretaría Nacional de Planificación y Desarrollo*, SENPLADES) out of the fusion of the National Council of Modernization of the State (CONAM) and the old SENPLADES, an office within the presidency, which was established in 2004 (Executive Order No. 103, published

---

153 Among the new nine secretariats was the *Secretaría del Buen Vivir*. For comparison, Germany has 15 ministries, including the Federal Chancellery (*Bundeskanzleramt*) (Matthes 2019, 178).

154 President Lenín Moreno (2017-2021) dismantled the ministries of coordination during his very first day in office (Executive Order No. 7, May 24, 2017). This and other shutdowns of state entities added to several measures enforced by Moreno to take distance from his predecessor.

in the Official Gazette No. 26, February 22, 2007). The new secretariat was meant to prioritize national and local development projects through neutral techno-economic tools, thus granting the state's developmental endeavor an apolitical appearance. Though, just as in Ferguson's (1994) "anti-politics machine"[155], the task of SENPLADES was imprinted by politics from the very first day on, only the elimination of CONAM meant a blatant political measure directed to break with the previous planning scheme, which prevailed during the crisis of the end of the twentieth century. The central government-based allocation scheme and the alleged technocratic prioritization of development projects resulted in an overall boost of physical infrastructure (Table No. 23). As during the first oil boom, particularly relevant was the construction of roads, which was comparable with the total amount of investments in social infrastructure. The domestic energy sector (like in the first oil boom) was meant to become a main beneficiary of the provision of infrastructure. At least seven hydropower plants, including 1,500 MW Coca Codo Sinclair (the nowadays biggest single plant, inaugurated in 2016), were meant to become the masterpiece in the expansion of the country's electricity supply[156]. The *Refinería del Pacífico*, was meant to be constructed by a joint venture between Petroecuador and Venezuelan national PdVSA (*Petróleos de Venezuela S.A.*). The refinery was declared a national priority at the beginning of Correa's government, its inauguration was planned for 2017 (Arias 2014, 36). Despite an outlay amounted to over US$ 1.5 billion, the construction of the refinery never begun[157] (Pacheco 2019).

---

155 In *The Anti-Politics Machine. "Development", Depoliticization, and Bureaucratic Power in Lesotho*, Ferguson (1994) argues that development projects are "sold" in underdeveloped countries "under cover of neutral, technical missions to which no one can object" (Ferguson 1994, 256). Though, the author argued, they have profound implications in politicizing the state and poverty.

156 The Coca Codo Sinclair hydropower plant was built by China-based Synohidro Corporation. The construction was bankrolled by a Chinese loan of US$ 1,682 million. Chinese funding bankrolled at least other eight energy projects (hydropower and wind energy) until 2016 for further US$ 1,500 million (Zapata, Castro, and Benzi 2018, 15). According to Villavicencio (2014, 277), the government's plan of induction stoves (*cocinas de inducción*), which consisted in replacing domestic gas by electricity for cooking, responded rather to the need of justifying overinvestment in the energy sector, rather than to the country's demand of electricity. The plan *cocinas de inducción* did not succeed and was cancelled by Lenín Moreno's government.

157 In August 2017, President Lenín Moreno declared that the project was to continue exclusively with private investment. In January 2018, 21 foreign investors visited the project and questioned basic conditions, e.g. the location, which was

Table No. 23: Sectorial composition of public investment (percent), Ecuador
             2008-13

	2008	2009	2010	2011	2012	2013
Production sectors	**6.0**	**11.0**	**4.0**	**3.0**	**3.0**	**2.0**
Agriculture	6.0	11.0	4.0	3.0	3.0	2.0
Natural resources	**n.a.**	**3.0**	**19.0**	**18.0**	**20.0**	**23.0**
Petroleum and electricity	n.a.	3.0	19.0	18.0	20.0	23.0
Physical infrastructure	**27.0**	**45.0**	**30.0**	**24.0**	**22.0**	**26.0**
Roads	27.0	45.0	30.0	24.0	22.0	26.0
Social infrastructure	**52.0**	**28.0**	**29.0**	**34.0**	**29.0**	**31.0**
Urban equipment	23.0	6.0	6.0	5.0	8.0	12.0
Social welfare	6.0	8.0	8.0	7.0	4.0	3.0
Health	8.0	3.0	6.0	6.0	7.0	4.0
Education	15.0	11.0	9.0	16.0	10.0	12.0
Other sectors	**15.0**	**12. 0**	**18.0**	**21.0**	**25.0**	**18.0**
Internal affairs	n.a.	2.0	2.0	3.0	7.0	4.0
Central administration	2.0	2.0	9.0	9.0	7.0	6.0
National defense	2.0	3.0	2.0	5.0	4.0	n.a.
Environmental protection	3.0	n.a.	n.a.	n.a.	n.a.	n.a.
Other investments	8.0	5.0	5.0	4.0	7.0	8.0

Source: Gachet and Carrión (2014, 64)

In order to channel oil rent to territories influenced by the exploitation of non-renewable natural resources, e.g. the Amazon region and the Esmeraldas province, Correa's government established the public company of local development Ecuador Estratégico (*Empresa Pública de Desarrollo Estratégico Ecuador Estratégico EP*) in 2011. A main duty of Ecuador Estratégico was to provide infrastructure and community amenities[158] to backward regions

---

allegedly to far from the coast. By the beginning of 2019, President Moreno cancelled the project (Pacheco 2019).

158 The objectives of Ecuador Estratégico changed throughout time. By 2015, the president required the company to build health and education infrastructure, as well as police stations (Executive Order No. 753, published in the Official Gazette No. 573, August 26, 2015). Since 2016, Ecuador Estratégico is assigned to support the post-earthquake reconstruction process (Executive Order No. 1004, published in the Official Gazette No. 760, May 23, 2016). The magnitude 7.8 earthquake of April 2016 mostly affected the provinces of Manabí and Es-

(Executive Order No. 870, published in the Official Gazette No. 534, September 14, 2011). The principal source of the company's funding was the 12 percent of the profit of private oil companies (Executive Order No. 1135, published in the Supplement of the Official Gazette No. 699, May 9, 2012). According to a former head of Ecuador Estratégico in the Sucumbíos Province, such funding was mainly used in education infrastructure, health infrastructure, urban equipment, and electricity supply. The provision of infrastructure was "not free of conflict with local governments", since the public company intersected their competences[159] (Ángel Sallo, former head of Ecuador Estratégico in Sucumbíos, interview with Dr. Stefan Peters, September 18, 2015). Until 2015, the bulk of the investments of Ecuador Estratégico was channeled to education infrastructure, mainly to the construction of the so-called Millennial Educational Units (*Unidades Educativas del Milenio*), i.e. schools in backward territories (Pablo Ortiz, former General Manager of Ecuador Estratégico, interview with Dr. Stefan Peters, September 8, 2015). Widespread criticism of Ecuador Estratégico denounced that the company delivered infrastructure in conflict-prone territories in order to dampen opposition to extractivism. Besides, specific criticism of the *Unidades Educativas del Milenio* denounced that 1) the schools were regarded as a "recompense" for natural resources extraction, and 2) new schools were built without participation of locals in educational planning as old community schools were dismantled (Ivette Vallejo, lecturer at FLACSO Ecuador, interview with Dr. Stefan Peters, September 22, 2015).

Nevertheless, state's recovery of the national oil sector, which indeed served public social spending, was not accompanied by a long-term oil pol-

---

meraldas. The liquidation of Ecuador Estratégico is expected on 2021 (Tapia 2018).

159 According to a former General Manager of Ecuador Estratégico, the duties of the company have "nothing to do with *asistencialismo*", they rather have to do with bringing state benefits to backward regions (Pablo Ortiz, former General Manager of Ecuador Estratégico, interview with Dr. Stefan Peters, September 8, 2015). During the crisis of the end of the twentieth century, and particularly during the 1990s, when the state's absence from key economic and social arenas became palpable, private oil companies provided remote villages in the Amazon region with infrastructure and community amenities, "local leaders bargained with foreign oil companies, with their corporate social responsibility units, to become what they called *proyectos*, mainly infrastructure, for example, a soccer field, a pickup truck, school facilities, in exchange for preventing disturbances or local's demonstrations against extractivism" (Synneva Geithus Laastad, interview, December 6, 2018).

icy aimed at getting around the risks of international price volatility and ensuring the sustainability of the oil sector (Villavicencio 2014, 272). Conventional oil policy generally entails two main components, 1) increasing oil extraction, and 2) at least maintaining (if not increasing) reserve levels through exploration of new oil fields. Table No. 24 shows the volume of oil extraction for the period 2002-16; besides the 30 percent increase observed between 2002 and 2004 due to the beginning of operations of the private pipeline OCP in 2003, there is no significant variation in the further levels of extraction. According to Villavicencio (2014, 270), the number of exploration wells drilled between 2000 and 2012 dramatically decreased, and thus no new oil reserves were confirmed. These facts speak for the failure of conventional oil policy. The failure of non-conventional oil policy, epitomized in the Yasuní-ITT initiative and the idea of "leaving oil under the ground" is approached in the section *Nature and the State: The Polyphonic Concept of* Buen Vivir.

Table No. 24: Volume of extraction of oil, thousands of barrels, Ecuador 2002-16

	Extraction of oil (thousands of barrels)
2002	143,121
2004	192,383
2006	195,651
2008	184,728
2010	177,422
2012	184,323
2014	203,142
2016	200,711

Source: BCE (2017, 192)

The State and Development: Amazonian Oil and the Rentier National Construction

The consequence of the stagnation of the oil sector is dependence on imports of oil products. Figure No. 9 depicts the skyrocketing increase in imports of oil products, which jumped from 2.1 million barrels in 1978, the first year of operations of the *Refinería Estatal de Esmeraldas*, to the historical peak of 57.1 million in 2014. The bulk of the imports has been tradi-tionally composed by diesel, gasoline, and domestic gas (liquefied petroleum gas, LPG), which are broadly used by households; in public transportation[160] (diesel), in family cars (gasoline), and in cooking (LPG). Despite widespread consensus among high-ranking government officials about the "economic distortions introduced by fuel imports", subsidies have been maintained since the first oil boom due to the "potential high political cost of their elimination" (Luis Manzano, interview, January 23, 2019).

Table No. 25 shows the average imports of oil products for the period 1981-2016. Remarkably, the amount of oil products imported during the first decade of the twenty-first century tripled the imports of the previous decade. A significant example of the country's dependence on imports of oil products is gasoline. In absence of sufficient domestic refining capacity, the Ecuadorian state imported 10 percent of the country's demand in 2000; by 2015 imported gasoline amounted to 70 percent of domestic demand (Espinoza and Guayanlema 2017, 7). Like other oil products (e.g. diesel and LPG[161]), the Ecuadorian state purchases gasoline at international prices and markets it domestically at a fixed subsidized price; with about US$ 0.49 per liter, gasoline in Ecuador is the second cheapest in South America[162] (GlobalPetrolPrices 2020).

---

160 The public transportation fare in Quito has remained unchanged since 2003 at US$ 0.25.

161 Imports of diesel jumped from 17 percent of the total domestic demand in 2000 to 69 percent in 2015, and of LPG from 60 to 87 percent (Espinoza and Guayan-lema 2017, 7).

162 The world's cheapest gasoline is found in Venezuela (less than US$ 0.01 per liter). For comparison a liter gasoline costs US$ 0.54 in Bolivia and US$ 1.53 in Germany (La Razón 2019). Liquefied petroleum gas (LPG) for cooking consti-tutes another significant example of a subsidy that benefits households. The 15 kg-cylinder is marketed domestically at a fixed price of US$ 1.60; the Ecuadori-an state pays at least ten times more for the same amount of LPG in internation-al markets.

Figure No. 9: Imports of oil products, thousands of barrels, Ecuador 1978-2016

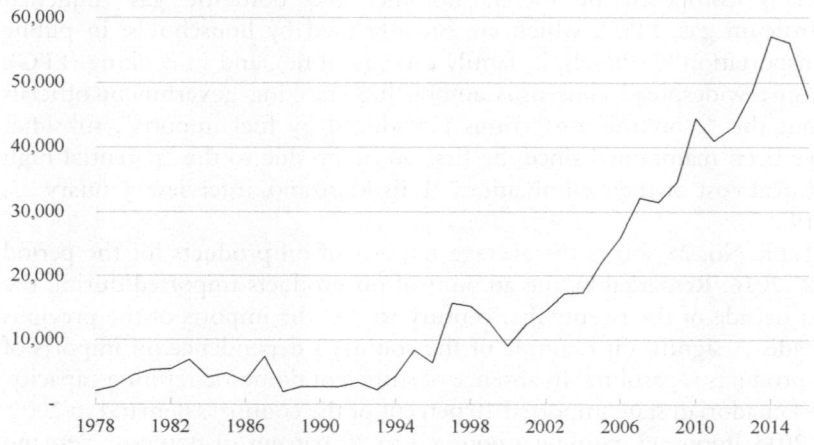

Source: Own diagram based on BCE (2017, 197)

Table No. 25: Average imports of oil products, thousands of barrels per year, Ecuador 1981-2016

	Imports of oil products (thousands of barrels per year)
1981-90	4,529
1991-2000	8,078
2001-10	25,256
2011-16	48,821

Source: BCE (2017, 197)

Hence, the state's expenditure in subsidizing oil products for domestic consumption is astronomical (Table No. 26); the cost of importing oil products (gasoline, LPG, and diesel) jumped from circa 1.7 percent of GDP by the beginning of the twenty-first century to 5.4 percent of GDP during the period 2011-15 (Table No. 26). Currently, subventions on oil products constitute by far the largest subsidy granted by the state. By 2010, 55 percent of all state subsidies were subventions on oil products (Orozco 2012, 87); the cost of all subsidies, which included newly introduced financial assistance programs, amounted to 7.3 percent of GDP (MCPE 2012,

52)[163]. For comparison, that same year, public expenditure of the central government in education and health amounted 4.1 and 1.5 percent of GDP, respectively (CEPALSTAT 2019c).

Table No. 26: Imports of oil products as percentage of GDP (average) and value, Ecuador 2001-15

	Imports of oil products (percentage of GDP)	Imports of oil products (billions of US$)
2001-05	1.7	n.a.
2006-10	4.6	13.35
2011-15	5.4	24.54

Source: Espinoza and Guayanlema (2017, 13-17)

Subsidies on oil products for domestic consumption unveil an unequal distribution of oil rent. Whereas upper and middle classes, as owners of one or more family cars, benefit from a larger portion of the oil rent entailed in the subsidy on gasoline, lower classes benefit from a smaller portion of oil rent entailed in the subsidy on diesel for public transportation[164]. Figure No. 10 aims to depict the booming fleet of motor vehicles in Ecuador. Whereas by the beginning of the century about 19 thousand new motor vehicles were introduced (assembled domestically and imported), by 2011, during the second Ecuadorian oil boom, about 140 thousand new motor vehicles were sold. Circa 70 percent of the new motor vehicles were sold in the cities of Quito and Guayaquil[165] (AEADE 2019, 48). At least three quarters of the new vehicles introduced to the Ecuadorian market serve as private cars in families, who benefit from the swollen subsidy on gasoline.

---

163 For comparison, the cost of all subsidies granted by the state in 2006 amounted to 4.8 percent of GDP (MCPE 2012, 52).

164 Parsing the problems associated with the consumption of fossil fuels in Quito, Alarcón (2011) drew attention to the environmental inequalities linked to this kind of subsidies. Owners of private cars (which are used practically as individual cars in Quito) are responsible for a larger portion of emissions of global and local contaminants to the atmosphere.

165 Since the bulk of the new vehicles introduced to the Ecuadorian market is composed by family cars, local sales of motor vehicles might serve as a barometer of final household consumption expenditure. Remarkably, whereas during the bonanza period, the number of motor vehicles sold followed an increasing trend, after the decline of international oil prices in 2014, the number of motor vehicles sold dipped.

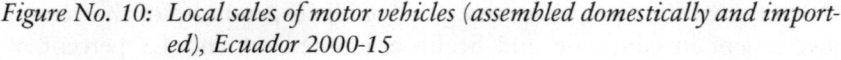

Figure No. 10: Local sales of motor vehicles (assembled domestically and imported), Ecuador 2000-15

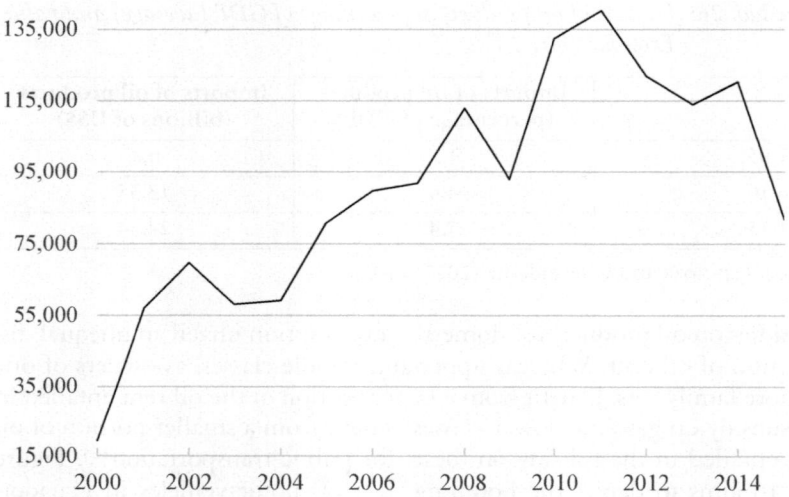

Source: Own diagram based on AEADE (2019, 48)

Besides subsidies, other meaningful components of financial assistance granted by the state are social security and retirement pensions. These forms of rent transfer to society amounted to 20 percent of total subsidies in 2010 (MCPE 2012, 52). According to Gachet et al. (2017, 342), between 2005 and 2015, the amount paid for social security and retirement pensions increased as well as the number of beneficiaries. In 2009, the Bank of the Social Security Institute (*Banco del Instituto Ecuatoriano de Seguridad Social*, BIESS) was established (Asamblea Nacional 2009); between October 2010 and December 2015, the bank channeled state resources amounted to circa US$ 5.6 billion (US$ 5,583 million) through mortgage loans to about 130,000 households (El Telégrafo, February 11, 2016). A further 15 percent of all subsidies in 2010 corresponded to other "traditional" mechanism of financial assistance, particularly the Human Development Grant (*Bono de Desarrollo Humano*), a cash transfer program established in 1998 to support lower classes during the crisis of the end of the twentieth century. Until 2005, the monthly grant amounted to US$ 15; it was raised to US$ 30 in 2007, to US$ 35 in 2009, and finally to US$ 50 in 2013 during Correa's re-election campaign (Matthes 2019, 162). The number of beneficiaries increased significantly between 2007 and 2013, after that, it shrunk (Gachet et al. 2017, 342). The set of subsidies completed in 2010 with newly introduced financial assistance mechanisms aimed at supporting lower income and disadvantaged groups as well as small agricultural enterprises. Further subsidies on electricity (e.g. for elderly citizens and low consumption households), the program Joaquín Gallegos Lara destined to disabled persons and its families, subsidies on agricultural inputs (e.g. urea), and subsidized credits up to US$ 5,000 for small farmers counted among new financial assistance mechanisms introduced by Correa's government (Orozco 2012, 88). The wider coverage of subsidies among society not only reinforced the social imaginary of the presence of a strong landlord-arbiter state, but also "legitimated the government by popular and political support" (Gudynas 2012, 134). Subsidies were central to gain popular backing for state's enhanced natural resources extraction[166] (Gudynas 2012, 136) and to mobilize lower classes in favor of governmental decision-making. Hence, a larger number of beneficiaries of subsidies granted by the state might be correlated with the enhancement of clientelistic networks[167].

However, in the same way as during the first oil boom, an utmost effective way to channel state's resources to middle classes was the creation of employment opportunities in the public sector with corresponding pay raises. Orozco (2012, 85) argued that the number of public servants in 2010 was about 496 thousand, circa 65 percent more than in 2001; for the author, the rate of growth in the number of public servants between 2009 and 2010 was ten times larger than that between 2002 and 2008. In this line, Ospina (2013, 236) estimated 98,784 new hires between December 2006 and December 2010. Though, Correa's government launched an offensive against unionization in the public sector in particular, and in general, unionization was subject of co-optation. However, the bulk of new public servants during the second oil boom was non-tenured, i.e. hired by

---

166 For Gudynas (2012, 144), cash transfers indeed allude to social re-distributive justice; though, as the economic dimension of justice is highlighted, other dimensions, such as environmental justice and representation and participation are veiled.

167 Other more "refined" mechanisms of ensuring society's support for governmental decisions might be also mentioned. During Correa's government, the financial crisis (*crisis bancaria*) of 1999 was revived. A commission was established with the duty of investigating the *feriado bancario* in order to determine responsibilities (Executive Order No. 263, published in the Official Gazette No. 67, April 19, 2007). Such measure appealed to the memory of the middle classes and even to the people's feelings.

contract. According to Orozco (2012, 85), whereas about 3 thousand public servants were hired by contract in 2001, circa 110 thousand new public servants were non-tenured by 2010; 80 percent of these persons worked for the central government in the new and old ministries and state's entities in the sectors of 1) education, 2) defense, 3) internal affairs, and 4) public health (Orozco 2012, 86). "Consultants [*consultores*]…, consulting professionals and consulting companies were commonsense in the ministries, with six-months-, one-year-contracts. Together with state contractors working in infrastructure, they created the illusion of a booming private sector besides the booming public sector" (former consultant at SENPLADES, interview, March 16, 2017).

With the state pouring oil rent into society, the majority of the population benefited asymmetrically, as during the first oil boom. Between 2006 and 2014 per capita GNI doubled from US$ 3,110 to US$ 6,276 (Cypher and Alfaro 2016, 168). The minimum wage steadily increased from 2001 on, together with the remunerations of public servants; by 2016, the minimum wage reached US$ 426.9 (BCE 2017, 178). Household final consumption expenditure grew at an annual average rate of 4 percent between 2003 and 2014, the period of the second oil boom (compared to 8 percent during the first oil boom) (World Bank 2019b). Besides, enrollment in tertiary education outstripped levels of the previous oil boom (compared to the peak of 34.1 percent in 1981); after dipping below 20 percent during the crisis of the end of the twentieth century, the gross enrollment ratio in tertiary education surpassed 40 percent by 2013 (World Bank 2019g), which means that about two out of five persons of the age group that officially corresponds to the tertiary level was actually enrolled in that year. Table No. 27 aims to depict the beneficiaries of the second Ecuadorian oil boom. According to Gachet et al. (2017, 330), economic growth generated by the oil bonanza was the main responsible for the "rise of the middle class", whose population share[168] doubled from 18.6 percent to 37.4 percent during the period 2005-15. Consistent with this improvement was the

---

168 Gachet et al. (2017, 331) adopt a rather orthodox "economic view and identify the middle class based on household per capita income". This narrow definition converges upon the broader approach proposed in this book, in which a social class is regarded as "a way of talking about the interconnections between people's individual attributes and their material conditions of life" (Wright 2009, 102). In order to understand middle classes, this book highlights the access to higher education as the key individual attribute (Wright 2009, 13), on the one hand. On the other hand, people's opportunities and choices in a market economy are epitomized by their "market capacities" (Wright 1996, 694). Hence, mid-

decline of the disadvantaged stratum, whose population share dropped 26 points from 46.3 percent in 2005 to 19.8 in 2015. Though, the other side of the coin (i.e. the bad news) was the growth of the "vulnerable" layer[169] (Table No. 27).

Table No. 27: Share in total income by population strata (percent), Ecuador 2005-15

Population strata	Share in total income (Share in total population)					
	2005	**2007**	**2009**	**2011**	**2013**	**2015**
Disadvantaged	13.1 (46.3)	9.6 (38.4)	9.8 (35.5)	6.5 (26.4)	5.1 (22.2)	4.2 (19.8)
Vulnerable	27.8 (33.9)	24.9 (36.6)	29.5 (40.1)	26.6 (41.2)	23.6 (41.4)	22.7 (40.8)
Middle	45.1 (18.6)	47.2 (23.2)	49.0 (23.2)	56.6 (31.0)	55.5 (34.2)	58.7 (37.4)
Upper	14.1 (1.3)	18.4 (1.8)	11.8 (1.2)	10.2 (1.4)	15.8 (2.1)	14.5 (2.0)

Source: Gachet et al. (2017, 335)

Pioneering in the study undertaken by Gachet et al. (2017) is the inclusion of the vulnerable stratum understood as the share of the population with a "larger-than-10-percent probability of falling into poverty" (Gachet el al. 2017, 332). Thus, the vulnerable stratum draws attention to the permanence of the social achievements reaped during the second Ecuadorian oil boom. According to Gachet et al. (2017, 330), "the rise of the middle class is likely to be ephemeral as it was dependent on the oil boom and the specific dynamics that were in play during the period analyzed". Otherwise, an analysis of the growth of the upper strata during the second oil boom, and particularly during Correa's government, is beyond the scope of this

---

dle classes are identified as the portion of the population, "who have enough education and money to participate fully in some vaguely defined mainstream way of life (which might include particular consumption patterns)" (Wright 2009, 103).

169 For the authors, households in the middle class have a daily income per capita of at least US$ 10 and less than US$ 50, and in the vulnerable strata a daily income between US$4 and US$ 10 (2005 US$) (Gachet et al. 2017, 333).

book[170]. Though, according to CEPALSTAT (2019d), the Gini coefficient, as a measure of income inequality, improved during the second Ecuadorian oil boom from 0.513 in 2004 to 0.452 in 2014. These values outstripped the average performance of the Latin American region, which improved from 0.547 in 2002 to 0.491 in 2014.

The other side of the coin of expanding middle classes and reduction of inequality during the second oil boom was, as during the first oil boom, growing dependence on 1) imports of consumer goods, which nearly tripled (in thousands of US$) between 2003 and the historical peak of 2014 (BCE 2017, 119), and on 2) internationally borrowed funds. Total debt doubled between 2003 and 2016 (BCE 2017, 131-132), as external debt decreased as percentage of gross national income (GNI) from 64.5 percent to 35.8 during the same period (World Bank 2019a). Though, different from the first oil boom, 1) increasing demand for imported consumer goods took place within the framework of a growing balance of payments deficit (Calderón and Stumpo 2016, 15; Meireles and Martínez 2013, 91; Orozco 2012, 55), and 2) Correa's government bargained credits with foreign oil companies (Chinese companies PetroChina Co. Ltd. and Sinopec Corp., and Thailand's state-run PTT) in exchange of presale orders of Amazonian oil since 2009. As a result, Asian oil companies take a large part of Ecuadorian crude exports as debt agreements that are repaid with oil (Orozco 2018; Valencia 2017; Valencia 2015). Biddings were conducted in secrecy; this, added to the volatile nature of international oil prices might have caused underestimation of the country's external debt.

First, the Ecuadorian balance of payments has been deteriorating since 2009 (Calderón and Stumpo 2016, 15) despite high international oil prices. According to Calderón and Stumpo (2016, 15), the balance of payments' current account dropped from a surplus of 2.4 percent of GDP for the period 2005-09 to a deficit of 1.1 percent of GDP for the period 2010-15. Since the main component of the Ecuadorian balance of payments' current account is its balance of trade (which registers the country's exports versus its imports), a deficit in the current account is related to an increasing expenditure in imports. By 2015, the deficit in the balance of trade peaked at US $ 2.1 billion (US$ 2,116 million) (BCE 2017, 109), and counted as the main component of the current account's total deficit of US$ 2.2 billion

---

170 Prosperity of economic elites and further concentration of wealth seem to be a constant in Latin America during the youngest oil boom. *Progresista* governments were unable or unwilling to break the trend effectively (Peters 2019, 179).

(or 2.2 percent of GDP) (Calderón and Stumpo 2016, 15). To cope with the problem, Correa's government imposed a tariff on imports in March 2015. The tariff was imposed on about one third of all imported goods, and charged consumer goods (such as televisions) up to 45 percent *ad valorem* (Calderón 2016, 113; Domínguez and Caria 2016, 104; El Comercio, March 6, 2015). Until February 2017, when the protectionist measure ended[171], the revenue collected by the state was about US$ 1.5 billion (Revista Líderes, May 31, 2017), a value below the 2015 deficit. Though, the imposition of tariffs did not stop consumption addiction. Between October 2010 and December 2015, only the state's Bank of the Social Security Institute (BIESS) provided about 6.5 million consumption credits (*préstamos quirografarios*) amounted to circa US$ 7.7 billion (compare with US$ 5.6 billion in mortgage loans provided during the same period) (El Telégrafo, February 11, 2016). The elimination of extra imports tariffs in February 2017 and the entering into force of the free trade agreement with the European Union in January 2017 (which mirrored in less tariffs and hence cheapened imported goods) boosted the demand for consumption credits[172] (El Comercio, May 26, 2018). Between January and November 2017, the BIESS provided loans for consumption amounted to circa US$ 2.1 billion (González 2018).

Second, consumption addiction (particularly of imported consumer goods) grew parallel to the government's greed for fresh petrodollars. By 2017, Correa's government oversold Amazonian oil. After clinching oil-for-loans deals with Chinese oil companies since 2009, which significantly reduced the country's exports stocks[173], Correa's government signed an oil supply deal with Thailand's state-run PTT. As a part of the agreement, Ecuador had to deliver 124 million barrels of oil in 2017, which the country did not totaled anymore (Orozco 2018). Unfavorable contracts with

---

171 The duration of protectionist measures, like tariffs, is determined by the treaties on free trade to which Ecuador is signatory. As mentioned before, the WTO (at global level), and the CAN (at regional level) promote free trade, i.e. the elimination of import tariffs.

172 Booming demand for consumption credits in 2017 might also be related to increasing unemployment (González 2018). As mentioned before, by 2017, the newly elected President Lenín Moreno began his administration dismantling a series of state entities created during Correa's government (e.g. the ministries of coordination).

173 In rough numbers, Ecuador extracts about 200 million barrels of oil per year. Since circa one quarter of that amount is destined to the local refinery, three quarters, i.e. about 150 million barrels of oil constitute the country's exports stocks.

foreign companies that precluded the state from benefiting from its natural resources (Valencia 2017), together with 1) pending legal actions taken by multinational oil corporations against the Ecuadorian state in international courts as the International Centre for Settlement of Investment Disputes (ICSID), 2) the Chinese dominance in energy projects, and 3) the failure in the conventional oil policy (section *Overture to the Return of the State: The Recovery of the National Oil Sector* approached these three issues) remind of a state class acting as a "comprador bourgeoisie" (Amin 1990) in favor of foreign interests. These, added to the rumors of Ecuador's withdrawal from OPEC[174] by 2020, in turn, might speak for an ongoing (re-)denationalization of the oil sector.

However, the amount of beneficiaries of the capitalist system increased as an outcome of the state's recovery of a larger portion of oil rent during the second Ecuadorian oil boom (Table No. 27). The strong presence of the state in the economic arena boosted the ongoing modernization process as the construction of the rentier state gained momentum. Remarkably, the Ecuadorian rentier state configuration assimilates the characteristics of what Amin (1990) called the "bourgeois state". According to the author, the bourgeois state has two main characteristics, 1) it is a suitable partner in the world capitalist system, and 2) it is pursued by the local hegemonic class throughout the contemporary Third World, i.e. the bourgeoisie in power (Amin 1990, 15). It might be argued that he role of the "bourgeoisie in power" is played by the Ecuadorian state class, which held high positions in government and public entities during the long second oil boom. Hence, the rentier national construction in Ecuador had a twofold nature that neared it to a bourgeois state configuration. *First*, increasing levels of household final consumption expenditure, enrollment in tertiary education, and, particularly, booming imports of consumer goods speak for a strengthened integration of middle classes into the dynamics of the capitalist world system through "market capacities" (Wright 1996, 694). As during the first oil boom, the strengthening and consolidation of middle classes lacked in class consciousness; instead, expanding middle classes try to imitate the middle classes of the Global North and their mate-

---

174 During the closure of this book, rumors confirmed and "Ecuador is to leave OPEC by January 1st, 2020". According to the Ministry of Non-Renewable Resources, the measure "aims at reducing public spending and generating new income" (El Universo, October 1, 2019). The purpose of "generating new income" reminds of Ecuador's previous withdrawal from the cartel during the crisis of the end of the twentieth century.

rial consumption levels (as during the first oil boom they mimicked the decaying *latifundista* oligarchy). *Second*, the belief that the process of building a bourgeois state "does not demand popular initiative in the first place, but merely popular support for state actions" (Amin 1990, 15). The lack of *participation* of lower classes and, instead, its *mobilization* in favor of state or government measures not only unveils their subsidiary role in the construction of the bourgeois state, but also signalizes the ultimate departure of the national project from any possible popular construction.

Development and Nature: The Resource Curse Revisited

Aggregate demand boosted by available petrodollars (due to high international oil prices and galloping external debt) further mirrored in a swollen tertiary sector (Table No. 28); though, resembling the first oil boom, Correa's government announced the intention of supporting other sectors of the economy. The idea of "sow the oil", which was translated into a state-led industrialization endeavor during General Rodríguez Lara's "revolutionary nationalist" government, was revived[175] by the "citizen's revolution". Indeed, Domínguez and Caria (2016, 104) argued that the industrial policy during the second oil boom aimed mainly at replicating the ISI scheme of incentives (without penalizations) of the 1970s but its enforcement mirrored in "disappointing results in the non-oil balance of payments". However, an approach to "classic" industrialization (i.e. a boost to the manufacturing sector), as it was understood during the ISI consensus, was highly unlikely during the epoch of the *consenso de los* commodities.

---

175 Andrade (2015, 12) argued that industrial policy was "abandoned" during the last decades of the twentieth century. According to the perspective of this book, the abandonment of industrial policy by successive governments added up to the "internal circumstance" during the crisis of the end of the twentieth century. The "external constraints" were shaped mainly by international low commodities' prices within the new governance scheme of economic globalization. Internal circumstance and external constraints mirrored in the diversification of the portfolio of natural resources exports (Table No. 14). Andrade (2015, 12) also argued that the abandonment of industrial policy had "high costs"; deindustrialization provoked unemployment and the dismantling of unions: "without industry, the material and political space for the workers class formation disappeared and other social actors emerged taking its place". The argument is consistent with the rise of the indigenous movement and the environmental movement, which had an increasing influence on Ecuadorian politics since the last decades of the twentieth century.

External conditions as well as domestic circumstances provided a new scenario for the state's attempt to "sow the oil" during the second Ecuadorian oil boom. *First*, economic globalization became a growing hindrance to the enforcement of state's protectionist measures in countries like Ecuador, which are integrated into the world system through their natural resources. *Second*, as technological advance increasingly sets the pace for industrial development, the incorporation of technology (together with an increase in productivity) became the measure of competitiveness within the globalized world economy. *Third*, the irruption of the environmental factor (mirrored in the discourse of sustainable development) into economic planning meant for productive sectors the obligation to comply with a series of environmental standards in order to compete in the globalized world economy, which were unthinkable during the ISI consensus. Even tough, state's embracement of the discourse of sustainable development hypothetically entailed the possibility of access to a market of "environmental or ecological goods and services" (Domínguez et al. 2019, 156).

The prevalence of market rules over state regulation, the growing technological gap, and the inclusion of the environmental factor, all legacies of the epoch of the Washington Consensus, have been approached in a rather separate way by contemporary scholars leading to different policy implications in Latin America. On the one hand, the renewed integration into the world economy, based on natural resources and increasing technological backwardness, advocated a "new balance between the [agency of the] state and the market in the context of globalization" (Sunkel 2006, 24 in Domínguez et al. 2019, 162). On the other hand, the inclusion of the environmental factor into state's economic planning opened the gates to a broader discussion on economic diversification, i.e. the actual possibilities of promoting other sectors of the economy (e.g. tourism). Thus, the quest of "sow the oil" during the twenty-first century commodities boom translated into the enforcement of a diverse set of policies aiming at a twofold objective: 1) carrying out a thorough search of new *comparative* advantages (sometimes even based on traditional natural resources exports), and 2) chasing after *competitive* advantages.

There is wide consensus among researchers of contemporary Ecuador around the idea that the decade of Correa's government ought not to be assessed as a unitary period, but as several phases depending on the analyzed subject. Regarding economic diversification, a successive mix-up of policies was discursively prioritized throughout different periods. Though, elements of the dichotomy between competitive and comparative advantages can be found in the national development plans; incidentally, the

National Development Plan 2009-2013 defines *cambio de la matriz producti-va* (transformation of productive structure) as "[...] the transit from a primary exporter and extractivist model to a scheme which privileges diversified eco-efficient production, as well as services based on knowledge and biodiversity" (Secretaría Nacional de Planificación y Desarrollo 2009, 329), and the National Development Plan 2013-2017, declares the intention of "using extractivism to exit extractivism" (Secretaría Nacional de Planificación y Desarrollo 2013, 82). Such idea has to do, so the plan, with "sowing the oil in order to reap the productive structure of the knowledge society" (Secretaría Nacional de Planificación y Desarrollo 2013, 17). Hence, in order to assess the scope of the "sow the oil" attempt during the second Ecuadorian oil boom and the niche assigned to the environmental factor in Correa's government, it is necessary 1) to examine the role of nature in the government's economic diversification proposal, and 2) to delve into a possible relationship of such proposal with neo-*estructuralismo*.

First, reliance on natural resources, i.e. comparative advantages, was accepted as "using extractivism" in order to bankroll the quest for competitive advantages, i.e. the "exit from extractivism". According to the view of a faction of the government that prioritized a knowledge-based economic diversification, the exit road of extractivism headed to the utopia of biotechnology industry and the "bio-knowledge society" (Ramírez 2012, 38 in Alarcón and Mantilla 2017, 102). Resembling the orthodox view of economic development and the Rostownian transit from the traditional society to the mass consumer society (Rostow 1990), the transit from extractivism to biotechnology industry is envisioned through a series of intermediate stations including the promotion of "ecotourism services and agroecological products"[176], in which the pursuit of comparative advantages remains unchanged. *Second*, stemming from Latin American *estructuralismo*[177], neo-*estructuralismo* remains constrained to the epistemic pattern of neoclassical economics; though, different from its antecessor, neo-*estructuralismo*'s mindset explicitly accepts the inevitability of market rules in a globalized economy, and promotes economic openness. Therefore, Sotelo (2005, 21) argued that neo-*estructuralismo* converges upon "the ideological, psychological and cultural superstructure of contemporary capitalist society". In this line, Braña (2016, 41) neared neo-*estructuralismo* to a "human face" of ne-

---

176 For a critique of such proposal see Alarcón and Mantilla (2017, 102).

177 Braña (2016) lingered over the origins of neo-estructuralismo in *El pensamiento desarrollista y neodesarrollista en América Latina y el buen vivir. Continuidades y cambios.*

oliberalism[178]. The neo-*estructuralista* strategy of finding comparative advantages applied during Correa's government was characterized by Andrade (2015) as "selective industrialization and commerce" (SIC), in which selective industrialization alluded to state's backing to certain productive sectors. The selection of benefited sectors was a source of conflict between contrary factions within the government. On the one hand, a group of state entities headed by the Ministry of Production advocated a more ISI-like classic industrialization process based on strategic industries such as refineries, shipyards, copper metallurgy, petrochemical industry, and iron and steel industry, backed by mariculture, biofuels, and wood products (Secretaría Nacional de Planificación y Desarrollo 2012, 11 in Cypher and Alfaro 2016, 170). On the other hand, state agencies led by the Secretariat of Higher Education, supported the integration of the concepts of "knowledge", "science and technology", or "research and development" into the discussion on economic diversification.

The Law of Creation of the University of Research of Experimental Technology *Yachay* (knowledge) (Asamblea Nacional 2013a) signaled the governmental faction that resulted victorious of the dispute and, hence, the groups that were to be granted significant state's resources (in form of a larger portion of oil rent and Chinese loans) to support their vision on economic diversification. The university[179] was preceded by the establishment of the public enterprise Yachay EP (*Empresa Pública Yachay EP*), which was in charge of "managing the Project of the City of Knowledge", *Ciudad Yachay* (Executive Order No. 1457, published in the Official

---

178 In a similar way as Latin American *estructuralismo* provided economic rationalization to *desarrollismo*, neo-estructuralismo might be regarded as a theoretical underpinning of neo-*desarrollismo* or new developmentalism, a "new theoretical system that is being created" (Bresser-Pereira 2016, 31). According to Bresser-Pereira (2016, 341), central to new developmentalism is the prevalence of the market. The definition of economic development in new developmentalism basically does not differ from that in the developmental state theory: "the process of capital accumulation with the incorporation of technical progress [...]; it involves increasing productive sophistication combined with the transference of labor from low to high income per capita industries" (Bresser-Pereira 2016, 341).

179 Other three universities were created in December 2013: 1) the Regional Amazonian University Ikiam (*Universidad Regional Amazónica Ikiam*), which was meant to focus on biotechnology, 2) the University of the Arts (*Universidad de las Artes*) in Guayaquil, and 3) the National University of Education UNAE (*Universidad Nacional de Educación UNAE*), in the South of the country, with the purpose of training the next generation of school teachers (Asamblea Nacional 2013b; Asamblea Nacional 2013c; Asamblea Nacional 2013d).

Gazette No. 922, March 28, 2013). The project was initially planned in an area of 4,462 ha, which is equivalent to 13 times the Central Park in New York, with a gradual investment of US$ 5.7 billion in 33 years (El Comercio, April 6, 2018). According to a former consultant at Yachay EP, the duty of the public enterprise was to build a technology hub in the province of Imbabura (about 130 km north of Quito) in a territory that was traditionally destined to agriculture and farming, "the university was imagined as the epicenter of *Ciudad Yachay*... the city was sold as a new Silicon Valley projected to house the world's top technology companies, which were meant to undertake research at the university" (former consultant at Yachay EP, interview, September 16, 2018). The imitative nature of the project became plain when the university was re-baptized *Yachay Tech* and Correa successively alluded to it as "our MIT [Massachusetts Institute of Technology]". Existing public universities were excluded from the project. Allegedly, the idea stuck to the tenet of the East Asian developmental state of the 1950s (Japan) and 1960s (Taiwan and Korea), which advocated building industrial science and technology institutes, networked into private firms (Wade 2018, 528). Yachay EP contracted with a set of private companies (mostly Chinese) to erect the city. Among the first buildings that arose counted *Yachay Tech*'s campus facilities, which included university's buildings, labs, and dormitories. The university was inaugurated in March 2014 with half-finished public services and amenities; streets were still in progress. The construction of the campus was tainted by corruption since its start (Heredia 2018); by the beginning of 2018, the Comptroller General's office had conducted already 14 audits in *Yachay Tech* and Yachay EP (El Universo, February 8, 2018), which reflected losses for US$ 31.4 million in the construction of the campus (Heredia 2018), and alleged mismanagement of state's resources through excess payments, irregular recruitment of staff, payment of excess travel allowances in favor of a family unit, etc. (El Universo, February 14, 2018). After the oil boom, Moreno's government decided to resize the project of *Ciudad Yachay* to a more feasible goal of 382 ha (El Comercio, April 6, 2018), more than ten times smaller than initially projected. By the beginning of 2018, *Yachay Tech* functioned as a public polytechnic university[180]. Whilst, Yachay EP employed 618 persons in 2018; its liquidation is expected on 2021 (Tapia 2018).

---

180 "It is well known that the construction of education infrastructure does not mean automatically better education. The decision of a pompous intervention in higher education [and not in elementary education, for example] followed clearly populistic criteria" (Pablo Lucio Paredes, former member of the Asam-

Another landmark of the intention to match the vision of economic diversification with the concepts of "knowledge", "science and technology", or "research and development" was the program of international scholarships. Between 2007 and 2018, the government granted more than 13 thousand scholarships for Ecuadorian nationals to attend higher education abroad, more than three-quarters of the scholarships were granted between 2011 and 2015 (10,830 out of 13,312 scholarships). An important number of bursaries was channeled to master and doctoral programs (Figure No. 11); scholarship holders are meant to return after completing their studies and work two years in Ecuador for every year they spent abroad in order to "become the carriers of economic diversification" (former Deputy Secretary of the Ecuadorian Secretariat of Higher Education, interview, July 6, 2017). In order to comply with the necessity of incorporating science and technology into the envisioned transformation of the productive structure (*cambio de la matriz productiva*), more than half (about 58 percent) of the scholarships were granted in the fields of natural sciences, mathematics and statistics, engineering, and health sciences (SENESCYT 2019b). The possibilities of highly-qualified scholarship holders to be involved in economic diversification or even to find a job in Ecuador at their return will be a constant matter for discussion during the next years, as the bulk of beneficiaries continues completing their studies and starts its journey back.

---

blea Constituyente, lecturer at USFQ Ecuador, interview with Dr. Stefan Peters, September 21, 2016).

Figure No. 11: International scholarships for higher education granted by the Ecuadorian government, 2007-18

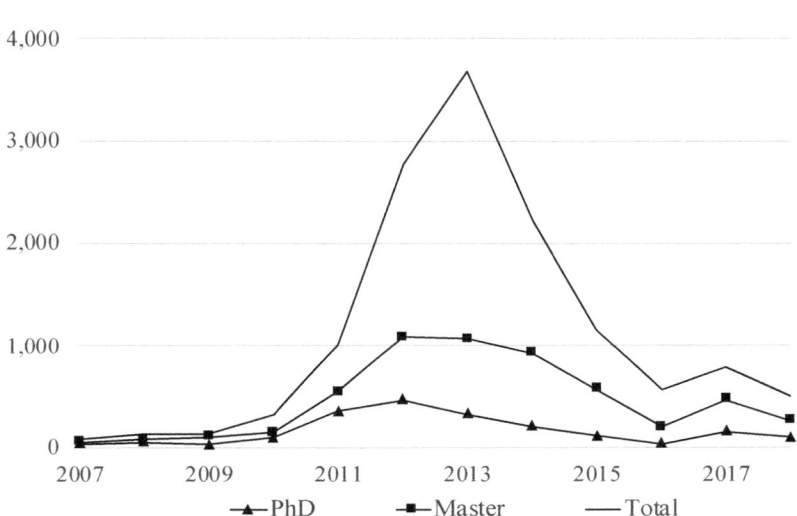

Source: Own diagram based on SENESCYT (2019a)

The private sector did not participate in the formulation of the economic diversification policymaking of Correa's government (Sergio Sáenz, former Communication Director at the Pichincha Chamber of Small and Medium-Sized Enterprises, interview with Dr. Stefan Peters, September 14, 2016; Eduardo Cadena, former Executive Director of the Quito Chamber of Commerce, interview with Dr. Stefan Peters, September 14, 2015). Further, there was no specific policy regarding the significant sector of the small and medium-sized enterprises, neither an articulation with the intended *cambio de la matriz productiva* (Sergio Sáenz, former Communication Director at the Pichincha Chamber of Small and Medium-Sized Enterprises, interview with Dr. Stefan Peters, September 14, 2016). In a similar fashion as did the "revolutionary nationalist" dictatorship with the old oligarchy, Correa's government cultivated a populist[181] anti-elite rhetoric against what the president called "the chambers", targeting the chambers of commerce and industries. Despite the confrontational atmosphere, eco-

---

181 The rhetoric reminded of a classic populist distinctive: The Manichaean discourse of people versus elites (de la Torre 2010, 140).

nomic sectors controlled by traditional local elites counted among the principal beneficiaries of the overall boost of the economy triggered by public investment during the second oil boom. According to a former Executive Director of the Quito Chamber of Commerce, "elites were far from being aligned with the government policies"; though, they mostly benefited from state contracts during the second oil boom (Eduardo Cadena, former Executive Director of the Quito Chamber of Commerce, interview with Dr. Stefan Peters, September 14, 2015). Thanks to public spending-based growth, and not necessarily to economic diversification policies, 1) the financial sector (mainly banks), 2) the commerce sector (mainly importers), and 3) the construction sector mostly profited from the second oil boom (Pablo Lucio Paredes, former member of the Asamblea Constituyente, lecturer at USFQ Ecuador, interview with Dr. Stefan Peters, September 21, 2016).

Table No. 28 depicts the value added by different sectors of the economy to GDP for the period 1972-2016. The table shows a traditionally strong tertiary sector with a participation of more than the half in the total value added. In contrast, in nearly all industrialized countries, the manufacturing sector "represents between one fourth and one third of GDP, and absorbs about 90 percent of the resources destined to research and development" (Fajnzylber 1992, 25). Whereas the petroleum and mining sector maintained its relative weight during the Ecuadorian oil era, the manufacturing sector showed a downward path that began with the twenty-first century; the contribution of the manufacturing sector during the second oil boom was smaller than that during the 1980s decade. Regarding non-oil GDP, the value added of the manufacturing sector (as percentage share) amounted circa 20 percent during the 1970s and 1980s decades; during the 1990s, the value added of the manufacturing sector peaked at an average of about 23 percent. With the beginning of the twenty-first century, the contribution dropped to circa 15 percent for the period 2001-10 and 14 percent for the period 2011-18 (World Bank 2019c). Otherwise, the counterpart of the shrinkage of the construction sector during the 1990s might be found in the expansion of the manufacturing sector during that decade. Nonetheless, the construction sector recovered and appeared as one of the winners of the second oil boom.

Table No. 28: Gross value added by sector (as percentage of GDP), 2007 U.S. dollars, selected years, Ecuador 1972-2016

Economic sector	Value added (percent)						
	1972	1981	1988	1994	2000	2007	2016
Agriculture (includes live-stock, fishing, and forestry)	10.7	6.7	7.4	8.3	9.4	9.4	9.4
Petroleum and mining	6.0	9.3	11.7	12.2	10.2	11.7	10.2
Manufacturing	12.6	13.8	13.4	14.3	15.2	13.7	13.2
Construction	16.0	9.8	7.7	6.3	6.0	7.9	9.4
Utilities	0.9	0.2	1.2	1.1	1.4	1.1	2.8
Tertiary sector (includes commerce, government services, transport, other services)	53.8	60.2	58.6	57.8	57.8	56.2	55.0

Source: BCE (2019a)

Throughout the Ecuadorian oil era, the decreasing trend in the gross value added by the manufacturing sector mirrored in the downward path of the gross fixed capital formation (GFCF) (Table No. 29). Since GFCF comprises private and public investments in (rather than consumption of) fixed assets, e.g. infrastructure, machines, real state, it might be understood as a suitable proxy for the new value added. Through the lens of GFCF, the plummeting participation of the manufacturing sector in GDP appears more sharply. Following the logic of the contraction of the manufacturing sector, Andrade (2015, 16) argued that current "levels of industrialization are less than those forty years ago". The decreasing trend in the GFCF of the manufacturing sector (Table No. 29) might also be regarded as a proxy of the lack of investments in (new) technology. According to Cimoli and Porcile (2015, 235), investments in innovation and diffusion of technology are the only effective way to avoid technological backwardness. In this line, so the authors, successful examples of catching up with industrialized countries "are based on a continuous effort to use foreign technology as an input for local learning and not as a substitute" (Cimoli and Porcile 2015, 235). But, hardly an Ecuadorian manufactured product with a certain level of technology has enjoyed until present day considerable demand (Matthes 2019, 347) nor acknowledgment.

Table No. 29: Average gross fixed capital formation (GFCF) by sector (as percentage of total), 2007 U.S. dollars, Ecuador 1971-2017

Economic sector	GFCF by sector (as percentage of total)				
	1971-80	1981-90	1991-2000	2001-10	2011-17
Agriculture (includes livestock, fishing, and forestry)	3.0	4.2	7.9	6.9	5.4
Petroleum and mining	18.6	15.2	9.4	8.2	9.2
Manufacturing	18.4	14.1	16.4	12.7	12.1
Construction	4.3	2.5	3.5	3.8	2.5
Utilities	4.5	5.1	10.4	12.9	14.1
Tertiary sector (includes commerce, government services, transport, other services)	51.2	58.9	52.4	55.4	56.8

Source: BCE (2019b)

However, consistently with the relative high GFCF attained during the 1970s decade (Table No. 29), Table No. 30 shows a historical highpoint in the share of Ecuadorian manufactured exports (i.e. exports that include a certain level of technology) around 1980. The peak might be related to the significant boost of the industrial sector experienced during the first oil boom (which also puts the thesis of the resource curse into question). Though, the manufactured exports coefficient has been steadily declining since then and has been unable to keep pace with other South American countries. In Latin America, only Venezuela, the "textbook case of a rentier society" (Peters 2017a, 54), shows a poorer performance (Table No. 30).

Table No. 30: Manufactured exports coefficient (percent), South America (selected countries) 1970-85

	1970	1975	1980	1981	1982	1983	1984	1985
Argentina	7.0	2.9	3.9	4.5	5.6	4.5	3.8	5.5
Brazil	2.8	3.0	5.3	6.1	5.0	7.4	17.3	28.4
Bolivia	2.6	3.5	3.2	2.1	1.6	n.a.	n.a.	n.a.
Colombia	2.0	4.9	4.9	5.0	4.5	3.5	3.6	4.6
Chile	2.2	5.4	6.1	4.4	5.1	5.4	6.0	6.6
Ecuador	1.9	5.4	9.8	7.4	6.6	2.4	4.4	n.a.

	1970	1975	1980	1981	1982	1983	1984	1985
Peru	0.5	0.5	5.1	3.3	3.5	2.5	3.1	n.a.
Uruguay	2.3	4.8	7.8	6.6	7.6	11.3	11.7	10.3
Venezuela	0.6	0.8	1.0	1.3	1.0	0.7	1.9	5.0

Source: Fajnzylber (1990, 18)

The null growth of the manufacturing sector, and even the stagnation of the tertiary sector, mirror the ineffectiveness of the set of policies aiming at the *cambio de la matriz productiva*. Also, the sluggishness of the tertiary sector might mirror the failure of the intended increase in ecotourism services. Such symptoms speak rather for a rare kind of Dutch disease, in which the construction sector expanded during the oil bonanza (Table No. 28). An expanding construction sector during the second Ecuadorian oil boom might suggest that private investors temporarily crossed the limits of their own comfort zone (mainly in the tertiary sector) and participated increasingly in construction. In other words, in a context of galloping household consumption expenditure, and taking into account the volume of the mortgage loans provided by the Bank of the Social Security Institute (BIESS), the transient growth of the construction sector might be regarded as the natural outcome of the boost of the economy (triggered by public investment) coupled with expectations of high return private investments. Hence, once the state provided the conditions for economic growth, it might be argued that the rentier character of local investors became evident. During the second oil boom, in absence of market incentives (for capitalists) to invest in the manufacturing sector, the rentiers benefited from the construction sector and the tertiary sector (commerce sector, financial sector, imports, among others), which were swollen by public investment. The state's hand was also visible in the improvement of the utilities sector. Its increasing GFCF value during the second oil boom (Table No. 29) mirrors the government's investments in hydropower plants. Whilst, the stagnation of the petroleum and mining sector during the last decades might be coupled with the failure of the conventional oil policy, which was referred to in the section *Overture to the Return of the State: The Recovery of the National Oil Sector*. However, both facts regarding GFCF (the improvement of the utilities sector and the stagnation of the petroleum and mining sector) expose the state's hand in the economy.

As the Ecuadorian state further relied on oil rent basically from state companies (Figure No. 12), the public sector became the motor of the economy. Despite neo-*estructuralista* authors stressed on the importance of the private sector to the achievement of economic diversification (Cimoli and Porcile 2015), the role of private initiative in economic planning was overlooked during Correa's government. Despite the benefits received from the overall growth of the economy, the Ecuadorian private sector was overshadowed by the public sector, and contributed with less than the half to the economy during the second oil boom (Pablo Lucio Paredes, former member of the Asamblea Constituyente, lecturer at USFQ Ecuador, interview with Dr. Stefan Peters, September 21, 2016). From the viewpoint of the private sector, the Ecuadorian state is not a reliable business partner, the high country risk "discourages domestic and foreign investments" (Eduardo Cadena, former Executive Director of the Quito Chamber of Commerce, interview with Dr. Stefan Peters, September 14, 2015). Besides, the "constant change of the regulatory framework [e.g. fiscal regulations], the high rotation of ministers and other authorities, and a hefty bureaucratic burden [i.e. red tape] do not contribute to the creation of an adequate business environment in the long term" (Sergio Sáenz, former Communication Director at the Pichincha Chamber of Small and Medium-Sized Enterprises, interview with Dr. Stefan Peters, September 14, 2016).

Figure No. 12: Oil output, million US$, Ecuador 1991-2010

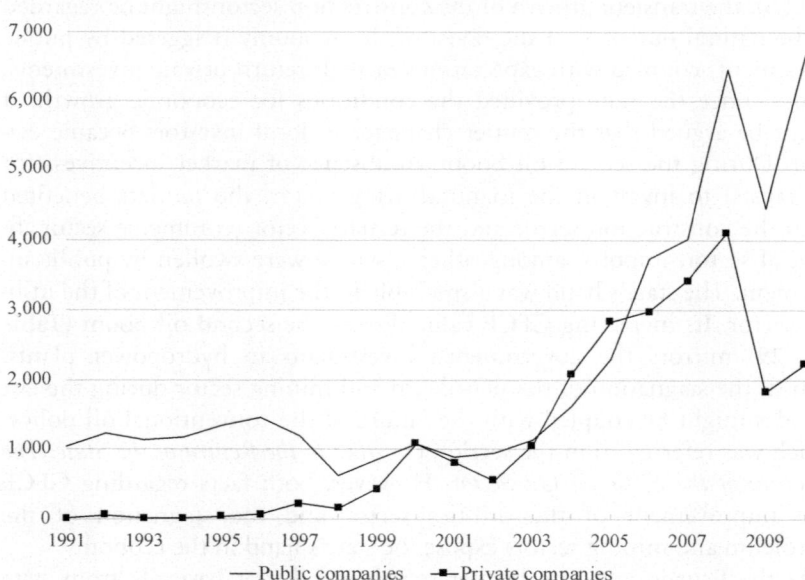

Source: Own diagram based on BCE (2017, 193)

The renewed bet on natural resources is depicted in Table No. 31 and Figure No. 13. The stagnation of non-traditional exports (the possible place for the incorporation of manufactured products) reinforces the idea of the failure of any economic diversification attempt during the second oil boom. Whilst, any decline in oil exports was covered by an increase in traditional exports.

Table No. 31: Average share of export products (percent), Ecuador 1996-2016

Export product	1996-2002	2003-09	2010-16
Oil products (mainly crude oil)	35.9	54.9	49.8
Traditional products (banana and plantain, coffee and coffee products, shrimp, cocoa and cocoa products, tuna and fish)	38.3	20.5	25.4
Non-traditional products (mainly natural flowers, canned sea food and mining products)	25.8	24.6	24.8

Source: BCE (2017, 111)

Figure No. 13: Average share of export products (percent), Ecuador 1972-2016

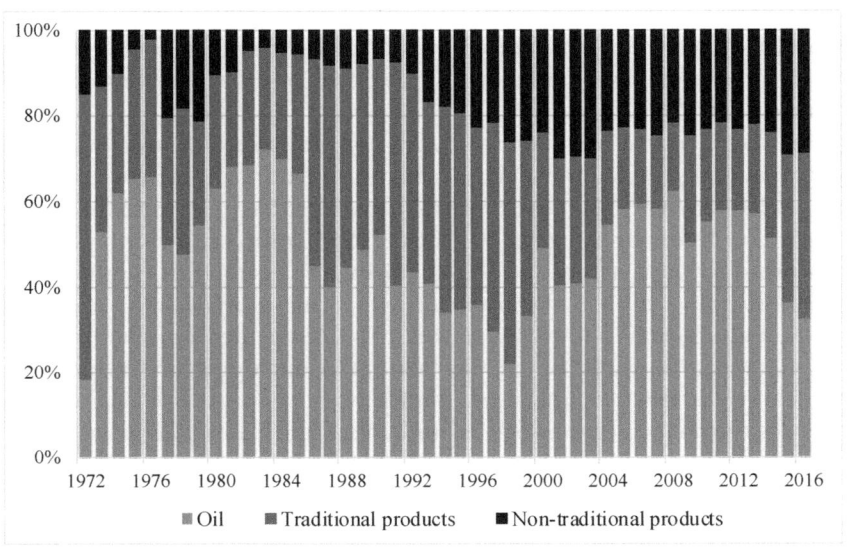

Source: Own diagram based on BCE (2017, 111)

Nature and the State: The Polyphonic Concept of Buen Vivir

Whereas the external conditions for the return of the state were shaped by high international oil prices, the internal circumstance for its comeback was molded by mainly two social settings that were highly unlikely during the 1970s. *First*, indigenous peoples were firmly entrenched in national politics, as opposed to the 1970s decade when they were doomed to social invisibility. Indígenas irrupted in national politics during the 1990s as the spearhead of the protests against the enforcement of neoliberal policies; in 2000 and 2005, their role was decisive in the overthrow of President Jamil Mahuad (1998-2000) and President Lucio Gutiérrez (2003-2005), respectively. *Second*, the environmental discourse of sustainable development was rooted in the Ecuadorian sociopolitical arena, in contrast with the 1970s when any allusion to the environmental factor was absent from the discussions on the national development project. During the 1990s, three events signalized the ultimate incorporation of the environmental discourse of sustainable development into the logic of the Ecuadorian state, 1) the issuance of the Basic Environmental Policies (*Políticas básicas ambientales del Ecuador*) in 1994 (Executive Order No. 1802, published in the Official Gazette No. 456, June 7, 1994), 2) the creation of the Ministry of Environment (*Ministerio del Ambiente*) in 1996, and 3) the inclusion of five articles regarding "environmental protection and the right of Ecuadorian citizens to live in a healthy environment" in the 1998 Constitution (Fontaine and Narváez 2007, 25).

The state's embracement of the international discourse of sustainable development contributed to weld the concepts of nature and development in the social imaginary and was a central ingredient in the construction of a scenario of "semiotic struggles" (Escobar 1995b) aimed at revisiting the relationship between nature and society during the twenty-first century. The Ecuadorian environmental movement, which increasingly influenced domestic politics since the 1980s, (Lewis 2016, 55) gained momentum and the vigor necessary to critique the natural resources-based development model; at the dawn of the new century negative socioecological consequences of monoculture associated to banana and palm plantations were denounced as well as the destructive effects on mangrove of farmed shrimp (Larrea 2013, 12), the landmark of the "diversification of exports" attained during the height of neoliberalism. Nonetheless, oil extraction was principally under scrutiny. Judith Kimerling's (1991) *Amazon Crude* blatantly exposed the negative socioecological impacts on the Amazon region of Texaco's extractivist activities undertaken since 1964. The book was called

"Ecuador's Silent Spring" (Brooke 1993) in reference to Rachel Carson's (1962) celebrated "Silent Spring", which "popularized modern ecology and ignited the environmental movement" (Griswold 2012). *Amazon Crude* became promptly a milestone to the production of an environmental discourse *à la* Ecuadorian (Alarcón and Mantilla 2017, 96). Suzana Sawyer (2008, 324) argued that Kimerling's opus became a main driver of the start of legal action against Texaco in 1993; a group of victims of oil exploitation in northern Amazon region, in representation of about 30,000 plaintiffs (Kimerling 2000, 54; Yanza 2004, 38), took the multinational corporation to court in the state of New York and accused it of intentionally using technology "based on minimal investment and maximal profit criteria" (Yanza 2004, 37). Initially, the case was known as Aguinda vs Texaco, in reference to María Aguinda, one of the plaintiffs of the *kichwa* indigenous peoples; when Chevron Corporation acquired Texaco in 2001, the process was nicknamed "the trial of the century". Despite the 2011 verdict against the company, the case is currently in force.

However, the Chevron process not only generated further society's awareness of the consequences of extractivism, but also provided concrete motives to draft a timid moratorium proposal. The environmental organization *Acción Ecológica*, established in the mid-1980s, advocated for moratorium on new oil exploration in the Amazonia in *El Ecuador post petrolero* in 2000; "local and global ecological impacts" wielded as principal reasons besides the necessity of "slow extraction" of finite resources (Martínez-Alier 2000, 12). By the time it was proposed, the idea of a moratorium on oil activities was not new. Indeed, the purpose of "leaving oil in the ground" might be traced in the late 1990s as non-governmental organizations' avant-garde strategy to cope with climate change. The possibility of induced global climate change due to anthropogenic emissions of greenhouse gases urged Greenpeace's *Fossil Fuels and Climate Protection: The Carbon Logic* (Hare 1997), which presented the "carbon budget" as "a total amount of CO_2 emissions computed for ecological goals' achievement" (Hare 1997, ix). The report advised that "estimated economically recoverable volumes of gas and oil [i.e. proven reserves] are sufficient alone to breach the carbon budget". Hence, it recommended that "national governments should be taking steps to stop plans to allow the expansion of exploration for oil and gas reserves" (Hare 1997, 57-58). Also by 1997, during alternative negotiations of the Kyoto Protocol, Oilwatch propositioned carbon credits as fair compensation for leaving oil in the ground (Martínez-Alier and Temper 2007, 18).

These and other proposals of multinational non-governmental organizations echoed in Ecuadorian environmental movements, which in 2006 integrated into the coalition of social forces that led the PAIS Movement (now Alianza País) to win the presidential election. Alongside with the backing of environmental activists, PAIS added up support of the indigenous movement; environmental protection theses as well as largely postponed indigenous vindications converged upon the draft of the *Government Plan of the PAIS Movement 2007-2011* (PAIS 2006). *Buen vivir*, which was allegedly inspired in the indigenous cosmovision of *sumak kawsay* (good living), arose from PAIS' government plan and became the guiding thread of the new government's developmental project. Whereas *buen vivir* impregnated the 2008 Constitution, *sumak kawsay* still echoed in official documents such as the 2009-2013 National Development Plan nicknamed "Building a Plurinational and Intercultural State" (*Plan Nacional para el Buen Vivir 2009-2013: Construyendo un Estado Plurinacional e Intercultural*) (Secretaría Nacional de Planificación y Desarrollo 2009). However, the demands of the Ecuadorian environmental movement promptly converged upon the influential socioecological dimension of *buen vivir*, which is founded on the imperative of a harmonious relationship between society and nature; the stream of *buen vivir* that underscores an ecological approach has been referred to as "utopian *buen vivir*" (Domínguez, Caria, and León 2017, 138).

The materialization of "utopian *buen vivir*" and its underscored harmonious relationship between society and nature could have taken place through the Yasuní-ITT initiative, a plan to "leave oil in the ground" in a sensitive region of the Ecuadorian Amazonia. Nonetheless, the failure of the initiative epitomizes the rise and fall of the discourse of *buen vivir*. The Yasuní-ITT initiative was meant to withdraw to the exploitation of about a quarter of the country's total oil reserves, i.e. circa 850 million barrels contained in field 43 (Ishpingo-Tambococha-Tiputini or ITT). That volume, which is essential for the Ecuadorian economy, is only enough to satisfy one week of world's demand. Thereby, the consumption of such amount of oil sets 407 million tons of CO_2 into the atmosphere (Larrea 2010, 10). Besides its contribution to avoid global impacts of fossil fuel consumption, the initiative was central to the conservation of the Yasuní National Park (YNP), created in 1979, and since 1989 within the World Biosphere Reserves of the United Nations Educational, Scientific and Cultural Organization (UNESCO). The YNP reserve is "habitat of various indigenous nationalities, including uncontacted peoples"; therefore, a portion of the national park was marked off in 2006 as Intangible Zone Tagaeri Taromenane in recognition of these peoples' ancestral territory (Narváez, de Marchi, and Pappalardo 2013, 9). About 80 percent of the area of the YNP overlaps with six oil fields, including field 43, where extraordinary biological and cultural diversity are found.

In exchange for leaving oil in the ground *sine die*, the Ecuadorian state applied for an international compensation based on "the principle of differentiated co-responsibility" (Alberto Acosta, interview, February 12, 2016), which amounted to "at least US$ 3,6 billion or half of the total the state would obtain in case of oil exploitation [i.e. US$ 7,2 billion]" (Larrea 2010, 8). By this means, Ecuador appeared as the first contributor to the initiative by assuming up to half of the opportunity cost of leaving the oil underground. Correa's government launched the Yasuní-ITT initiative as a state policy in June 2007, on World Environment Day. Beforehand, the project was introduced to Correa's cabinet by Alberto Acosta, even before he was appointed Minister of Energy and Mines. The counterpoint between antagonist positions inside the government mirrored in the March 2007 Resolution of the Board of Petroecuador, which comprised two options for field 43. The Yasuní-ITT initiative was option A: "[the Board of the oil state company] accept[s] the option of leaving oil unexploited under the ground [...]". Option B was oil exploitation (Resolution No. 25DIR-2007-03-30 of March 30, 2007). It was remarkable that the national authority responsible for conventional oil policy[182] (i.e. the Minister of Energy and Mines) supported option A. The president, instead, supported option B (Alberto Acosta, interview, February 12, 2016). A couple of days after, the Ministry of Energy and Mines[183] (MEM) released the Energy Agenda 2007-2011, in which option A explicitly highlighted (Acosta and Villavicencio 2007, 51).

Though, after its initial thrust in MEM, Correa moved the initiative to the Ministry of Foreign Affairs. The chosen platform for the promotion of the initiative was the international forum for climate change. Even though the alternative-to-development vein[184] of the Yasuní-ITT initiative originally breached the liberal epistemic pattern of sustainable development

---

182 As mentioned before, conventional oil policy generally entails two main components, 1) increasing oil extraction, and 2) at least maintaining (if not increasing) reserve levels through exploration of new oil fields.

183 Now Ministry of Non-Renewable Natural Resources.

184 An alternative-to-development inspiration of the Yasuní-ITT initiative becomes recognizable as the project critiques the current development model based on the consumption of fossil fuels and the emission of greenhouse gases to the atmosphere, i.e. the "conceptual foundations of development, as well as the insti-

and the master narrative of the Kyoto Protocol, the Ecuadorian government strove to fit the initiative into such mainstream schemes. By September 2007, Correa presented the Yasuní-ITT initiative to the United Nations General Assembly and made reference to "climate justice international policy" (Acosta et al. 2009, 450), which, in turn, alluded the "common but differentiated responsibilities" made explicit in article 10 of the Kyoto Protocol (United Nations 1998, 10). In a further attempt to harmonize the Ecuadorian proposal to official climate change mechanisms, the Minister of Foreign Affairs presented the initiative during the thirteenth meeting of the Conference of the Parties (COP 13) of the United Nations Framework Convention on Climate Change (UNFCCC) in December 2007.

By the beginning of 2008, Correa issued two Executive Orders meant to outline an organizational chart for the Yasuní-ITT initiative. On the one hand, he established the Energy Transition Trust Fund in order to "allocate the contributions of the international community for investment in energy efficiency and renewable energy plans" (Executive Order No. 847, published in the Official Gazette No. 253, January 16, 2008). On the other hand, the president created the Technical Secretariat of the Yasuní-ITT Initiative inside the Ministry of Foreign Affairs to "foster the initiative and outline international negotiation strategies" (Executive Order No. 882, published in the Official Gazette No. 269, February 9, 2008). Only six months after, the Administrative and Directive Council of the Yasuní-ITT Initiative (ADC) was established to supervise the Technical Secretariat (Executive Order No. 1127, published in the Official Gazette No. 401, August 12, 2008). Until November 2009 the ADC outlined the proposal of a trust fund for the initiative's contributions to be administered by the United Nations Development Programme (UNDP). The agreement with UNDP was to be signed during the COP 15 in December 2009, but Correa argued that the mechanism was "not aligned with the sovereignty principles" of the Ecuadorian government and vetoed it (Álvarez 2013, 92). The cancelation of the agreement provoked the resignation of the members of the ADC and the Minister of Foreign Affairs.

---

tutions and practices that legitimate them" (Gudynas 2014, 65). Though, the National Development Plan 2007-2010 (*Plan Nacional de Desarrollo 2007-2010*) incorporated the initiative within a national strategy of "alternative and sustainable use of biodiversity, with special attention to indigenous peoples and culture, [...]" (Secretaría Nacional de Planificación y Desarrollo 2007, 156). Hence, the official document places the Yasuní-ITT initiative within an orthodox narrative that makes refence to rather sustainable development and human development (Alarcón and Mantilla 2017, 101; Cortez 2014, 338).

After the impasse, the resurrection of the initiative was to come by the hand of the Ministry of Coordination of Natural and Cultural Patrimony (MCP)[185] in 2010. The memorandum of agreement between the Ecuadorian government and UNDP was finally signed in August 2010 (Executive Order No. 596, published in the Official Gazette No. 356, January 6, 2011), thereby establishing an additional mechanism to manage contributions to the initiative besides the national trust fund created in 2008. The new UNDP-administered trust fund was meant to bankroll "sustainable development and human development strategies", mainly conservation and reforestation, and social development in the Amazon region (UNDP 2010, 5). MCP's guardianship of the initiative was imprinted by the creation of an Administrative Negotiation Commission (ANC) with the key duty of fundraising under the direction of Ms. Ivonne Baki (Executive Order No. 241, published in the Official Gazette No. 132, February 19, 2010). Under this scheme, the initiative was to be bankrolled with 1) contributions of governments, private and public entities, including intergovernmental and non-governmental organizations, and individuals, and 2) the issuance of Yasuní Guarantee Certificates (CGYs) (UNDP 2010, 6). Yasuní Guarantee Certificates were meant to add to the long list of emission permits such as carbon credits, and other mechanisms that refer to emissions *reduction*; though, CGYs strictly denoted *avoided* emissions (i.e. emissions that would never take place whilst oil is kept in the ground). Since the logic of CGYs differed from UNFCCC's schemes, the Yasuní certificates could not be traded in carbon markets. Thus, CGYs acted only as guarantee provided by the Ecuadorian government of keeping the oil underground. In the event of oil exploitation, CGYs entitled the holders to be reimbursed by the Ecuadorian state (UNDP 2010, 13). By December 2010, during the COP 16, in a further attempt to comply with the logic of UNFCCC, Correa plead for the inclusion of ampler compensation schemes and introduced the concept of Net Avoided Emissions (*Emisiones Netas Evitadas*, ENE) as

---

185 The *Ministerio de Coordinación de Patrimonio Natural y Cultural* (MCP) was inaugurated and disbanded during Correa's government. Its establishment in February 2007 responded to the need of coordination of "policies and actions regarding intangible capital" of various ministries (Executive Order No. 117-A, published in the Official Gazette No. 33, March 5, 2007). Though, in May 2013, only three months before the termination of the Yasuní-ITT initiative, the MCP was dissolved. The bulk of its responsibilities, including the coordination of the Ministry of Environment, was transferred to the Ministry of Coordination of Strategic Sectors. The move later recalled the transit of the notion of nature from patrimony to strategic resources.

"the emissions that could be released by a country, but are not produced, or the emissions that exist in a country that are reduced". The Ecuadorian president further stated that the Yasuní-ITT initiative was based on ENE and advocated for the adoption of the mechanism under the Framework Convention on Climate Change, since existing instruments, as Reducing Emissions from Deforestation and forest Degradation (REDD+), were "insufficient, inefficient, and inconsistent" (Rafael Correa, presidential address, December 8, 2010). REDD+, which aims to compensate developing countries for the "environmental service of reducing deforestation" (Lovera 2009, 46), was a principal incentive being discussed during COP 16.

The "erratic wander-around" (Martínez 2009, 36) of the initiative through different government dependencies and chairpersons seemed to come to an end by the beginning of 2011. The budget of the initiative was transferred to the Office of the President, and Mrs. Ivonne Baki was appointed "Plenipotentiary Representative of the Yasuní-ITT Initiative" and chair of the negotiation team in charge of fundraising (Executive Order No. 648, published in the Official Gazette No. 391, February 23, 2011). One year later, in 2012, Mrs. Baki was appointed "Secretary of State for the Yasuní-ITT Initiative" (Executive Order No. 1030, published in the Official Gazette No. 637, February 9, 2012). Since her first designation in 2010 until August 2013, Mrs. Baki and her team of about fifteen persons spent US\$ 7.3 million in the fundraising campaign around the world (El Universo, August 22, 2013). By that time, the contributions in the international trust fund amounted for about US\$ 11 million, and US\$ 2 million in the national Energy Transition Trust Fund (Executive Order No. 74, published in the Official Gazette No. 72, September 3, 2013). Whilst, the minimum threshold to be reached by 2011 was established in US\$ 100 million (UNDP 2010, 13).

Despite the duration of the project was indefinite (Executive Order No. 1572, published in the Official Gazette No. 530, February 17, 2009) and the term to materialize the international compensation was agreed in thirteen years beginning in 2011 (Executive Order No. 74, published in the Official Gazette No. 72, September 3, 2013), in August 2013, the Ecuadorian government announced the unilateral termination of the Yasuní-ITT initiative and the start of oil extraction in the YNP. "The world has failed us", stated the fresh reelected[186] President Correa as announcement of the end of the initiative, while dozens of protesters gathered in front of the Presidential Palace. Correa further argued that the opportunity cost of oil exploitation raised to US$ 18,000 million, i.e. nearly US$ 11,000 million more than initially expected; so the beggars realized the sack of gold they were sitting on. Such fresh oil revenues were meant to fight poverty, the president offered (Rafael Correa, presidential address, August 15, 2013). Alberto Acosta, who stood against Correa in the 2013 presidential election with a derisory result, anticipated the end of the initiative after Correa's victory as he stated that "the infrastructure[187] needed to extract oil from field 43 is already in place" (The Guardian, February 14, 2013). An additional spark to the announcement of the beginning of oil drilling in field 43 might be related to the hefty debt burden under the oil-for-loans scheme; just one month before the drop of the Yasuní-ITT initiative, "Ecuador obtained a $2 billion loan from the China Development Bank in exchange for nearly 40,000 barrels a day [about 8 percent of national oil extraction] over two years" (Kraus 2013).

The president petitioned the National Assembly to declare of national interest[188] the exploitation of oil fields within YNP. In order to support the request, Correa ordered the ministers of environment and of non-renewable natural resources to assess the feasibility of oil drilling in the YNP within five days (Executive Order No. 74, published in the Official Gazette No. 72, September 3, 2013). The approbatory resolution of the National Assembly, with majority of Alianza País, was issued in the first days of October in record time: "[The National Assembly...] declares of national interest the exploitation of oil field 43, [...], in order to accomplish funda-

---

186 Correa was re-elected for a next four-year period in February 2013, only six months before the announcement of the cancelation of the Yasuní-ITT initiative.

187 Infrastructure projects, mostly bankrolled with Chinese funding, accounted for the main concern of the new Correa administration. Correa assigned the task to the new Vice-president Jorge Glas. The assignment of the vice-president's duties confirmed the shift of government's priorities previously imprinted by social investment led by former vice-president (and current president for the period 2017-2021) Lenín Moreno.

188 Article 407 of the 2008 Constitution prohibits "activities for the extraction of non-renewable natural resources [...] in protected areas and in areas declared intangible assets", but also states that "exceptionally, these resources can be tapped at the substantiated request of the President of the Republic and after a declaration of national interest issued by the National Assembly" (Asamblea Constituyente 2008a).

mental tasks of the state, assure individuals', peoples', and nature's rights, to achieve *buen vivir* [...]" (Resolution of the National Assembly, October 3, 2013). Successive mentions of "infantile ecologists" made by Correa in the following days to allude supporters of the Yasunít-ITT initiative accomplished another step to legitimize the government's 'new' extractivist proposal. Along with the unilateral termination of the Yasuní-ITT initiative, the discourse of *buen vivir* ultimately departed from its alternative-to-development stance, and signalized the state's capitulation to Latin American neo-extractivism (Alarcón 2020, 222). As an "empty signifier" (Laclau 2014, 256; Domínguez, Caria, and León 2017, 143), *buen vivir* could successively be filled in with diverse meanings. Once, it echoed in nature's rights (granted in the 2008 Constitution) and in the prohibition to extract oil from sensitive territories. Then, coinciding with the government's termination of the Yasuní-ITT initiative, *buen vivir* was related to a milestone of neo-extractivism: strategic resources extraction to fight poverty. The meaning of nature, as well, shuttled back from natural heritage and ancient peoples' habitat to strategic resources, a more functional concept to address economic growth and material welfare.

The cancellation of the Yasuní-ITT initiative not only "highlighted government's hostility toward its own constitutional principles" (Conaghan 2016, 115), but also disclosed the 2008 Constitution as a straitjacket against neo-extractivist policies, which can be activated by civil society. Article 407 of the Constitution mandates regarding non-renewable natural resources located in sensitive territories that "exceptionally, these resources can be tapped at the substantiated request of the President of the Republic and after a declaration of national interest issued by the National Assembly, which can, if it deems advisable, convene a referendum" (Asamblea Constituyente 2008a). A "handful of people", which met during the protests against the government's cancellation of the Yasuní-ITT initiative, decided to undertake the petition of a referendum in order to prevent oil drilling in the Yasuní National Park, "as convened in the Constitution... this was the beginning of Yasunidos", a group of activists originated in urban middle classes (Pato Chávez, spokesperson Yasunidos, interview, April 13, 2016). The petition of a referendum entailed the presentation of about 600,000 supporting signatures, i.e. five percent of the national electorate, to the National Electoral Council (*Consejo Nacional Electoral*, CNE). The task implied for the novel collective of the Yasunidos the mobilization countrywide. The collective undertook the enterprise successfully with the backing of other social movements, but the CNE alleged fraud and disqualified the signatures, thus rejected the petition. Though, the significance of Yasunidos as a domestic social force, which contested the government's neo-extractivist strategy, was sealed with the decision to seek a referendum on the Yasuní-ITT initiative (O'Connell 2016, 50). Yasunidos nurtured of the rupture between the government and the environmental movement and embodied a new generation of urban activists for whom the meaning of development is indissoluble from that of nature. Voices of social movements, indigenous and peasants' organizations, and groups of intellectuals who advocate for a post-oil era converged into the critique of the renewed bet on natural resources commodification to support the national development project led by the state (Alarcón, Rocha, and Di Pietro 2018, 70). In this logic, Ortiz (2016, 61) advocated a "qualitative leap in the character of social movements opposed to government" and argued that a "polycentric social movement" emerged[189].

However, opposition to neo-extractivism as the government's favored developmental strategy had been cooking since the beginning of 2012, one year before Correa's reelection in February 2013. The "March for Water, Life, and the Dignity of the Peoples" (*Marcha por el agua, la vida y la dignidad de los pueblos*) was summoned by most heterogeneous opposition factions led by the Confederation of Indigenous Nationalities of Ecuador (*Confederación de Nacionalidades Indígenas del Ecuador*, CONAIE) and local governments against mining. The *marcha por el agua* took place between March 8 and 22, through a 700 km journey from southern Ecuador, a region menaced by mining activities, to the capital. About 70,000 persons participated in the *marcha* and in the demonstration held at its arrival to Quito on World Water Day (Ortiz 2016, 51). Alberto Acosta was one of the head protestors and embodied popular support to the Yasuní-ITT initiative during the march. Though, opposition to neo-extractivism did not achieve to turn into an electoral platform, so the outcome of Acosta's presidential candidacy in 2013, he obtained about three percent of the votes among eight candidates. If not in electoral successes, the legacy of the *marcha por el agua* is to be found elsewhere, in the organized critique of the state's

---

189 Consequences of the government's termination of the Yasuní-ITT initiative were not only to be found in the domestic arena. The cancellation of the initiative led to an impasse with the German government, which supported the Yasuní-ITT initiative. Germany has been a traditional partner in international cooperation; only with the special programme "Biosphere Reserve Yasuní" (*Sonderprogramm Biosphärenreservat Yasuní*), the German government channeled 34.5 million Euro to protection of the Yasuní National Park during a five-year period (BMZ 2013, 2). For a detailed relation of the impasse, see Alarcón, Rocha, and Di Pietro (2018).

neo-extractivist developmental strategy. Such critique outlived the polyphonic concept of *buen vivir*, and is evoked in the Yasuní-ITT initiative as a fissure within the [current] development model (Fernando Fajardo, member Yasunidos, interview, May 6, 2016).

Postlude to Nature and the State: Towards a Political Ecology of Rentierism

By August 2019, renowned field 43 ITT reported record oil extraction, circa 80 thousand barrels per day or nearly one fifth of the extraction undertaken by the state-owned companies (El Comercio, August 17, 2019). Though, it proved to be crumbs from the rich man's table to deal with the devastating consequences of the end of the last "commodities super-cycle" (Alarcón and Peters 2020; Erten and Ocampo 2013). Indeed, plummeting oil prices meant for Ecuador a budget gap of circa US$ 7 billion due to less revenues in 2015, i.e. about 7 percent of GDP (former Minister of Coordination of Economic Policy, interview, October 7, 2015). Thereby, liquidity from Chinese loans provided oxygen for a couple of years and contributed to the illusion that the brink of the crisis was far to be reached. Nonetheless, even before the COVID-19 pandemic arrived in 2020 to checkmate the economy and unveil clear signals of a humanitarian catastrophe, Ecuador was facing a severe social and economic crisis; by October 2019, escalating social discontent exploded into political turmoil. After failing to renegotiate debt conditions with China, Moreno's government reverted to traditional international financial institutions (IFI) and reached a US$ 4.2 billion deal with the International Monetary Fund (IMF) (Reuters 2019; Long 2019). In order to meet targets agreed with lenders, Moreno announced a set of economic measures that included scrapping subsidies on transportation fuels on October 1st 2019 (Executive Order No. 883, October 1, 2019; El Comercio, October 2, 2019). According to government officials, the measure aimed at saving the country about US$ 1.3 billion a year (Long 2019); though, eliminating subsidies on domestic fuels has proven to be like tossing a stick of dynamite into a tinder box in contemporary Ecuadorian history. When President Abdalá Bucaram eliminated the subsidy on domestic gas for cooking in 1997, the National Assembly declared him "mentally incapacitated" (*loco*), and deposed him within a few days. With hindsight, it might be argued that herein Moreno found a good reason to maintain domestic gas untouched. However, the elimination of subsidies on transportation fuels did trigger nationwide protests, which could not even be stopped by repression or the declaration of a state of emergency, and Moreno was forced to repeal the measure on October 15, after two weeks of street pressure.

The origin of the protests was certainly not monocausal; yet, Alarcón and Peters (2020) argued that political turmoil was the consequence of questioning the foundations of the rentier bargain and therefore trying to alter state-society relations. Central to the "rentier bargain" between the state and society in oil-rich countries is peoples' claim on their portion of oil rent in the form of subsidies on oil products, i.e. the expression of a quasi-naturalized right derived from living in a natural resources-rich country (Peters 2017a, 58). Reclaim on oil rent, in the form of access to subsidies, proved to be central to assess the limits of reform, and even government's room for maneuver when trying to impose changes to the current development model. Analogously, reclaim on natural resources rent might gain momentum in further debates on tightening the fiscal contract, or discussing what Atria, Biehl, and Labarca (2019) called the "fiscal sociology" applied to natural resources-rich countries. The elimination of subsidies on transportation fuels reminded of the loss of state's autonomy from international financial institutions (IFI) and unveiled the process of dismantling of the landlord-arbiter state configuration. As the sociopolitical atmosphere resembled the end of the first oil boom (and even reminded of the crisis of the end of the twentieth century), debates on the alternatives to the elimination of subsidies took place in an economy that traditionally followed procyclical tendencies. Conservative economists consider Keynesian policymaking (i.e. state's intervention to boost aggregate demand during crisis) as the paradigm of countercyclical economic policy. Though, the country study of Ecuador proved to be unsuitable to access the enforcement of countercyclical economic policy. On the one hand, crises coincided with the state's loss of relative autonomy based on the appropriation of a larger portion of oil rent and with the dismantling of the landlord-arbiter state configuration. On the other hand, subsidies on fuels remain since the beginning of the oil era, they outlived booms as well as crises.

However, the elimination of subsidies on transportation fuels was not the first measure taken by Moreno's government to cope with the budgetary gap after assumption in May 2017. Besides trying to renegotiate oil deals with China clinched by his predecessor (Valencia 2017), and returning to traditional creditors, particularly the IMF, a significant action was the dismantling of the ministries of coordination and other state entities established during the last decade[190] (such as sectorial ministries, national secretariats, technical secretariats, public enterprises, agencies, councils, research institutes). These measures were also directed to signalize an alleged rupture with Correa. A hard hit was the dismantlement of the National Secretariat of Planning and Development (SENPLADES). Despite oil rent allocation was driven by political criteria (rather than by neutral, economic criteria) during the second oil boom, SENPLADES epitomized the return of the faith in state's economic planning. Though, by preserving the bulk of SENPLADES payroll, its elimination was regarded as rather symbolic. Instead, Lenín Moreno established the Technical Secretariat of Planning "Planifica Ecuador" (*Secretaría Técnica de Planificación "Planifica Ecuador"*) subordinated to the Office of the President (Executive Order No. 732, May 13, 2019); such a configuration reminded of the old SENPLADES, an office within the presidency between 2004 and 2007.

The elimination of state entities was at the cost of about 12,000 dismissals until the beginning of 2019 (El Comercio, March 13, 2019). The ongoing pursuit of a smaller state counted already 16,000 layoffs in the public sector by the beginning of August 2019 (El Comercio, August 4, 2019), and further set its sights on public enterprises. Between December 2018 and July 2019, about 6,500 public servants have been removed from public companies in an alleged "optimization". According to government officials, the payroll of circa 33,500 employees at public enterprises (by August 2019) is "still obese" (Montenegro 2019). As the public sector continues shrinking, highly qualified manpower resulting from the international scholarships granted by the Ecuadorian government (Figure No. 11) will increasingly become a loose end. PhD- and master scholarship holders (mostly with a middle class origin), who returned to Ecuador during the last years of the oil bonanza applied for the academia in absence of a consolidated private sector, and with an already saturated public sector. But job hunting in the academia implied competing with states classes, which regarded public universities as a lifeline or a "plan B" during the reduction of the high-ranking bureaucracy, "already by 2016, public universities were overflowed by former high-ranking government officials, who served, or were still serving in ministries" (former scholarship holder of the Ecuadorian government, interview, August 8, 2018). By October 2019, in average

---

190 Another significant measure at domestic level was the prosecution of Correa and his close allies for corruption allegations. Though, an estimation of the contribution of corruption (e.g. embezzlement, bribery) to the budget gap is beyond the scope of this book.

for newly hired lecturers, the salary payed by public universities was double so high than that payed by private universities. Ecuadorian public universities are well-known for their above-average remunerations compared to Latin American levels. By 2012, during a height of international oil prices, the Council of Higher Education (*Consejo de Educación Superior*, CES) resolved upward adjustments in wages of public university lecturers ranging from 131 percent to 300 percent. With that, the average wage of a full-time lecturer in public universities reached circa ten 2012 minimum wages (Resolution No. RPC-SO-037-265-2012 of October 31, 2012). Whilst, "private universities did not catch up with upward adjustments in wages [...] work conditions were less attractive, for the few offers" (former scholarship holder of the Ecuadorian government, interview, August 8, 2018). Another impact on higher education of the loss of employment opportunities in the public sector was university desertion, mainly from middle class private universities, "particularly in the social sciences, less students matriculated... some students deserted due to the economic situation, they were removed from their jobs in the public sector, or their parents were" (lecturer at private university in Quito, interview, January 24, 2019). Consequently, "demand for public education has been increasing" (María Augusta Espín, Vice President of Academic Affairs at the Central University of Ecuador, interview, March 8, 2019).

Empty state coffers and menaced middle classes revived the faith in natural resources rent; like his predecessor, President Moreno reiterated his high hopes for mining as a future pillar of the economy (Tapia 2019; Astudillo 2019; León and Domínguez 2017, 129). Moreno's vice-president, Otto Sonnenholzner, publicly guaranteed support for private investments and assured that the Ministry of Transport "will work on the roads required for mineral exports" (Astudillo 2019). In this line, "bridges nearing camps of mining companies have been designed for heavy traffic during the last years in order to support loaded trucks" (Pepe Vásquez, interview, October 11, 2018)[191]. From 2012 until May 2019, the Ecuadorian state received circa US$ 270 million for mineral royalties (Astudillo and Castillo 2019). Until 2021, the government expects about US$ 3,660 million in

---

191 Governments' backing of private mining companies has also taken other forms. In the same way as heads of the oil sector have been traditionally former managers of multinational oil corporations, high-ranking officials of the mining sector, and even of the environmental sector (the national authority granting environmental licenses), have been working or are connected with mining companies (Jessica López Pérez, interview, November 13, 2018).

mineral exports and US$ 800 million in tax revenues (Tapia 2019). With that, the share of mining in GDP would jump from 0.6 percent in 2017 to 4.0 percent in 2021 (Astudillo 2019). Different from the case of oil rent, where state's participation has traditionally been ensured by a national company, state's pursuit of a larger portion of mineral rent seems to follow a planned scheme founded on private companies' taxation and royalties. Table No. 32 depicts a comparison between the weight in GDP of oil rent and mineral rent for the period 1971-2017 (data entails exclusively rent, not tax revenues). The participation of mineral rent in GDP shows an upward trend, and averaged 0.21 percent for the period 2011-17 (World Bank 2019k). Though, such values are still far behind the benchmark case of oil rent. As percentage of GDP, oil rent averaged two digits during the twenty-first century commodities boom, and peaked at 18.5 percent by 2006 (World Bank 2019d). The upward trend was only altered by the 2014 drop of international oil prices.

Table No. 32: Oil rent and mineral rent as percentage of GDP (average), Ecuador 1971-2017

	Oil rent (percentage of GDP)	Mineral rent (percentage of GDP)
1971-80	5.6	0.01
1981-90	8.0	0.09
1991-2000	7.3	0.0
2001-10	13.0	0.05
2011-17	9.4	0.21

Source: World Bank (2019d; 2019k)

In a context of increased awareness of the negative socioecological consequences of extractivism, optimism about mining among society is related to the promise of development, particularly to the promise of employment opportunities, which have been proven central to the consolidation and strengthening of middle classes. On September 3rd 2019, supporters of mining led by public servants of the Ministry of Energy and Non-Renewable Resources[192] marched on Quito exhibiting posters in which mining was placed in the core of development: *"YES* to mining, *YES* to develop-

---

192 By 2007, Correa split the Ministry of Energy and Mines (MEM) into the Ministry of Mining and Oil and the Ministry of Electricity and Renewable Energy (Executive Order No. 475, published in the Official Gazette No. 132, July 23,

ment, *YES* to employment, *NO* to poverty" (*SI a la minería, SI al desarrollo, SI al trabajo, NO a la pobreza*) or "Mineral Royalties = Health, Education, and Employment Opportunities" (*regalías mineras = salud, educación y oportunidades*). Faith in the potential impacts of mining on the economy (found in government and at least in a significant portion of society[193]), as well as further reliance on oil, take place in Ecuador in an scenario shaped by increased awareness of the negative socioecological consequences of extractivism and with the involvement of new stakeholders, who defend antagonist meanings of nature and development. Such a cocktail speaks for the need of a political ecology approach of natural resources rentierism, which nurtures from previous academic contributions like 1) the evidence of semiotic struggles (Escobar 1995b) over a prevailing meaning of nature and development, 2) the struggle over natural riches that takes place in natural resources exporting societies, where the generation of value is based on the capture of rents (Coronil 2008, 20), and 3) society's claims on rent as a quasi-naturalized right to participate in the benefits generated by natural riches (Alarcón and Peters 2020; Peters 2017a, 63). Hence, the proposed political ecology approach of rentierism *à la* Ecuadorian comprises *first*, the evidence left by the termination of the Yasuní-ITT initiative of antagonist meanings of development defended by the state and society, which are founded on different visions of nature; *second*, the validity of an approach to the state's strategies to capture a larger portion of natural resources rent (e.g. through a state-owned company and the renegotiation of contracts in the case of oil extraction, or through taxation and royalties in the case of mineral extraction); and *third*, the necessity of stressing on the struggle of different society sectors to access to a portion of rent captured by the state, not as a struggle over natural riches itself, but as a pursue of benefits granted by the state on the basis of rent allocation (e.g. funding for local development projects, subsidies, employment opportunities in the public sector, access to public health and education).

2007). The Ministry of Mines and the Ministry of Hydrocarbons resulted from the division of the Ministry of Oil and Mining (Executive Order No. 578, published in the Official Gazette No. 448, February 28, 2015). By 2018, Moreno fused 1) the Ministry of Mines, 2) the Ministry of Hydrocarbons, 3) the Ministry of Electricity and Renewable Energy, and 4) the Secretariat of Hydrocarbons into the Ministry of Energy and Non-Renewable Resources (Executive Order No. 399, May 15, 2018).

193 Following Eisenstadt and Jones West (2017), inhabitants of natural resources-rich backward territories, where extractivist activities have not been undertaken yet, add to a portion of society that has high hopes for mining.

Conclusion: Beyond the Ecuadorian Case

"According to Marx, history repeats once as tragedy and
once as farce, nonetheless there is another possibility: it can
endlessly replay as slapstick comedy" (Latour 2017, 147).

Key Findings

The diachronic comparative approach of the two Ecuadorian oil booms, 1)
1972-1980 and 2) 2003-2014, unveiled continuities and ruptures in the
state's developmental enterprise. On the one hand, the state's appropriation of a larger portion of oil rent was central to rentier modernization
during the last fifty years. On the other hand, the irruption of environmental thinking exposed the flaws of the state's endeavor as it contributed to
erode the hegemonic developmental discourse. The approach of the
Ecuadorian oil booms through the prism nature-state-development allowed the discussion of the role of the state within an scenario framed by
1) external constraints (the position of Ecuador in the international division of nature) and 2) domestic circumstances (debatable outcomes of
economic diversification and temporary improvements of social and economic indicators).

An English proverb says "as you sow, so shall you reap". The Ecuadorian
desarrollista state had the intention to "sow the oil" during both oil booms,
and expected to reap economic diversification. In this line, the inspirations
of this book were twofold. On the one hand, it was motivated by the different visions of economic diversification, which stemmed from the evolution of the meaning of development during the last half century. The vision of economic diversification during the first oil boom was different
from that of the second oil boom; a main rupture was introduced by the
irruption of environmental thinking. On the other hand, the persistent impact on the Ecuadorian economy of the volatility of international oil prices
(the external constraint) speaks for the validity of discussing the scope and
the outcomes of the state-driven economic diversification attempts (the domestic circumstance). Assessing *how* was oil sown and *what* was reaped
throughout half century, led to the question of *where* are the outcomes of
the state's developmental efforts to be found, *who* reaped them.

Key Findings: The State and Development

The endeavor of the Ecuadorian *desarrollista* state during both oil booms has been characterized through the "Poulantzas' reformulation" of the developmental state theory. The landlord-arbiter state configuration was presented as central to this theoretical elaboration since oil rent was not outright at the state's disposal at the beginning of the oil era. Thus, the Ecuadorian *desarrollista* state became a landlord only after its struggle with multinational oil corporations for the appropriation of a larger portion of oil rent. The seminal struggle, which took place during the first Ecuadorian oil boom, configured the state as a landlord henceforth, and might also have contributed to forge the state's authoritarian character. In this line, Karl (1999, 34) argued that the initial bargaining with foreign oil companies left a legacy of "overly-centralized political power". After controlling a larger portion of oil rent, the state became an arbiter of its allocation among society. This granted the state the main role as political actor in the economy during oil booms. As the bourgeoisie was split into factions that pursued diverse objectives, the state arose as what Poulantzas (1978, 121) called a "subject" of development, with its own power, and with relative autonomy from social classes. Such a state form exists outside social classes and might force divergent interests within the bourgeoise to converge into "the politics of the bureaucracy or the politics of the political elites" (Poulantzas 1978, 121). During the first Ecuadorian oil boom, when environmental thinking was practically absent from the discussion on development, the discourse on the central role of natural resources to economic development was hegemonic. Then, the developmental endeavor of the state might be considered as widely supported "politics of the bureaucracy". Contrarily, during the second Ecuadorian oil boom, when the state's interpretation of the role of nature in development found opposition among society, the state's developmental project might be regarded as the imposition of "the politics of the political elites".

Nevertheless, the landlord-arbiter state configuration gave rise to a political regime in which the state 1) directed the national economy, with the public sector as its motor, and 2) allocated oil rent during bonanza periods. The *desarrollista* state grasped at different mechanisms of rent distribution; on the one hand, during the first oil boom, oil revenues were earmarked for specific state entities. On the other hand, during the second oil boom, control of oil revenues was centralized in the hands of the government, which channeled them through diverse ministries. The distribution schemes enforced during bonanza periods resulted in the state pouring rent into society. Every social class benefited from the oil booms in what might be called a general "(up)lift effect" (Burchardt and Dietz 2014); though, the mechanisms of state's sponsorship were different. Whereas upper classes profited from mechanisms as the reduction of the tax burden, subsidized credits, access to lucrative and sometimes inflated state contracts and business opportunities, and even from overvaluation of the currency, lower classes benefited from diverse kinds of state benefits as subsidies on basic goods, creation of low-skill government jobs and public spending in social policy programs. Nonetheless, middle classes were the winners of the Ecuadorian oil booms as they expanded and consolidated unprecedently thanks to the distribution of oil wealth. The *desarrollista* state endowed middle classes with market capacities (Wright 1996, 694) and improved their possibilities to access to tertiary education. Central to the strengthening of middle classes during oil boom periods was the expansion of the state apparatus; oil windfalls were used to bankroll the creation of employment opportunities in the public sector. In fact, the first Ecuadorian oil boom witnessed the rise *modern urban* middle classes at the cost of the *hacendado* class, the epitome of the crumbling oligarchical state. The rise of modern urban (rentier) middle classes and the fall of the oligarchical state remained as the landmark and legacy of the 1970s. The magnitude of the earthquake provoked by the first oil boom in the Ecuadorian social formation remained unparalleled until present day.

Key Findings: Development and Nature

The successful modernizing effort led by the Ecuadorian *desarrollista* state, which mirrors in the social formation, contrasts with the failure in attaining structural change in the economy. During oil booms, the state devoted itself to economic planning in order to attain economic diversification. According to Larrain (1989, 87), traditional societies are supposed to follow 1) the industrial society paradigm, and 2) the ideal typical process of transition, which is constructed on the basis of the fact that certain societies have already industrialized. In this line, industrialization is regarded as the foundational myth of progress, which promises access to a new era of consumption standards comparable with those of developed countries. Technocratic planning agencies epitomized the Ecuadorian state's developmental effort during oil booms as they were intended to guide the process of transition to industrialized societies. Though, Ferguson (1994, 255) already warned that "the development apparatus is a *machine* for reinforcing and expanding the exercise of bureaucratic state power". In Ferguson's (2004) case study, Lesotho, the development apparatus took poverty as its point of entry, but had insignificant effects on its reduction. Significant effects of the development apparatus' agency are to be found elsewhere (not in economic diversification), but in "ugly [governmental] buildings", and "expensive road building and construction work" (Ferguson 1994, 251). Analogously, it may be argued that in Ecuador the development machine driven by the state incidentally took economic diversification as its point of entry. As a result, infrastructure projects were boosted and also "white elephants" (Robinson and Torvik 2005) testify the squander of petrodollars.

A common aspect observed in either boom periods is that strong planning agencies contributed less to economic diversification than to the strengthening of middle classes, by the creation of new employment opportunities in the public sector. Economic planning proved to be a political task instead of a neutral tool, as touted by development economics. Whereas during the first Ecuadorian oil boom, governments intended to channel state resources to promote a faction of the bourgeoisie to become a modern industrialist class, during the second oil boom, the government overlooked the options in the private sector and, instead, supported a faction within government itself with a certain vision on the way how to conduct the process of transition to an industrialized society. Central to explain the emergence of different visions on economic diversification during the second oil boom are 1) the inclusion of the environmental factor in development thinking, and 2) the pursue of integration into the current stage of capitalism. Notwithstanding, the creation of an "University of Research of Experimental Technology" named *Yachay Tech* and the intention to build a technology hub signaled the predominant vision on economic diversification and, hence, the faction that collected a larger portion of oil rent within government. The ill-conceived and imitative project remained of the imposition of "the politics of the political elites" since 1) it resulted from internal struggle within government for positioning a view on economic diversification as predominant, 2) existing public universities did not participate, and 3) the private sector was excluded from the design of the project. However, the enforcement of economic diversification policy during oil booms mirrored neither in a significant upsurge in manufactured exports nor in the incorporation of new technology into the Ecuadorian export portfolio. In a context where no significant change of the export structure is observed, a key finding is that the contribution of the manufacturing sector to economic growth has been following a declining trend since the beginning of the twenty-first century commodities boom and cannot stand comparison with levels attained during the years that succeeded the beginning of the Ecuadorian oil era.

The predominance of raw material in the Ecuadorian export portfolio during the last half-century signalizes the blatant failure of economic diversification attempts. This is only the icing on the cake of dependency. During oil booms, the developmental agency of the Ecuadorian state endowed social classes with market capacities, which found correlation in increasing demand for imported manufactured goods; the *desarrollista* state indeed consolidated and strengthened the domestic market, but for imported products. At the end of the oil booms, external debt became an inexorable way to sustain levels of consumption and standards of living that remain of wealthy classes of the Global North. However, oil rent might have endowed the *desarrollista* state with relative autonomy from domestic social classes to impose its developmental project (as the politics of the bureaucracy), and even a vision on economic diversification (as the politics of the political elites). But oil rent definitely did not provide the state with autonomy from external funding sources or international financial institutions (IFI). At the end of the oil booms, as domestic funding sources appear as insufficiently diversified and external debt becomes tangible, debt service turns into an imperative to get access to more external debt, in a vicious circle.

The imperative of debt service, which detonated at the end of either oil booms, jeopardizes the landlord-arbiter state configuration. First, it erodes the "arbiter" capacity of the *desarrollista* state as a larger portion of oil rent has to be allocated to debt service rather than to developmental purposes. Then, it also threatens the "landlord" capacity of the state. Incidentally, when the first oil boom was passé, the pursuit of foreign investments in the oil sector resulted in a larger participation of multinational corporations and, hence, in a smaller portion of oil rent under control of the state. During the second oil boom, the "landlord" capacity of the state was early jeopardized as Correa's government contracted debt with China to be repaid with crude oil. In this line, Benzi (2017, 12) argued that "the recent marriage with China is neither sustainable nor *progresista* as it reinforces the rentier logic of Latin American societies and contributes to environmental devastation".

Key Findings: Nature and the State

Central to the representations of nature forged in the twenty-first century were disputed environmental discourses, which in turn became capable of molding the state-society relationship. On the one hand, the state embraced the environmental discourse of sustainable development that fitted well with its modernizing rationality and justified the extractive imperative, i.e. the legitimation of neo-extractivism on the basis of economic and social development. On the other hand, social movements accepted the challenge of searching alternative meanings of development on the basis of a representation of nature that opposed to that of the state, i.e. to the official vision of strategic resources at the service of the national modernization project. Representations of nature apart from the role of natural resources in economic development were absent during the 1970s. Whereas the legacy of the first oil boom introduced a big bang in the Ecuadorian *social arena* (the rise of middle classes), the second oil boom granted environmental thinking a permanent position in the Ecuadorian *political arena*. Ecuadorian middle classes, which outlived the crisis of the end of the twentieth century, became the carriers of social environmental awareness into the twenty-first century.

Despite the antagonist nature of the environmental discourses (one held by the state, and the other defended by socio-environmental movements) they converged upon the socioecological dimension of *buen vivir*, or its epitome, the Yasuní-ITT initiative. The failure of the initiative opened the gates for a wider understanding of the rise and fall of the discourse of *buen vivir*. Coinciding with its inclusion into the state logic, *buen vivir* failed as an ecologist ideology since it lacked of a "decisive political strategy" aimed at materializing its action plan (Dobson 1997, 59). Indeed, after the vanishing of the Yasuní-ITT initiative, *buen vivir* was left no other possibility to materialize. The fiasco of *buen vivir* in Ecuador unveiled Latin American neo-extractivism as the state's favored development strategy in the dawn of the twenty-first century, and added a further reason to argue that the struggle for positioning a meaning of nature as predominant takes place in the political arena. After the fall of *buen vivir*, the state upheld the environmental discourse of sustainable development; though O'Connor (1994, 16) warned beforehand that the official environmental discourse might serve to co-opt peoples and social movements in the "game of conservation".

The assessment of fifty years of recent Ecuadorian economic history showed that nature shifted from a concept to be grasped in the economic arena (natural resources), to a disputed meaning to be defined in the political arena. Land reform acted as a proxy during the first oil boom; its enforcement by the "revolutionary nationalist" dictatorship indeed impacted on the state-society relationship to such a conflictual degree that it became one of the triggers for the coup of 1975 and for the replacement of General Rodríguez Lara in 1976. During the second oil boom[194], opposition to the state's vision of nature (i.e. strategic resources at the service of the national modernization project) proved its capacity to activate social movements in the *Marcha por el agua, la vida y la dignidad de los pueblos* of 2012, and even to mobilize urban middle classes during the protests against government's unilateral termination of the Yasuní-ITT initiative in 2013. Though, the mobilization capacity did not mirror in an electoral success of the opposition to the official environmental discourse.

The transit of nature from the economic to the political arena demands an interdisciplinary research program. Political economy approaches that focus on the appropriation of the surplus generated by natural resources or by Madame la Terre might be complemented by the discussion on the access to the benefits derived from the state's allocation of oil rent among society, which stems from the rise of the *desarrollista* state with the landlord-arbiter configuration. Access to employment opportunities in the public sector, state contracts, subsidies, and other state benefits, suggest a race between rentiers rather than capitalists, on the one hand. On the other hand, access to sectoral budgets (e.g. the strategic resources sector vs. the environmental protection sector, or the classical industrialization faction vs the *Yachay*-clique) and to territorial budgets (e.g. state's funds for projects in backward territories or in natural resources-rich territories affected by extractivism) reinforce the idea of the need of a political ecology approach.

---

194 Pink tide governments announced land reform at the top of their political agendas. Different from previous experiences, which entailed a significant ideological component, central to the re-launching of land reform during the twenty-first century were food sovereignty and a social justice compromise. Whereas article 282 of the 2008 Ecuadorian Constitution pleads for "social and environmental function of land", and advocates a "national fund of land to ensure equal access", article 334-2 establishes the need of specific policy aimed at "eradicating inequality and discrimination against women in the access to factors of production" (Asamblea Constituyente 2008a). Nonetheless, the re-launching of land reform vanished in electoral campaign promises.

Hypotheses from Ecuador and Theoretical Implications

A number of hypothesis derived from the case study of Ecuador during its fifty-year oil era are valid for other natural resources-rich countries. Thereby, the pursuit of economic diversification became a contemporary task of the *desarrollista* state in the Global South. Consequences of the enforcement of developmental strategies aimed at coping with boom and bust cycles provoked by the volatility of commodity international prices are twofold. On the one hand, the enforcement of state strategies unveils the quest for a renovated integration into the capitalist world economy. On the other hand, the outcomes of state's economic diversification strategies are found in the domestic sociopolitical arena (rather than in the economic arena) as they benefited in different ways specific society sectors. However, in the long run, the irruption of social environmental awareness increasingly erodes the state's developmental discourse, in which natural resources are central to modernization, and deeply questions the neo-extractivist developmental strategy. Hence, social environmental awareness is central to the relationship between the state and society. Increasing social environmental awareness together with the irruption of environmental thinking into development theories present a real challenge for scholars during the twenty-first century: The approach of the relationship between nature and the state under such premises not only opens the gates for revisiting the state-society relationship, but also invites to rethink fundamental issues such as the ontology of nature. In a context where disputed environmental discourses proved to be central to the construction of representations of nature forged in the first decades of the twenty-first century, a revitalized approach to discourses becomes an imperative. An interdisciplinary research agenda on environmental discourses (as political discourses) ought to entail not only a comprehensive approach to their authors, but also to the actors of the development process (as political process) (van Dijk 1999, 14). The inclusion of authors as well as actors of antagonist environmental discourses underpins the need of a political ecology approach of the development process in natural resources-rich countries.

The innovative diachronic comparative approach used to explore two Ecuadorian oil booms shows processes of continuity and change in the developmental endeavor of the state, and also in the way how the concept of the rentier state itself has been treated until today. On the one hand, the findings of the country study confirmed the political allocation of natural resources revenues among society as a central characteristic of the rentier state (Karl 1997, 16). On the other hand, by highlighting a general "(up)lift effect", the findings of the country study question the link between the rentier state and a rather small or exclusive group of beneficiaries from rent allocation, such as "a minority of rentier capitalists" (Karl 1999, 37), or "governing elites" (Omeje 2008, 5) proposed in classical rentier theory. Thereby, the findings of the case study speak for the need of a critical rentier theory approach. Besides, the concept of relative autonomy from social classes proved to be central not only to a wider understanding of the state's boosted agency (i.e. its capacity to intervene in the national development process) during either Ecuadorian oil booms, but also to explain the presence of regimes (such as the "revolutionary nationalist" or the "citizen's revolution") that gave birth to political elites, which not necessarily stem from traditional economic elites. In this line, the country study calls into question or at least advocates a more refined treatment of the connection between the rentier state model and authoritarian regimes (Ross 2001, 357). During the first Ecuadorian oil boom, General Rodríguez Lara's "revolutionary nationalist" dictatorship (1972-1976) was the paradigmatic regime. Indeed, it was a military de facto regime that ascended to power after a coup d'état. Though, it was stranded between its adherence to reformism and its intention to be accepted as a democratic leadership with a "technocratic-*desarrollista*" imprint (Báez 1984, 96). The next military dictatorship, the triumvirate, drafted a new constitution and orchestrated the return of democracy. The "technocratic-military" (Báez 1984, 102) stance of General Rodríguez Lara's "revolutionary nationalist" dictatorship shifted to the "techno-populist" (de la Torre 2013, 24) mien of the "citizen's revolution" during the second oil boom. After winning consecutive elections, Correa's government devolved into authoritarianism as power was shifted to the executive branch through the 2008 Constitution and other legal changes to the detriment of the judiciary and the legislature (Conaghan 2016). In this line, Peters (2015, 159) advocated for "democratic rentierism" as an option to study the connection between rentier states and authoritarian regimes in contemporary Latin America.

The approach of two Ecuadorian oil booms also shows that certain forms of authoritarianism are present at the imposition of a state's developmental project on society. During the first oil boom, the "revolutionary nationalist" dictatorship excluded indigenous peoples from the formulation of its developmental project. During the second oil boom, the "citizen's revolution" government excluded the private sector from the construction of the economic diversification policy[195] and tilted the balance towards the proposal of a faction within government. Thereby, mobilization (in support of governmental measures) is officially promoted over participation. Hence, the case study shows that the notion of authoritarianism within critical rentier state theory might converge upon the "ambiguous relationship with democracy" that accompanies the Latin American populist state (de la Torre 2000, 140). Together, they round off the proposal highlighted in this book of state's relative autonomy from social classes (Poulantzas 1978) to impose a national developmental project. Following this logic, natural resources booms might be approached as classic populist interludes in many regions of the Global South.

Pending Questions and Further Research

A number of further research questions arise from the diachronic comparative approach used to explore half-century of Ecuadorian oil era, in which the state plays a central role in the national development process. Thereby, pending questions stress on the need of deepening the interdisciplinary approach proposed in the triad nature-state-development, and contained traditionally in Latin American (under)development thinking.

Further Research: The State and Development

The appropriation of a larger portion of oil rent was central to boost state's agency during either Ecuadorian oil booms. With oil revenues at its disposal, the state managed to steer the sociopolitical sphere as the public sector turned into the motor of the economy. Oil rent and external debt bankrolled the "(up)lift effect", in which every social class benefited to different degrees. Though, external debt turned into the booms' nemesis, as it increasingly jeopardizes socioeconomic improvements attained during bonanza periods. External debt came as a rude awakening to the loss of autonomy from international financial institutions (IFI) straight after the oil booms. The debt crisis of the 1980s *década perdida* heralded the Ecuadorian state's withdrawal from key economic and sociopolitical arenas after the

---

195 It might be discussed if the exclusion of the private sector from the construction of the economic diversification policy is an authoritarian act *per se*, or if it corresponds to an authoritarian behavior towards the political opposition.

first oil boom. Few years after the twenty-first century commodities boom, the Ecuadorian government announced the return of the International Monetary Fund (IMF) after failing to renegotiate debt deals with China. As the fiscal deficit grew, the shrinkage of the state apparatus became an imperative of external creditors. The loss of employment opportunities in the public sector also compromises the living standard of modern urban middle classes, which arose as winners of the "(up)lift effect" of either Ecuadorian oil booms. This recurring threat suggests the necessity of getting a closer look at what Ouaissa (2014, 14) called the "political origin" of middle classes in the Global South (rather than its economic origin), and at its potential role in social protests or regime changes that might follow bonanza periods, on the one hand. On the other hand, blooms of Ecuadorian middle classes, that temporarily matched them up to those of the Global North, contrast with the enduring realization of state classes.

As economic elites unceasingly benefit from the prevailing export-led outward-oriented development model, state classes epitomize political elites, which seek to reproduce their power by defining the terms of national development during bonanza periods and by outlining and imposing a state's developmental discourse on society. In this line, this book advocates a further strand of research to delve into the mechanisms grasped by state classes in order to access to high ranking governmental positions and other state benefits in the long run (even after bonanza periods). Further research might include revisiting governments as "autonomous state elites" (Mann 2003, 55), and the "extent to which state-administrative activity is enjoying relative autonomy vis-à-vis the potentials of influence and conflict linked to elitist, particular interests" (Burchardt and Weinmann 2012, 19). Such investigation does not exclude the approach to the mechanisms of access to state benefits in natural resources-rich countries like kinship, crony capitalism, and rent-seeking behavior.

The analysis of the country study shows that the state's modernizing logic translated into the pursuit of a bourgeoise national construction in the long-term. With boosted capacity to intervene in the national development process during oil booms, the Ecuadorian *desarrollista* state endowed middle classes with enhanced consumption possibilities, which decisively contributed to improve their market capacities, thus to integrate them into the globalized economy. Consequences of the state-led integration of middle classes into the globalized economy are twofold. On the one hand, with improved market capacities, domestic middle classes tend to mimic consumption standards of those in the Global North. On the other hand, the illusion of higher living standards did not result in the maturing of class consciousness but rather in middle classes' dependence on governmental decisions. Otherwise, a closer look at the role of lower classes might also corroborate the state's departure of any popular project, and might confirm its pursuit of a bourgeois national construction. Oil rent allowed the Ecuadorian state to attend to historically overlooked demands of popular sectors. Though, this does not mirror in enhanced *participation* of lower classes but instead in their *mobilization* in favor of governmental measures. The main role of rentier middle classes in the bourgeois national construction, as well as the subsidiary role of lower classes, also advocate further exploration into the connections between the authoritarian vein of the rentier state and the "ambiguous relationship with democracy" (de la Torre 2000, 140) that traditionally accompanied the Latin American populist state. In this vein, Svampa (2016, 63) anticipated the emergence of "non-anti-elite middle-class populisms that are not interested in promoting participation".

Further Research: Development and Nature

In his 1977 classic *El desarrollo del capitalismo en América Latina*, Cueva (2013, 150) already denounced the apparent dichotomy between the primary sector of the economy and other sectors. The author pointed out that the take-off of advanced economic sectors in Latin America does not suppose the abolition of the primary sector, since economic diversification hinges on the appropriation of surplus generated precisely by it (Cueva 2013, 150). Following this logic, it might be argued that in natural resources-rich countries, the promotion of the industrial sector (or any other more advanced sector of the economy) turns into a race for access to a larger portion of natural resources rent. The case study of Ecuador shows that even the definition of the national economic diversification policy within the government might turn into a competition for a larger portion of state's swollen budget during oil booms. Regardless of the preferred mechanisms of state's rent allocation, either the earmarks for specific state entities of the first boom or the distribution of a general budget among ministries of the second boom, oil windfalls are put at the disposal of selected state actors, which use them to bankroll public spending in specific ways. As the public sector becomes the motor of the national economy, the private sector might be regarded as a secondary cog in the big machine. However, in such scenario is nothing new that economic elites might profit from the economic sectors prioritized by the administration. Also political elites might develop different mechanisms to take advantage of boom periods. Whereas economic elites grasp lucrative state contracts, subsidized credits and low taxation, political elites (sometimes detached from economic elites) come to enjoy the foretaste of becoming state classes with access to high ranking governmental positions and over-average remunerated academic positions in public universities, as well as higher possibilities of political participation and decision-making. Hence, state-led promotion of further sectors of the economy underlined the rentier nature of domestic elites (economic as well as political elites). In this line, this books advocates for broadening investigation on current possibilities of accessing rental income (and on the types of rental income) even after the initial allocation of natural resources rent made by the state. Standing (2016) argued that since the 1980s, chief mechanisms of wealth accumulation have been shifting from "hard work or productive activity" to rental income.

The dissection of fifty years of economic diversification attempts in natural resources-rich Ecuador exposed the metamorphosis of the role of the state in the economy. The role of the state wavered according to the scenario provided by the current "stage of capitalism" (Poulantzas 1978, 15) from steering the economy to stepping aside from key economic decisions in favor of 1) free market regulations, 2) directives of supranational organizations, and/or 3) impositions of international creditors. In this line, the approach to recent economic history also attests the development of a global governance scheme to underpin the idea of free trade; the resulting regulatory corpus, to which the Ecuadorian state is signatory, castrates any initiative of protection of nascent domestic industry and, further, turns unviable the mere idea of delinking from the capitalist world market. The latter speaks for the necessity of revisiting *dependentismo*, the Latin American school of dependency theory. Where exports of natural resources account for the main source of state's non-tax revenue (as in Ecuador), one of the *façades* of dependency materializes when fluctuations of international commodity prices impact on the structure of public finances. The validity of Latin American (under)development thinking surpasses the current strand of neo-structuralism and its proposal of a more "strategic" integration into the globalized economy; it is rather founded on a theoretical corpus that might help to understand contemporary problems related to local economic diversification under conditions imposed by the evolutional trajectory of global capitalism.

As the slope toward further dependence on natural resources rent becomes more slippery, orthodox development economists tend to think of the resource curse (often confounded with the Dutch disease) as a *deus ex machina* that explains any failure in economic diversification attempts. By doing so, they disregard two main aspects of a comprehensive analysis, 1) a complete branch of research that originated in what Bernstein (1971, 143) called the "non-economic barriers of economic growth", and 2) that economic theories inspired in the reality of the Global North may lack of the universal character needed to approach manifold cases of natural resource-rich countries of the Global South. The scope of a long-term analysis, such as the undertaken in this book, 1) might surpass the study of the economic effects of *transient* natural resources boom periods, that are highlighted in the Dutch disease, and 2) might include an approach to the *enduring* sociopolitical consequences of living in a natural resources-rich country that are underscored in the paradox of plenty. Then, the integration of the economic and the sociopolitical strands of the resource curse might lead to its demystification. The analysis of fifty years of recent Ecuadorian economic history indeed presented optimistic outcomes, such as the rise of the middle classes. In this line, this book might be regarded as an important contribution to the current academic debate if natural resources abundance is a blessing or a curse.

Further Research: Nature and the State

The country study attests to the incorporation of the concept of nature into Latin American development thinking. During the 1970s, and particularly during the first Ecuadorian oil boom, nature was regarded as mere *natural resources* to serve the national modernization project. By the hand of multilateral organizations, the concept of *environment* permeated the discussion on development during the last decades of the twentieth century, and deeply influenced the official agenda of Latin American states. By the dawn of the twenty-first century the environmental movement was deeply entrenched in Ecuadorian society and politics. One the one hand, the rising environmental movement helped to catalyze the already growing social environmental consciousness of the negative socioecological consequences of nearly fifty years of oil extraction in the Ecuadorian Amazonia. On the other hand, positions embraced by the environmental movement began to influence the state's official environmental discourse. Thus, during the second Ecuadorian oil boom, the concepts of nature and development were joined at the hip. The approach to the rise and fall of the Yasuní-ITT initiative in Ecuador shows, on the one hand, that the defense of environmentalist theses entails a critique to the current natural resources-based development model. On the other hand, the analysis of the Yasuní-ITT initiative suggests that the defense of environmentalist theses might turn into a defense of democracy or established democratic institutions. Since the Ecuadorian 2008 Constitution grants nature rights, the defense of environmentalist theses might be regarded as a demand for compliance with the constitution. The latter is a challenge for the peripheral authoritarian state and its intention to impose on society a natural resources-based development project. In this line, the approach of the second Ecuadorian oil boom suggests that governments of any color might grasp the populist strategy of co-optation in order to gain adherents among social/environmental movements.

As nature increasingly became a core concept to the construction of the meanings of development during the twenty-first century, debates on post-development gained momentum. South American *buen vivir* and African *ubuntu* have often been cited as examples of alternatives to development. Though, the dissolution of the Yasuní-ITT initiative rounded up the impossibility of setting into force *buen vivir* in harmony with nature. This also holds true for *ubuntu*. Conceived as an appeal to "rekindle an original, pre-colonial, authentic African philosophy", *ubuntu* succumbed to Western discourses and "reproduced precisely those dichotomies it aimed to fight" (Matthews 2018, 178). In this line, Matthews (2018, 178) made an appeal, which is easily transferable to any region of the Global South: "Instead of engaging in romanticizing projections about an Africa [or Latin America] beyond development, people's views and needs should be taken as the starting point for the struggle against injustice and inequality". Hence, the quest for alternative meanings of development (or alternatives to development) turned into a "search-out imperative" (Table No. 6) for contemporary socio-environmental movements. Nonetheless, as alternatives to development mushroomed in academic literature and even in official documents, Latin American neo-extractivism prevailed as the paradigm of successful development in natural resources-rich countries. The "extractive imperative" (Table No. 6) followed by so-called *progresista* governments was legitimated by economic and social development. Whilst, the current official discourse of Latin American national states converged in the stream of development alternatives (rather than alternatives to development) inaugurated by sustainable development. The evolution of developmental and environmental discourses as well confirms that neoliberalism has never been the *last* development theory, on the one hand; on the other hand, it draws attention to the intention of UN's sustainable development to turn into a Barthesian narrative, i.e. "international, trans-historic, trans-cultural" (Barthes 1977, 65). As a dominant paradigm with hegemonic pretensions, sustainable development currently provides the problems and the solutions to the scientific community (Kuhn 1971, 13). Only to cite a couple of examples of the powerful master narratives of sustainable development, the UN's Sustainable Development Goals (SDG), formerly Millennium Development Goals (MDG), have been widely embraced by national policy agendas, and the UN's Human Development Index (HDI) has become a widely accepted way of measuring development.

However, nature proved to be the magic word that transformed the state's modernizing logic in the long-term and increasingly shapes the relationship between the state and society. Further issues that evoke the notion of nature, such as reaching peak oil (i.e. exhausting oil reserves) or meeting climate change international commitments, will continue to demand the re-formulation of state's discourses and practices. Another powerful word that has been increasingly shaping state's agency is gender. Analogously with nature, discourses on gender have been appropriated by either the state and social movements. Despite numerous gender vindications that stem from social demands have been incorporated into the state logic, discourses are not necessarily convergent, and the official discourse is currently under scrutiny of social movements. Hence, different gender discourses might as well shape the relationship between the state and society in the twenty-first century.

The approach to half-century of recent economic history confirms that the modernizing logic of the peripheral state demands what Svampa (2013, 34) called "sacrifice zones". Despite consecutive attempts to channel oil rent to the Ecuadorian Amazonia (through earmarks or through a public enterprise in charge of infrastructure building), the spring of national oil remains as one of the most backward regions of the country. The country study shows that the Ecuadorian state "arrived" to the Ecuadorian Amazonia only after multinational oil corporations did; the townships of Shell Mera or Lago Agrio (Sour Lake) might tell the story. The President of the Confederation of Indigenous Nationalities of Ecuador (CONAIE) argued that nearly fifty years of oil extraction brought misery to the rich Amazon region; "[…] they made us poor. The poor now life in cities, surrounded by delinquency, prostitution, alcoholism, corruption. They even lack of rivers to bathe" (Jaime Vargas, President of the Confederation of Indigenous Nationalities of Ecuador, interview with La Jornada, January, 2020). The acknowledgement of the statement demands further research on the "sacrificed peoples" (even surpassing "sacrifice zones") that have been historically relegated by the state and its apparent successful neo-extractivist strategy.

Particularly in natural resources-rich backward regions, the presence of the state as "the majestic agent of country's transformation" (Coronil 1997, 239) might continue polarizing public opinion into two competing positions, namely, development versus preservation of nature. The promise of development offers access not only to state benefits and public infrastructure bankrolled by oil rent, but also to enhanced employment opportunities and thus market capacities. As the dichotomy heightens, the state might dip into corporative mechanisms, and also into outright repression, in order to impose its developmental endeavor. Besides unveiling the flaws of the state's modernization logic, further study might be aimed at scrutinizing the successive incorporations of natural resources-rich countries into the world-system. The study of half-century of recent economic history exposes Ecuador's reinsertions into the capitalist world-economy through its natural resources, and suggests that other conditions might be further imposed for a next reinsertion due to the cyclical nature of capitalism. By the closure of this book, mining seems to be the next bet of the Ecuadorian state for a new reinsertion into the globalized economy, as the foretaste of "development" gradually gains adherents to the state's project. At global level, the pursuit of cleaner energy sources (or a *Energiewende*), or even the proximity of peak oil (the end of cheap oil), invite natural resources-rich countries of the Global South to revisit their possibilities of a new reinsertion into the capitalist world-economy and even to fear the consequences of a possible long-term demand drop in the Global North (Peters 2020). However, the next bet of the Ecuadorian state will revitalize dilemmas linked to what Peters (2017a, 47) called a "crisis-prone development model of boom and bust cycles provoked by low economic diversification combined with the high volatility of commodity prices on the world market". Besides, the state might face an enormous challenge by trying to impose its developmental project on society more due to increased social environmental awareness of the negative socioecological consequences of neo-extractivism than to the validity of a legal framework that protects nature.

Epilogue

A happy ending is by far not in the plans of this book, it would not fit. Though, at the closure, the consolidation and strengthening of middle classes and the enduring position of environmental thinking in the discussions on the development process must be highlighted as the actual good news over the failed economic diversification attempts. With that, the quest if natural resources abundance is a blessing or a curse in the Global South is by far not solved. The issue is more topical than ever, particularly in the middle of the twenty-first century crisis, where the peripheral state prepares for hibernation, as it yearns for the next perfect storm.

References

Acosta, Alberto. 2011. "La reforma a la ley de hidrocarburos y la renegociación de los contratos petroleros." *La tendencia. Revista de análisis político* 11: 95–103.

———. 2004a. "Del libre comercio o la vieja práctica de quitar la escalera." In *Libre comercio: Mitos y realidades. Nuevos desafíos para la economía política de la integración latinoamericana*, edited by Alberto Acosta and Eduardo Gudynas, 81–110. Quito: Abya-Yala. ILDIS-FES, D3e.

———. 2004b. "Dolarización o desdolarización, esa no es toda la cuestión!." *Íconos. Revista de Ciencias Sociales* 19: 54–65.

———. 2001. *Breve historia económica del Ecuador*. Segunda edición. Quito: Corporación Editora Nacional.

Acosta, Alberto, Eduardo Gudynas, Esperanza Martínez, and Joseph Vogel. 2009. "Dejar el crudo en tierra o la búsqueda del paraíso perdido. Elementos para una propuesta política y económica para la iniciativa de no explotación del crudo del ITT." *Polis. Revista de la Universidad Bolivariana*, 8 (23): 429–452.

Acosta, Alberto, and Arturo Villavicencio. 2007. *Agenda energética 2007-2011. Hacia un sistema energético sustentable*. Quito: Ministerio de Energía y Minas.

Acosta, Alberto, Susana López, and David Villamar. 2004. "Ecuador: Oportunidades y amenazas económicas de la emigración." In *Migraciones: Un juego con cartas marcadas*, edited by Francisco Hidalgo, 259–302. Quito: Abya-Yala. ILDIS-FES, Plan Migración, Comunicación y Desarrollo.

Acosta, Alberto, and Jürgen Schuldt. 2000. "Dolarización: Vacuna para la hiperinflación?." *Ecuador Debate* 49: 25–41.

Acosta, Alberto, Alexandra Almeida, Milton Balseca, Elizabeth Bravo, Fernando Carrión, Judith Kimerling, Carlos Larrea, and Esperanza Martínez. 2000. *El Ecuador post petrolero*. Quito: Acción Ecológica, ILDIS, Oilwatch.

AEADE (Asociación de Empresas Automotrices del Ecuador). 2019. *Anuario 2018*. Quito: AEADE.

AfDB (African Development Bank), OECD (Organization for Economic Co-operation and Development), UNDP (United Nations Development Programme), and UNECA (United Nations Economic Commission for Africa). 2013. *African Economic Outlook 2013: Structural Transformation and Natural Resources*. Tunis, Paris, New York, Addis Ababa: OECD Publishing.

Agénor, Pierre-Richard. 2004. *The Economics of Adjustment and Growth*. Cambridge: Harvard University Press.

Alarcón, Pedro. 2020. "Latin American Environmental Thinking Revisited: The Polyphony of Buen Vivir." *Diálogos Revista Electrónica de Historia* 21 (2): 215–236.

————. 2011. "Movilidad urbana, consumo de energía y calidad del aire." *Letras verdes. Revista Latinoamericana de Estudios Socioambientales* 8: 15–17.

————. 2008. "Petróleo, economía neoclásica o economía ecológica: El retorno del Ecuador a la OPEP." *Entre voces. Revista del Grupo Democracia y Desarrollo Local* 14: 24–26.

Alarcón, Pedro, and Stefan Peters. 2020. "Ecuador After the Commodities Boom: A Rentier Society's Labyrinth." *Cadernos do CEAS Revista crítica de humanidades* 250 (45): forthcoming.

Alarcón, Pedro, Katherine Rocha, and Simone Di Pietro. 2018. "Die Yasuní-ITT-Initiative zehn Jahre später: Entwicklung und Natur in Ecuador heute." *Peripherie: Politik, Ökonomie, Kultur* 149 (38): 55–73.

Alarcón, Pedro, and Renata Mantilla. 2017. "El discurso ambiental en el gobierno de la revolución ciudadana." *Iberoamérica social. Revista-red de estudios sociales* 7 (4): 91–107.

Almeida, María Dolores, Verónica Gallardo and Andrés Tomaselli. 2006. *Gobernabilidad fiscal en Ecuador*. Santiago de Chile: ILPES, CEPAL, GTZ.

Álvarez, Yomar. 2013. "Una propuesta desde el ecologismo para proteger a una parte del Parque Nacional Yasuní." In *Yasuní, zona de sacrificio: análisis de la Iniciativa ITT y los derechos colectivos indígenas*, coordinated by Iván Narváez, Massimo de Marchi, and Eugenio Pappalardo, 80–101. Quito: Flacso Ecuador.

Amin, Samir. 1990. *Delinking: Towards a Polycentric World*. London: Zed Books.

Amsden, Alice. 1985. "The state and Taiwan's economic development." In *Bringing the State Back In*, edited by Peter Evans, Dietrich Rueschemeyer, and Theda Skocpol, 78–106. New York: Cambridge University Press.

————. 1989. *Asia's Next Giant: South Korea and Late Industrialization*. Oxford: Oxford University Press.

————. 2001. *The Rise of "The Rest": Challenges to the West from Late-Industrializing Economies*. Oxford: Oxford University Press.

Andrade, Pablo. 2015. *Política de industrialización selectiva y nuevo modelo de desarrollo*. Quito: Corporación Editora Nacional, Universidad Andina Simón Bolívar sede Ecuador.

Aravena, Claudio, and Juan Alberto Fuentes. 2013. *El desempeño mediocre de la productividad laboral en América Latina: una interpretación neoclásica*. Santiago de Chile: CEPAL.

Arbatli, Ekim. 2018. "Resource nationalism revisited: A new conceptualization in light of changing actors and strategies in the oil industry." *Energy Research & Social Science* 40: 101–108.

Arias, Karla. 2014. "Gobernanza energética y neonacionalismo. Caso Refinería del Pacífico: Implicaciones en política energética, económica, social y ambiental." Master's thesis, Facultad Latinoamericana de Ciencias Sociales sede Ecuador.

Arsel, Murat, Barbara Hogenboom, and Lorenzo Pellegrini. 2016. "The extractive imperative in Latin America." *The Extractive Industries and Society* (3): 880–887.

Artola, Verónica, and María Fernanda Pazmiño. 2007. "Análisis de los fondos petroleros en el Ecuador." *Apuntes de Economía* 53: 1–31.

Asamblea Constituyente. 2008a. *Constitución política de la República del Ecuador*. Official Gazette No. 449 of October 20.

———. 2008b. *Ley Orgánica para la Recuperación del Uso de los Recursos Petroleros del Estado y Racionalización Administrativa de los Procesos de Endeudamiento*. Supplement of the Official Gazette No. 308 of April 3.

———. 2007. *Ley Reformatoria para la Equidad Tributaria en el Ecuador*. Supplement of the Official Gazette No. 242 of December 29.

Asamblea Nacional. 2013a. *Ley de Creación de la Universidad de Investigación de Tecnología Experimental Yachay*. Supplement of the Official Gazette No. 144 of December 16.

———. 2013b. *Ley de Creación de la Universidad Regional Amazónica Ikiam*. Supplement of the Official Gazette No. 144 of December 16.

———. 2013c. *Ley de Creación de la Universidad de las Artes*. Supplement of the Official Gazette No. 145 of December 17.

———. 2013d. *Ley de Creación de la Universidad Nacional de Educación UNAE*. Supplement of the Official Gazette No. 147 of December 19.

———. 2010. *Ley Reformatoria a la Ley de Hidrocarburos y a la Ley de Régimen Tributario Interno*. Official Gazette No. 244 of July 27.

———. 2009. *Ley del Banco del Instituto Ecuatoriano de Seguridad Social*. Official Gazette No. 587 of May 11.

Atria, Jorge, Andrés Biehl, and José Tomás Labarca. 2019. "Towards a Fiscal Sociology of Latin America." *European Review of Latin American and Caribbean Studies* (107): 139–150.

Auty, Richard. 1993. *Sustaining Development in Mineral Economies: The Resource Curse Thesis*. London: Routledge.

Báez, René. 1989. "Petróleo, capitalismo y dependencia." In *La investigación económica en el Ecuador*, edited by Amalia Mauro, 141–53. Quito: ILDIS.

———. 1984. *Dialéctica de la economía ecuatoriana*. Tercera edición. Quito: Editorial Alberto Crespo Encalada.

Balassa, Bela. 1981. *The newly industrializing countries in the world economy*. New York: Pergamon Press.

Banco Central del Ecuador (BCE). 2019a. *Cuentas Nacionales No. 24. A precios de 2007*. Quito: Banco Central del Ecuador, https://contenido.bce.fin.ec/document os/PublicacionesNotas/Catalogo/CuentasNacionales/Anuales/Dolares/indicecn1. htm, last accessed: 13.07.2019.

———. 2019b. *Formación bruta de capital fijo por industria. Miles de dólares de 2007*. Quito: Banco Central del Ecuador, https://contenido.bce.fin.ec/documentos/Pub licacionesNotas/Catalogo/CuentasNacionales/Anuales/Dolares/indiceFBKF.htm, last accessed: 13.07.2019.

———. 2017. *Noventa años del Banco Central del Ecuador. Series estadísticas históricas 1927-2017*. Quito: Banco Central del Ecuador.

Baptista, Asdrúbal. 2010 (1997). *Teoría económica del capitalismo rentístico*. Caracas: Banco Central de Venezuela.

Baran, Paul. 1968. *Unterdrückung und Fortschritt. Essays*. Second edition. Frankfurt am Main: Suhrkamp.

Bárcena, Alicia, and Antonio Prado. 2015. "Introducción." In *Neoestructuralismo y corrientes heterodoxas en América Latina y el Caribe a inicios del siglo XXI*, edited by Alicia Bárcena and Antonio Prado, 17–29. Santiago de Chile: CEPAL.

Bardhan, Pranab, and Christopher Udry. 1999. *Development Microeconomics*. Oxford: Oxford University Press.

Barsky, Osvaldo. 1984. *La reforma agraria ecuatoriana*. Quito: Corporación Editora Nacional.

Barthes, Roland. 1977 (1966). "Introducción al análisis estructural de los relatos." In *El análisis estructural*, edited by Silvia Niccolini, 65–101. Buenos Aires: Centro Editor de América Latina.

Batista, Arianni. 2013. "Arte contemporáneo en Ecuador: La producción femenina en la configuración de la escena (1990-2012)." Master's thesis, Facultad Latinoamericana de Ciencias Sociales sede Ecuador.

Beasley-Murray, Jon, Maxwell Cameron, and Eric Hershberg. 2010. "Latin America's Left Turns: A Tour d'Horizon." In *Latin America's Left Turns: Politics, Policies, and Trajectories of Change*, edited by Maxwell Cameron and Eric Hershberg, 1–20. Boulder: Lynne Rienner.

Becker, Joachim. 2008. " Der kapitalistische Staat in der Peripherie: politökonomische Perspektiven." *Journal für Entwicklungspolitik* 25 (2): 10–32.

Benavente, José Miguel. 2001. *Exportaciones de manufacturas de América Latina: ¿Desarme unilateral o integración regional?*. Santiago de Chile: CEPAL.

Benzi, Daniele. 2017. *ALBA-TCP. Anatomía de la integración que no fue*. Buenos Aires: Imago Mundi, Universidad Andina Simón Bolívar.

Bernstein, Henry. 1971. "Modernization Theory and the Sociological Study of Development." *Journal of Development Studies* 7 (2): 141–60.

Bielschowsky, Ricardo, and Antonio Carlos Macedo e Silva. 2016. "The UNCTAD system of political economy." In *Handbook of Alternative Theories of Economic Development*, edited by Erik Reinert, Jayati Ghosh, and Rainer Kattel, 291–306. Cheltenham: Edward Elgar.

BMZ (Bundesministerium für wirtschaftliche Zusammenarbeit und Entwicklung). 2013. *Sonderprogramm Biosphärenreservat Yasuní*. Berlin: BMZ.

Bocco, Arnaldo. 1987. *Auge petrolero, modernización y subdesarrollo: el Ecuador de los años setenta*. Quito: Corporación Editora Nacional.

Braña, Francisco Javier. 2016. "El pensamiento desarrollista y neodesarrollista en América Latina y el buen vivir. Continuidades y cambios." In *Buen vivir y cambio de la matriz productiva. Reflexiones desde Ecuador*, edited by Francisco Javier Braña, Rafael Domínguez, and Mauricio León, 15–83. Quito: Friedrich-Ebert-Stiftung (FES-ILDIS).

Bretón, Víctor. 2008. "From Agrarian Reform to Ethnodevelopment in the Highlands of Ecuador." *Journal of Agrarian Change* 8 (4): 583–617.

———. 2006. "Glocalidad y reforma agraria: ¿de nuevo el problema irresuelto de la tierra?." *Íconos. Revista de Ciencias Sociales* 24: 59–69.

Bresser-Pereira, Luiz Carlos. 2016. "Reflecting on new developmentalism and classical developmentalism." *Review of Keynesian Economics* 4 (3): 331–352.

Bulmer-Thomas, Victor. 2003. *The Economic History of Latin America since Independence*. Second edition. Cambridge: Cambridge University Press.

Burchardt, Hans-Jürgen, Rafael Domínguez, Carlos Larrea, and Stefan Peters. 2016. "Introducción." In *Nada dura para siempre. Neo-extractivismo tras el boom de las materias primas*, edited by Hans-Jürgen Burchardt, Rafael Domínguez, Carlos Larrea, and Stefan Peters, 7–17. Quito: Universidad Andina Simón Bolívar sede Ecuador, International Center for Development and Decent Work.

Burchardt, Hans-Jürgen, and Kristina Dietz. 2014. "(Neo-)extractivism – A New Challenge for Development Theory from Latin America." *Third World Quarterly* 35 (3): 468–486.

Burchardt, Hans-Jürgen, and Nico Weinmann. 2012. "Social Inequality and Social Policy Outside the OECD: A New Research Perspective on Latin America." *ICDD Working Papers No. 5*. Kassel: International Center for Development and Decent Work.

Bustamante, Fernando. 2001. "Economía, política y familia en la sociedad ecuatoriana: en torno a una crisis bancaria." *Ecuador Debate* 53: 61–72.

Bustamante, Teodoro. 2007. "La cortina de humo en torno a la actividad petrolera: algunas aproximaciones." In *Detrás de la cortina de humo. Dinámicas sociales y petróleo en el Ecuador*, edited by Teodoro Bustamante, 13–20. Quito: Flacso sede Ecuador.

Bustamante, Teodoro, and Óscar Zapata. 2007. "Características de los contratos petroleros." In *Detrás de la cortina de humo. Dinámicas sociales y petróleo en el Ecuador*, edited by Teodoro Bustamante, 97–165. Quito: Flacso sede Ecuador.

Calderón, Álvaro. 2016. "Política industrial y tecnológica de Ecuador: avanzando en la construcción de capacidades." In *Los desafíos del Ecuador para el cambio estructural con inclusión social*, edited by Álvaro Calderón, Marco Dini, and Giovanni Stumpo, 93–134. Santiago de Chile: CEPAL.

Calderón, Álvaro, and Giovanni Stumpo. 2016. "La evolución económica y social del Ecuador: las restricciones de la estructura productiva." In *Los desafíos del Ecuador para el cambio estructural con inclusión social*, edited by Álvaro Calderón, Marco Dini, and Giovanni Stumpo, 11–58. Santiago de Chile: CEPAL.

Campbell, Colin, and Jean Laherrère. 1998. "The End of Cheap Oil." *Scientific American* 278 (3): 78–83.

Cantamutto, Francisco. 2013. "Sobre la noción de Estado en Marx: un recorrido biográfico-teórico." *Eikasia Revista de Filosofía* 49: 99–115.

Cardoso, Fernando Henrique, and Enzo Faletto. 2002 (1969). *Dependencia y desarrollo en América Latina: Ensayo de interpretación sociológica*. Thirtieth edition. México D.F.: Siglo XXI.

Cardoso, Fernando Henrique. 1973. "Associated-Dependent Development: Theoretical and Practical Implications." In *Authoritarian Brazil. Origins, Policies, and Future*, edited by Alfred Stepan, 142–176. New Haven: Yale University Press.

————. 1971. *Ideologías de la burguesía industrial en sociedades dependientes (Argentina y Brasil)*. México D.F.: Siglo XXI.

Caria, Sara, and Rafael Domínguez. 2016. "Ecuador's Buen Vivir. A New Ideology for Development." *Latin American Perspectives* 43 (1): 18–33.

Carson, Rachel. 1962. *Silent Spring*. Boston: Houghton Mifflin Company.

CEPAL (Comisión Económica para América Latina y el Caribe). 2019. *Social Panorama of Latin America 2018*. Santiago de Chile: CEPAL.

————. 2017. *Statistical Yearbook for Latin America and the Caribbean 2016*. Santiago de Chile: CEPAL.

————. 2016. *Social Panorama of Latin America 2015*. Santiago de Chile: CEPAL.

————. 2014. *Cambio estructural para la igualdad. Una visión integrada del desarrollo*. Santiago de Chile: CEPAL.

————. 2002. *Economic survey of Latin America and the Caribbean 2000-2001*. Santiago de Chile: CEPAL.

————. 1993. *Preliminary overview of the Latin American and Caribbean Economy 1993*. Santiago de Chile: CEPAL.

————. 1979. *Ecuador: desafíos y logros de la política económica en la fase de expansión petrolera*. Santiago de Chile: CEPAL.

————. 1978. *Economic Survey of Latin America, 1977*. Volume Two. Santiago de Chile: CEPAL.

————. 1977. *The Economic and Social Development and External Relations of Latin America*. Third Meeting of the Committee of High-Level Government Experts to Appraise the International Development Strategy. Santo Domingo: CEPAL.

————. 1971. "Public enterprises: their present significance and their potential in development." *Economic Bulletin for Latin America* XVI (1): 1–70.

————. 1954. *El desarrollo económico del Ecuador*. México D.F.: CEPAL.

CEPALSTAT. 2019a. *Population living below the extreme poverty and poverty lines, by geographical area*. Santiago de Chile: CEPAL, https://cepalstat-prod.cepal.org/cep alstat/tabulador/ConsultaIntegrada.asp?idIndicador=182&idioma=i, last accessed: 13.03.2019.

————. 2019b. *Rate of growth of total annual gross domestic product (GDP) per capita at constant prices*. Santiago de Chile: CEPAL, https://cepalstat-prod.cepal.org/cep alstat/tabulador/ConsultaIntegrada.asp?idIndicador=2222&idioma=i, last accessed: 13.03.2019.

————. 2019c. *Public expenditure according to the classification of the functions of government (as a percentage of GDP)*. Santiago de Chile: CEPAL, https://cepalstat-pro d.cepal.org/cepalstat/tabulador/ConsultaIntegrada.asp?idIndicador=3127&idiom a=i, last accessed: 13.03.2019.

————. 2019d. *Gini coefficient*. Santiago de Chile: CEPAL, https://cepalstat-prod.ce pal.org/cepalstat/tabulador/ConsultaIntegradaProc_HTML.asp, last accessed: 13.03.2019.

Chiasson-LeBel, Thomas. 2016. "Neo-Extractivism in Venezuela and Ecuador: A Weapon of Class Conflict." *The Extractive Industries and Society* 3 (4): 888–901.

Childs, John. 2016. "Geography and resource nationalism: A critical review and re-framing." *The Extractive Industries and Society* 3 (2): 539–546.

Chiriboga, Manuel. 1985. "La crisis agraria en el Ecuador: Tendencias y contradic-ciones del reciente proceso." In *La economía política del Ecuador: campo, región, nación*, edited by Louis Lefeber, 91–132. Quito: Corporación Editora Nacional.

Cimoli Mario, and Gabriel Porcile. 2015. "Productividad y cambio estructural: el estructuralismo y su diálogo con otras corrientes heterodoxas." In *Neoestructural-ismo y corrientes heterodoxas en América Latina y el Caribe a inicios del siglo XXI*, edited by Alicia Bárcena and Antonio Prado, 225–42, Santiago de Chile: CEPAL.

Collier, Ruth Berins, and David Collier. 1979. "Inducements versus Constraints: Disaggregating 'Corporatism'." *The American Political Science Review* 73 (4): 967–86.

Comin, Diego. 2010. "Total factor productivity." In *Economic Growth*, edited by Steven Durlauf and Lawrence Blume, 260–3. London: Palgrave Macmillan.

CONADE (Consejo Nacional de Desarrollo). 1982. *Hidrocarburos: Estadísticas 1970-1981*. Quito: CONADE.

Conaghan, Catherine. 2016. "Ecuador Under Correa." *Journal of Democracy* 27 (3): 109–118.

———. 1988. *Restructuring Domination: Industrialists and the State in Ecuador*. Pitts-burgh: University of Pittsburgh Press.

Congreso Nacional. 2008. *Ley No. 2008-104 Ley Reformatoria a la Codificación de la Ley del Fondo para el Ecodesarrollo Regional Amazónico (ECORAE) y de Fortalec-imiento de sus Organismos Seccionales*. Official Gazette No. 245 of January 4.

———. 2006a. *Ley No. 42-2006 Reformatoria a la Ley de Hidrocarburos*. Supplement of the Official Gazette No. 257 of April 25.

———. 2006b. *Ley No. 57-2006 Ley Orgánica de Creación del Fondo Ecuatoriano de Inversión en los Sectores Energético e Hidrocarburífero -FEISEH-*. Official Gazette No. 386 of October 27.

———. 1996. *Ley de Régimen del Sector Eléctrico*. Supplement of the Official Gazette No. 43 of October 10.

———. 1994. *Ley General de Instituciones del Sistema Financiero*. Supplement of the Official Gazette No. 439 of May 12.

———. 1993. *Ley de Modernización del Estado, Privatizaciones y Prestación de Servicios Públicos por parte de la Iniciativa Privada*. Official Gazette No. 349 of December 31.

———. 1992. *Ley del Fondo para el Ecodesarrollo Regional Amazónico (ECORAE) y de Fortalecimiento de sus Organismos Seccionales*. Official Gazette No. 30 of Septem-ber 21.

———. 1989. *Ley especial de la Empresa Estatal Petróleos del Ecuador (Petroecuador) y sus empresas filiales*. Official Gazette No. 283 of September 26.

Corden, Max, and Peter Neary. 1982. "Booming Sector and De-Industrialisation in a Small Open Economy." *The Economic Journal* 92 (368): 825–848.

Coronil, Fernando. 2008. "It's the Oil, Stupid!!!." *ReVista. Harvard Review of Latin America* 8 (1): 19–20.

———. 1997. *The Magical State: Nature, Money and Modernity in Venezuela*. Chicago: The University of Chicago Press.

Cortez, David. 2014. "Genealogía del sumak kawsay y el buen vivir en Ecuador: un balance." In: *Post-crecimiento y buen vivir. Propuestas globales para la construcción de sociedades equitativas y sustentables*, coordinated by Gustavo Endara, 315–352. Quito: FES-ILDIS.

Cueva, Agustín. 2013 (1977). *El desarrollo del capitalismo en América Latina*. Second edition. México D.F.: Siglo XXI.

———. 2012 (1981). "El populismo como problema teórico-político." In *Ensayos sociológicos y políticos*, coordinated by Fernando Tinajero, 221–234. Quito: Ministerio de Coordinación de la Política y Gobiernos Autónomos Descentralizados.

Cuvi, Pablo. 1977. *Velasco Ibarra: El último caudillo de la oligarquía*. Quito: Instituto de Investigaciones Económicas.

Cypher, James, and Yolanda Alfaro. 2016. "Triángulo del neo-desarrollismo en Ecuador." *Problemas del Desarrollo* 185 (47): 163–186.

Daly, Herman. 2019. "Growthism: its ecological, economic and ethical limits." *Real-World Economics Review* 87: 9–22.

de la Cruz, Fernando. 2014. "Los estados desarrollistas en el este asiático: aportaciones institucionales y límites históricos" *Revista Iberoamericana de Estudios del Desarrollo* 3 (3): 26–49.

de la Torre, Augusto. 1987. "Macroeconomic aspects of a petroleum boom: Ecuador 1972-1980." PhD diss., University of Notre Dame.

de la Torre, Carlos. 2013. "El tecnopopulismo de Rafael Correa. ¿Es compatible el carisma con la tecnocracia?" *Latin American Research Review* 48 (1): 24–43.

———. 2010. "El gobierno de Rafael Correa: posneoliberalismo, confrontación con los movimientos sociales y democracia plebiscitaria." *Temas y debates* 20 (14): 157–172.

———. 2000. *Populist seduction in Latin America: The Ecuadorian experience*. Athens: Ohio University Press.

Dell, Gillian, and Andrew McDevitt. 2018. *Exporting Corruption. Progress Report 2018: Assessing enforcement of the OECD Anti-Bribery Convention*. Berlin: Transparency International.

Di John, Jonathan. 2009. *From Windfall to Curse? Oil and Industrialization in Venezuela, 1920 to the Present*. University Park, PA: The Pennsylvania State University Press. Kindle version.

Dobson, Andrew. 1997. *Pensamiento político verde*. Barcelona: Paidós.

Domínguez, Rafael, Mauricio León, José Luis Samaniego and Osvaldo Sunkel. 2019. *Recursos naturales, medio ambiente y sostenibilidad: 70 años de pensamiento de la CEPAL*. Santiago de Chile: CEPAL.

Domínguez, Rafael, Sara Caria, and Mauricio León. 2017. "Buen Vivir: Praise, Instrumentalization, and Reproductive Pathways of Good Living in Ecuador." *Latin American and Caribbean Ethnic Studies* 12 (2): 133–154.

Domínguez, Rafael, and Sara Caria. 2016. "Ecuador en la trampa de la renta media." *Problemas del Desarrollo* 47 (187): 89–112.

Domínguez, Rafael, and Sara Caria. 2014. "Cambio estructural y trampa de renta media en Ecuador." *Pre-textos para el debate No. 4*. Quito: Universidad Andina Simón Bolívar sede Ecuador.

Eccleston, Charles. 2008. "Climbing Hubbert's Peak: The Looming World Oil Crisis." *Environmental Quality Management* 17 (3): 25–30.

Eisenstadt, Todd, and Karleen Jones West. 2017. "Public Opinion, Vulnerability, and Living with Extraction on Ecuador's Oil Frontier: When the Debate Between Development and Environmentalism Gets Personal." *Comparative Politics* 49 (2): 231–251.

Elsenhans, Hartmut. 1987. "Dependencia, Underdevelopment, and the Third World State." *Law and State* 36: 65–94.

———. 1986. "Rente, strukturelle Heterogenität und Staat: Entwicklungsperspektiven der Staatsklassen in der Dritten Welt." *Journal für Entwicklungspolitik* 4: 21–36.

———. 1981. *Abhängiger Kapitalismus oder bürokratische Entwicklungsgesellschaft: Versuch über den Staat in der Dritten Welt*. Frankfurt am Main: Campus.

———. 1977. " Die Staatsklasse/Staatsbourgeoisie in den unterentwickelten Ländern zwischen Privilegierung und Legitimationszwang." *Verfassung und Recht in Übersee: Law and Politics in Africa, Asia, Latin America* 10 (1): 29–42.

Erten, Bilge, and José Antonio Ocampo. 2013. "Super-Cycles of Commodity Prices since the Mid-Nineteenth Century." *World Development* 44: 14–30.

Escobar, Arturo. 1995a. *Encountering Development. The Making and Unmaking of the Third World*. Princeton: Princeton University Press.

———. 1995b. "El desarrollo sostenible. Diálogo de discursos." *Ecología Política. Cuadernos de Debate Internacional* 9: 7–26.

Espinoza, Sebastián, and Verónica Guayanlema. 2017. *Balance y proyecciones del sistema de subsidios energéticos en Ecuador*. Quito: FES-ILDIS.

Evans, Peter. 1998. "Alternativas al Estado desarrollista. Lecciones de la crisis de Asia oriental." *Nueva Sociedad* 155: 142–156.

———. 1995. *Embedded Autonomy: States and Industrial Transformation*. Princeton: Princeton University Press.

———. 1989. "Predatory, Developmental, and Other Apparatuses: A Comparative Political Economy Perspective on the Third World State." *Sociological Forum* 4 (4): 561–587.

———. 1979. *Dependent Development: The Alliance of Multinational, State, and Local Capital in Brazil*. Princeton: Princeton University Press.

Evans, Peter, and James Rauch. 2007. "La burocracia y el crecimiento: un análisis transversal entre naciones de los efectos de las estructuras estatales 'weberianas' en el crecimiento económico." In *Instituciones y desarrollo en la era de la globalización neoliberal*, edited by Peter Evans, 67–96. Bogotá: ILSA.

Fajnzylber, Fernando. 1992. "Industrialización en América Latina. De la «caja negra» al «casillero vacío»". *Nueva Sociedad* 118: 21–28.

———. 1990. *Industrialización en América Latina: de la "caja negra" al "casillero vacío". Comparación de patrones contemporáneos de industrialización*. Santiago de Chile: CEPAL.

Ferguson, James. 1994. *The Anti-Politics Machine. "Development", Depoliticization, and Bureaucratic Power in Lesotho*. Minneapolis: University of Minnesota Press.

Fernández, Jorge. 1989. "Estado e industrialización." In *La investigación económica en el Ecuador*, edited by Amalia Mauro, 191–210. Quito: ILDIS.

Ferreira, Pedro Cavalcanti, Samuel de Abreu Pessoa, and Fernando Veloso. 2013. "On the Evolution of Total Factor Productivity in Latin America." *Economic Inquiry* 51 (1): 16–30.

Fontaine, Guillaume, and Iván Narváez. 2007. "Problemas de la gobernanza ambiental en el Ecuador." In *Yasuní en el Siglo XXI. El Estado ecuatoriano y la conservación de la Amazonía*, edited by Guillaume Fontaine and Iván Narváez, 13–31. Quito: Flacso Ecuador, IFEA, Abya-Yala, PETROBRAS, CEDA, WCS.

Foucault, Michel. 2002 (1969). *La arqueología del saber*. Buenos Aires: Siglo XXI.

Frank, André Gunder. 2006 (1966). "El desarrollo del subdesarrollo." *Monthly Review. Selecciones en castellano* 4: 144–57.

———. 1972. *Lumpenbourgeoisie: Lumpendevelopment: Dependence, Class and Politics in Latin America*. New York: Monthly Review Press.

Freidenberg, Flavia, and Simón Pachano. 2016. *El sistema político ecuatoriano*. Quito: Flacso Ecuador.

Friedman, Thomas. 2006. "The First Law of Petropolitics." *Foreign Policy* 154: 28–36.

Furtado, Celso. 1962 (1959). *Formación económica del Brasil*. Ciudad de México: Fondo de Cultura Económica.

Gachet, Francisco, and Diego Carrión. 2014. "Ámbito de la economía." In *Balance crítico del gobierno de Rafael Correa*, edited by Francisco Muñoz, 37–142 Quito: Universidad Central del Ecuador.

Gachet, Iván, Diego Grijalva, Paúl Ponce, and Damián Rodríguez. 2017. "The rise of the middle class in Ecuador during the oil boom." *Cuadernos de Economía* 36 (72): 327–352.

Galarza, Jaime. 1983. *Petróleo de nuestra muerte*. Quito: CEDIS.

———. 1978. "Ecuador, el oro y la pobreza." In *Ecuador, hoy*, coordinated by Gerhard Drekonja, 9–18. Bogotá: Siglo XXI.

———. 1972. *El festín del petróleo*. Quito: Solitierra.

Galeano, Eduardo. 2014 (1971). *Las venas abiertas de América Latina*. Third edition. Ciudad de México: Siglo XXI.

García, Santiago. 2016. *Sumak kawsay o buen vivir como alternativa al desarrollo en Ecuador. Aplicación y resultados en el gobierno de Rafael Correa (2007-2014)*. Quito: Abya-Yala.

Gelb, Alan. 1988. *Oil Windfalls: Blessing or Curse?*. New York: Oxford University Press, World Bank.

Gelb, Alan, and Jorge Marshall. 1988. "Ecuador: Windfalls of a New Exporter." In *Oil Windfalls: Blessing or Curse?*, edited by Alan Gelb, 170–95. New York: Oxford University Press, World Bank.

Gill, Indermit, and Homi Kharas. 2007. *An East Asian Renaissance: Ideas for Economic Growth*. Washington D.C.: World Bank.

GlobalPetrolPrices. 2020. *Gasoline prices, liter, 20-Apr-2020*. https://www.globalpetrolprices.com/gasoline_prices/, last accessed: 27.04.2020.

Gobierno Revolucionario y Nacionalista del Ecuador. 1972. *Filosofía y plan de acción del gobierno revolucionario y nacionalista del Ecuador: lineamientos generales*. Quito: sin editorial.

Gómez, Juan Carlos, Juan Pablo Jiménez, and Dalmiro Morán. 2015. *El impacto fiscal de la explotación de los recursos naturales no renovables en los países de América Latina y el Caribe*. Santiago de Chile: CEPAL.

Gondard, Pierre, and Hubert Mazurek. 2001. "30 años de reforma agraria y colonización en el Ecuador (1964-1994): Dinámicas espaciales." In *Dinámicas territoriales: Ecuador, Bolivia, Perú, Venezuela*, edited by Pierre Gondard and Juan León, 15–40. Quito: CGE, CEN, IRD, PUCE.

Gordon, Robert. 2017. *The Rise and Fall of American Growth: The U.S. Standard of Living since the Civil War*. Princeton: Princeton University Press.

Gudynas, Eduardo. 2014. "El postdesarrollo como crítica y el buen vivir como alternativa". In *Buena vida, buen vivir: imaginarios alternativos para el bien común de la humanidad*, coordinated by Gian Carlo Delgado, 61-95. Ciudad de México: UNAM.

———. 2012. "Estado compensador y nuevos extractivismos. Las ambivalencias de los progresismos sudamericanos." *Nueva Sociedad* 237: 128–146.

Hajer, Maarten, and Frank Fischer. 1999. "Introduction: Beyond Global Discourse: The Rediscovery of Culture in Environmental Politics." In *Living with Nature: Environmental Politics as Cultural Discourse*, edited by Maarten Hajer and Frank Fischer, 1–20. New York: Oxford University Press.

Hare, Bill. 1997. *Fossil Fuels and Climate Protection: The Carbon Logic*. Amsterdam: Greenpeace International.

Harris, John. 2014. "On Political Agency: An Appreciation of the Work of Adrian Leftwich (1940-2013)." *Journal of International Development* 26: 556–562.

Haslam, Paul, and Heidrich Pablo. 2016. "From neoliberalism to resource nationalism. States, firms and development." In *The Political Economy of Natural Resources and Development. From neoliberalism to resource nationalism*, edited by Paul Haslam and Pablo Heidrich, 1–32. New York: Routledge.

Herrero, Susana. 2019. "La influencia de la productividad y de los factores de producción en las exportaciones de manufacturas sudamericanas." *Regional and Sectoral Economic Studies* 19 (2): 79–102.

Hettne, Björn. 1987. "The Crises in Development Theory and in the World." *Journal für Entwicklungspolitik* 1: 5–25.

Hirschman, Albert. 1961 (1958). *La estrategia del desarrollo económico*. Ciudad de México: Fondo de Cultura Económica.

Hofman, André, Matilde Mas, Claudio Aravena, and Juan Fernández de Guevara. 2017. "Crecimiento económico y productividad en Latinoamérica. El proyecto LA-KLEMS." *El Trimestre Económico* 84 (334): 259–306.

Hout, Wil. 1993. *Capitalism and the Third World: Development, Dependency and the World System*. London: Edward Elgar.

Hurtado, Osvaldo. 2017. *Ecuador entre dos siglos*. Bogotá: Penguin Random House.

Jima, Alexandra, and Miguel Paradela. 2019. "The indigenous movement in Ecuador: Resource access and Rafael Correa's citizens' revolution." *Canadian Journal of Latin American and Caribbean Studies* 44 (1): 1–21.

Johnson, Chalmers. 1999. "The Developmental State: Odyssey of a Concept." In *The Developmental State*, edited by Meredith Woo-Cumings, 32–60. Ithaca: Cornell University Press.

———. 1982. *MITI and the Japanese Miracle: The Growth of Industrial Policy, 1925-1975*. Stanford: Stanford University Press.

Johnston, Ron. 1996. *Nature, State and Economy: A Political Economy of the Environment*. Chichester: Wiley.

JUNAPLA (Junta Nacional de Planificación y Coordinación Económica). 1972. *Plan integral de transformación y desarrollo 1973-1977*. Quito: JUNAPLA.

Karl, Terry Lynn. 1999. "The Perils of the Petro-State: Reflections on the Paradox of Plenty." *Journal of International Affairs* 53 (1): 31–48.

———. 1997. *The Paradox of Plenty: Oil Booms and Petro-States*. Los Angeles: University of California Press.

Kay, Cristóbal. 2005. "Celso Furtado: Pioneer of structuralist development theory." *Development and Change* 36 (6): 1201–1207.

———. 2002. "Reforma agraria, industrialización y desarrollo: ¿Por qué Asia oriental superó a América Latina?." *Debate Agrario* 34: 45–94.

———. 1989. *Latin American Theories of Development and Underdevelopment*. London: Routledge.

Kay, Cristóbal, and Robert Gwynne. 2000. "Relevance of Structuralist and Dependency Theories in the Neoliberal Period: A Latin American Perspective." *Journal of Developing Societies* 16 (1): 49–69.

Kimerling, Judith. 2000. "La Texaco en el Ecuador: informe del juicio". In *El Ecuador post petrolero*, edited by Esperanza Martínez, 51–65. Quito: Acción Ecológica

———.1991. *Amazon Crude*. New York: Natural Resource Defense Council.

Kingman, Manuel. 2012. *Arte contemporáneo y cultura popular: el caso de Quito.* Quito: Flacso sede Ecuador.

KSA (Kingdom of Saudi Arabia). 2016. *Saudi Vision 2030.* Riyadh: KSA.

Kuhn, Thomas. 1971 (1962). *La estructura de las revoluciones científicas.* Ciudad de México: Fondo de Cultura Económica.

Kuznets, Simon. 1973. "Modern Economic Growth: Findings and Reflections." *The American Economic Review* 63 (3): 247–258.

———. 1971. *Economic Growth of Nations.* Cambridge: Harvard University Press.

Laclau, Ernesto. 2014. "Lógicas de la construcción política e identidades populares". In *Reinventar la izquierda en el siglo XXI: hacia un diálogo Norte-Sur*, edited by José Luis Coraggio and Jean-Louis Laville, 253–265. Los Polvorines: Universidad Nacional de General Sarmiento.

Laclau, Ernesto, and Chantal Mouffe. 2001 (1985). *Hegemony and Socialist Strategy: Towards a Radical Democratic Politics.* Second edition. London: Verso.

Lal, Deepak. 1983. *The poverty of development economics.* Cambridge: MIT Press.

Larrain, Jorge. 1989. *Theories of Development: Capitalism, Colonialism and Dependency.* Cambridge: Polity Press.

Larrea, Carlos. 2013. *Extractivism, economic diversification and prospects for sustainable development in Ecuador.* Quito: Universidad Andina Simón Bolívar sede Ecuador.

———. 2010. "Petróleo o conservación en el parque Yasuní: una opción histórica." *UASB Digital* (Noviembre): 1–14.

———. 2006a. "Petróleo y estrategias de desarrollo en el Ecuador: 1972-2005." In *Petróleo y desarrollo sostenible en el Ecuador: las ganancias y pérdidas*, edited by Guillaume Fontaine, 57–68. Quito: Flacso sede Ecuador, FES-ILDIS, Petrobras.

———. 2006b. *Neoliberal Policies and Social Development in Latin America: The case of Ecuador.* Quito: Universidad Andina Simón Bolívar sede Ecuador.

———. 1987. "Auge y crisis de la producción bananera (1948-1976)." In *El banano en el Ecuador. Transnacionales, modernización y subdesarrollo*, edited by Carlos Larrea, 37–66. Quito: Corporación Editora Nacional.

Latour, Bruno. 2017. "Refugium Europa". In *Die große Regression. Eine internationale Debatte über die geistige Situation der Zeit*, edited by Heinrich Geiselberger, 135–148. Berlin: Suhrkamp.

Leff, Enrique. 1999. "On the social reappropriation of nature." *Capitalism Nature Socialism* 10 (3): 89–104.

———. 1986. *Ecología y capital: Hacia una perspectiva ambiental del desarrollo.* Ciudad de México: UNAM.

Leftwich, Adrian. 1993a. "Governance, Democracy and Development in the Third World." *Third World Quarterly* 14 (3): 605–624.

———. 1993b. "States of Underdevelopment: The Third World State in Theoretical Perspective." *Journal of Theoretical Politics* 6 (1): 55–74.

León, Mauricio, and Rafael Domínguez. 2017. "Contradicciones y tensiones en las políticas de desmercantilización de la Revolución Ciudadana en Ecuador." *Revista del CLAD Reforma y Democracia* 68: 113–134.

Levitsky, Steven, and Kenneth Roberts. 2011. "Latin America's 'Left Turn': A Framework for Analysis." In *The Resurgence of the Latin American Left*, edited by Steven Levitsky and Kenneth Roberts, 1–28. Baltimore: The John Hopkins University Press.

Lewis, W. Arthur. 1954a (1949). *The Principles of Economic Planning*. Second edition. London: Henderson & Spalding.

———. 1954b. "Economic Development with Unlimited Supplies of Labour." *Manchester School of Economic and Social Studies* 22 (2): 139–191.

Lewis, Tammy. 2016. *Ecuador's Environmental Revolutions. Ecoimperialists, Ecodependents, and Ecoresisters*. Cambridge: MIT Press.

List, Friedrich. 1955 (1841). *Sistema Nacional de Economía Política*. Madrid: Aguilar.

Llanes, Henry. 2011. "La reforma petrolera del gobierno de Rafael Correa." *La tendencia. Revista de análisis político* 11: 104–108.

Lovera, Simone. 2009. "REDD Realities." *Critical Currents* 6: 46–53.

Luna, Milton. 1993. *Modernización? Ambigua experiencia en el Ecuador: Industriales y fiesta popular*. Quito: IADAP.

Maldonado Lince, Guillermo. 1980. "La reforma agraria en el Ecuador." *Caravelle. Cahiers du monde hispanique et luso-brésilien* 34: 33–56.

Malloy, James. 1977. "Authoritarianism and Corporatism in Latin America: The Modal Pattern." In *Authoritarianism and Corporatism in Latin America*, edited by James Malloy, 3–19. Pittsburgh: University of Pittsburgh Press.

Mann, Michael. 2003. "The Autonomous Power of the State: Its Origins, Mechanisms and Results." In *State/Space: A Reader*, edited by Neil Brenner, Bob Jessop, Martin Jones, and Gordon MacLeod, 53–64. Malden: Blackwell Publishing.

Manzano, Osmel, and Francisco Monaldi. 2010. "The Political Economy of Oil Contract Renegotiation in Venezuela." In *The Natural Resource Trap: Private Investment without Public Commitment*, edited by William Hogan and Federico Sturzenegger, 409–466. Cambridge: MIT Press.

Marega, Magali. 2015. "Reconfiguración de la relación Estado-sindicalismo petrolero público en el Ecuador de la revolución ciudadana." *Ecuador Debate* 94: 31–42.

Marshall, Jorge. 1988. *Ecuador: cuantificación, distribución y efectos del ingreso petrolero 1972-1988*. Santiago de Chile: sin editorial.

Martínez, Esperanza. 2009. *Yasuní. El tortuoso camino de Kioto a Quito*. Quito: Abya-Yala.

Martínez-Alier, Joan. 2000. "Introducción." In *El Ecuador post petrolero*, edited by Esperanza Martínez, 11–12. Quito: Acción Ecológica.

Martínez-Alier, Joan, and Leah Termper. 2007. "Oil and Climate Change: Voices from the South." *Economic and Political Weekly* 42 (50): 16–19.

Martínez-Alier, Joan, and Jordi Roca. 2001. *Economía ecológica y política ambiental*. Second edition. Ciudad de México: Fondo de Cultura Económica.

Martínez-Alier, Joan, and Klaus Schlüpmann. 1991. *La ecología y la economía*. Ciudad de México: Fondo de Cultura Económica.

Martz, John. 1987. *Politics and petroleum in Ecuador*. New Brunswick: Transaction.

Marx, Karl. 1869 (1852). *Der achtzehnte Brumaire des Louis Bonaparte*. Second edition. Hamburg: Meissner. http://www.deutschestextarchiv.de/book/show/marx_bonaparte_1869, last accessed: 12.03.2018.

Marx, Karl, and Friedrich Engels. 1848. *Manifest der Kommunistischen Partei*. London: Office der Bildungs-Gesellschaft für Arbeiter. http://www.deutschestextarchiv.de/book/show/marx_manifestws_1848, last accessed: 12.03.2018.

Matthes, Sebastian. 2019. *Der Neo-Extraktivismus und die Bürgerrevolution. Rohstoffwirtschaft und soziale Ungleichheiten in Ecuador*. Wiesbaden: Springer.

Matthews, Sally. 2018. " Afrikanische Entwicklungsalternativen. Ubuntu und die Post-Development-Debatte." *Peripherie: Politik, Ökonomie, Kultur* 150-151 (38): 178–197.

Mayer, Jörg. 1999. "Introduction." In *Development Policies in Natural Resource Economies*, edited by Jörg Mayer, Brian Chambers, and Ayisha Farooq, 1–12. Cheltenham: Edward Elgar.

MCPE (Ministerio de Coordinación de la Política Económica). 2012. *Agenda de la Política Económica para el Buen vivir 2013-2017*. Quito: MCPE.

Meadows, Dennis, Donella Meadows, Erich Zahn, and Peter Milling. 1972. *Die Grenzen des Wachstums: Bericht des Club of Rome zur Lage der Menschheit*. Stuttgart: Deutsche Verlags-Anstalt.

Meireles, Mónika, and Mateo Martínez. 2013. "Crisis mundial e impactos en la economía ecuatoriana: un balance no-celebratorio de la Revolución Ciudadana." *Mundo Siglo XXI* 29 (8): 83–100.

Miliband, Ralph. 1969. *The State in Capitalist Society*. New York: Basic Books.

Mommer, Bernard. 2002. *Global Oil and the Nation State*. New York: Oxford University Press.

Moncada, José. 1989. *Ecuador: Los límites del (sub)desarrollo*. Quito: CEDEP.

———. 1975. *El desarrollo económico y la distribución del ingreso en el caso ecuatoriano*. Quito: sin editorial.

Moncayo, Patricio. 2017. *La planificación estatal en el interjuego entre desarrollo y democracia*. Quito: Flacso Ecuador.

Montúfar, César. 2019. "El ascenso del autoritarismo electoral en Ecuador (2007-2015)." In *Ecuador: Balance de una década. Crisis socioambiental, extractivismo, política e integración*, edited by César Montúfar, 359–75. Quito: Universidad Andina Simón Bolívar sede Ecuador.

MWV (Mineralölwirtschaftsverband e.V.). 2018. *Rohölpreisentwicklung jährlich*. Berlin: Mineralölwirtschaftsverband e.V., https://www.mwv.de/statistiken/rohoelpreise/, last accessed: 13.10.2018.

Narváez, Iván, Massimo de Marchi, and Eugenio Pappalardo. 2013. "Yasuní: en clave de derechos y como ícono de la transición para ubicarse en la selva de proyectos". In *Yasuní, zona de sacrificio: análisis de la Iniciativa ITT y los derechos colectivos indígenas*, coordinated by Iván Narváez, Massimo de Marchi, and Eugenio Pappalardo, 9–26. Quito: Flacso Ecuador.

Nederveen Pieterse, Jan. 2010. *Development Theory: Deconstructions/Reconstructions*. Second edition. London: Sage.

Nem Singh, Jewellord, and Jesse Salah Ovadia. 2018. "The Theory and Practice of Building Developmental States in the Global South." *Third World Quarterly* 39 (6): 1033–1055.

North, Liisa. 1985. "Implementación de la política económica y la estructura del poder político en el Ecuador." In *La economía política del Ecuador: campo, región, nación*, edited by Louis Lefeber, 425–57. Quito: Corporación Editora Nacional.

Nurkse, Ragnar. 1960 (1953). *Problemas de formación de capital en los países insuficientemente desarrollados*. Second edition. Ciudad de México: Fondo de Cultura Económica.

Ocampo, José Antonio. 2015a. "Tiempos de incertidumbre." *Finanzas y Desarrollo* septiembre.

———. 2015b. "América Latina frente a la turbulencia económica mundial." In *Neoestructuralismo y corrientes heterodoxas en América Latina y el Caribe a inicios del siglo XXI*, edited by Alicia Bárcena and Antonio Prado, 93–110, Santiago de Chile: CEPAL.

OCDE (Organización para la Cooperación y el Desarrollo Económicos), CEPAL, and CAF. 2016. *Perspectivas económicas de América Latina 2017: Juventud, competencias y emprendimiento*. Paris: OECD Publishing.

O'Connell, Chris. 2016. "Yasuni-ITT and Post-Oil Development: Lessons for Development Educators." *Policy and Practice: A Development Education Review* 22: 35–58.

O'Connor, Martin. 1994. "El mercadeo de la naturaleza. Sobre los infortunios de la naturaleza capitalista." *Ecología Política. Cuadernos de Debate Internacional* 7: 15–34.

O'Donnell, Guillermo. 1977. "Corporatism and the Question of the State." In *Authoritarianism and Corporatism in Latin America*, edited by James Malloy, 47–87. Pittsburgh: University of Pittsburgh Press.

Oleas, Julio. 2017. "Ecuador 1980-1990: Crisis, ajuste y cambio de régimen de desarrollo." *América Latina en la Historia Económica* 24 (1): 210–242.

———. 2013. "Ecuador 1972-1999: del desarrollismo petrolero al ajuste neoliberal." PhD diss., Universidad Andina Simón Bolívar sede Ecuador.

Omeje, Kenneth. 2008. "Extractive Economies and Conflicts in the Global South: Re-Engaging Rentier Theory and Politics." In *Extractive Economies and Conflicts in the Global South: Multi-Regional Perspectives on Rentier Politics*, edited by Kenneth Omeje, 1–26. Aldershot: Ashgate.

Öniş, Ziya. 1991. "The Logic of the Developmental State. Review of Asia's Next Giant: South Korea and Late Industrialization; the Political Economy of the New Asian Industrialism; MITI and the Japanese Miracle; Governing the Market: Economic Theory and the Role of Government." *Comparative Politics, Ph.D. Programs in Political Science, City University of New York* 24 (1): 109–126.

Orozco, Cristina. 2019. "Resource curse: The case of Ecuador." *Unpublished manuscript*.

Orozco, Mónica. 2012. "Una política sin rumbo: el caso de la política petrolera ecuatoriana 2005-2010." Master's thesis, Facultad Latinoamericana de Ciencias Sociales sede Ecuador.

Ortiz, Santiago. 2016. "Marcha por el agua, la vida y la dignidad de los pueblos." *Letras Verdes. Revista Latinoamericana de Estudios Socioambientales* 19: 45–66.

Ortiz, Jorge. 2011. *OCP Ecuador S.A.: primera década*. Quito: OCP Ecuador S.A.

Osorio, Jaime. 2014. *Estado, reproducción del capital y lucha de clases: la unidad económico/política del capital*. México D.F.: UNAM, Instituto de Investigaciones Económicas.

Ospina, Pablo. 2013. "Estamos haciendo mejor las cosas con el mismo modelo antes que cambiarlo. La revolución ciudadana en Ecuador (2007-2012)". In: *Promesas en su laberinto: cambios y continuidades en los gobiernos progresistas de América Latina*, 177–278. La Paz: IEE, CEDLA, CIM.

Ouaissa, Rachid. 2014. "Has the Middle Class Been a Motor of the Arab Spring? Thesis: The Misunderstandings about the Role of the Middle Classes." *Middle East – Topics & Arguments* 2: 12–16.

Ovadia, Jesse Salah. 2014. "Local Content and Natural Resource Governance: The Cases of Angola and Nigeria." *The Extractive Industries and Society* 1: 137–146.

———. 2013. "The Nigerian 'One Percent' and the Management of National Oil Wealth through Nigerian Content." *Science & Society* 77 (3): 315–341.

Oxilia, Victorio. 2013. "OLADE, 40 Years: Political Roots, Trajectory and Actuality of a Strategical Organism for Latin America and the Caribbean." *Enerlac* 5 (5): 9–50.

PAIS (Movimiento Patria Altiva i Soberana). 2006. *Plan de gobierno del Movimiento PAIS 2007-2011*. Quito: Movimiento PAIS.

Pérez, Carlos, and María Fernanda Solíz. 2014. "Territorio, resistencia y criminalización de la protesta." In *La restauración conservadora del correísmo*, edited by Juan Cuvi, 153–166. Quito: Montecristi Vive.

Pérez Alfonzo, Juan Pablo. 1976. *Hundiéndonos en el excremento del diablo*. Caracas: Lisbona.

Pérez Sáinz, Juan Pablo. 1984. "Industrialización y fuerza de trabajo en Ecuador." *Boletín de Estudios Latinoamericanos y del Caribe* 37: 19–43.

Peters, Stefan. 2020. "I can't live with or without you: Los desafíos de la transformación ambiental para las sociedades dependientes del petróleo." *Identidades*: forthcoming.

———. 2019. *Rentengesellschaften. Der lateinamerikanische (Neo)Extraktivismus im transregionalen Vergleich*. Baden-Baden: Nomos.

———. 2017a. "Beyond Curse and Blessing: Rentier Society in Venezuela." In *Contested Extractivism, Society and the State: Struggles over Mining and Land*, edited by Bettina Engels and Kristina Dietz, 45–68. London: Palgrave Macmillan UK.

———. 2017b. "Entwicklungsstaaten im 21. Jahrhundert." In *Entwicklungstheorie von Heute - Entwicklungspolitik von Morgen*, edited by Hans-Jürgen Burchardt, Stefan Peters, and Nico Weinmann, 85–110. Baden-Baden: Nomos.

———. 2015. "Mit Erdöl zur Entwicklung? Rentengesellschaften im 21. Jahrhundert." In *Der Staat in globaler Perspektive: Zur Renaissance der Entwicklungsstaaten*, edited by Hans-Jürgen Burchardt and Stefan Peters, 149–74. Frankfurt am Main: Campus.

———. 2014. "Post-crecimiento y buen vivir: discursos políticos alternativos o alternativas políticas?". In: *Post-crecimiento y buen vivir. Propuestas globales para la construcción de sociedades equitativas y sustentables*, coordinated by Gustavo Endara, 123-61. Quito: FES-ILDIS.

Peters, Stefan, and Hans-Jürgen Burchardt. 2015. "Der Staat in globaler Perspektive: Zur Renaissance der Entwicklungsstaaten." In *Der Staat in globaler Perspektive: Zur Renaissance der Entwicklungsstaaten*, edited by Hans-Jürgen Burchardt and Stefan Peters, 7–36. Frankfurt am Main: Campus.

Philip, George. 1979. "Oil and Politics in Ecuador, 1972-1976." *ISA Working Papers No. 1*. London: Institute of Latin American Studies.

Pinto, Aníbal. 1970. "Naturaleza e implicaciones de la «heterogeneidad estructural» de la América Latina." *El Trimestre Económico* 145 (37): 83–100.

Poulantzas, Nicos. 1978. *Staatstheorie: politischer Überbau, Ideologie, sozialistische Demokratie*. Hamburg: VSA.

Prebisch, Raúl. 1984. "Five stages in my thinking on development." In *Pioneers in Development*, edited by Dudley Seers and Gerald Meier, 175–191. New York: Oxford University Press.

———. 1950. *The Economic Development of Latin America and Its Principal Problems*. New York: United Nations Department of Economic Affairs.

Primera Comisión de Reestructuración Jurídica del Estado. 1979. *Constitución política de la República del Ecuador*. Quito.

Pryke, Sam. 2017. "Explaining Resource Nationalism." *Global Policy* 8 (4): 474–482.

Quijano, Aníbal. 2014 (1971). "Nacionalismo, neoimperialismo y militarismo en el Perú." In *Cuestiones y horizontes: De la dependencia histórico-estructural a la colonialidad / descolonialidad del poder*, edited by Danilo Assis Clímaco, 429–505. Buenos Aires: CLACSO.

Ramírez, René. 2012. *Socialismo del sumak kawsay o biosocialismo republicano*. Quito: SENESCYT.

Rist, Gilbert. 2008. *The History of Development: From Western Origins to Global Faith*. Third edition. London: Zed Books.

Robinson, James A., and Ragnar Torvik. 2005. "White Elephants." *Journal of Public Economics* 89 (2-3): 197–210.

Rodríguez, Octavio. 1977. "Sobre la concepción del sistema centro-periferia." *Revista de la CEPAL* primer semestre: 203–247.

Romano, Silvina, Julián Kelly, and Juan Lavornia. 2020. "Economy and Nature: Perspectives from South America." In Latin America in Times of Global Environmental Change, edited by Cristian Lorenzo, 107–33. Cham: Springer Nature.

Rosales, Antulio. 2019. "Structural constraints in times of resource nationalism: oil policy and state capacity in post-neoliberal Ecuador." *Globalizations* 17 (1): 77–92.

Rosenstein-Rodan, Paul. 1943. "Problems of Industrialization of Eastern and South-eastern Europe." *Economic Journal* 53 (210): 202–11.

Ross, Michael. 2012. *The Oil Curse: How Petroleum Wealth Shapes the Development of Nations*. Princeton: Princeton University Press.

———. 2001. "Does Oil Hinder Democracy?" *World Politics* 53 (3): 325–361.

Rostow, Walt Whitman. 1990 (1960). *The Stages of Economic Growth: A Non-Communist Manifesto*. Third edition. Cambridge: Cambridge University Press.

———. 1959. "The Stages of Economic Growth." *The Economic History Review* 12 (1): 1–16.

Saad-Filho, Alfredo, and John Weeks. 2013. "Curses, Diseases and Other Resource Confusions." *Third World Quarterly* 34 (1): 1–21.

Sachs, Jeffrey, and Andrew Warner. 1995. "Natural Resource Abundance and Economic Growth." *Working Paper* 5398. Cambridge: National Bureau of Economic Research.

Salgado, Germánico. 1978. "Lo que fuimos y lo que somos." In *Ecuador, hoy*, coordinated by Gerhard Drekonja, 19–58. Bogotá: Siglo XXI.

Sawyer, Suzana. 2008. "Suing Chevron Texaco." In *The Ecuador Reader. History, Culture, Politics*, edited by Carlos De la Torre and Steve Striffler, 321–28. Durham and London: Duke University Press.

Schuldt, Jürgen. 2004. "De la globalización selectiva a la glocalización cooperativa." In *Libre comercio: Mitos y realidades. Nuevos desafíos para la economía política de la integración latinoamericana*, edited by Alberto Acosta and Eduardo Gudynas, 189–232. Quito: Abya-Yala. ILDIS-FES, D3e.

Schumpeter, Joseph. 1911. *Theorie der wirtschaftlichen Entwicklung*. Leipzig: Duncker & Humblot.

SENESCYT (Secretaría Nacional de Educación Superior, Ciencia, Tecnología e Innovación). 2019a. *Total de becas internacionales por año de adjudicación, según tipo de beca y nivel de estudios*. Quito: SENESCYT, https://www.educacionsuperior.gob.ec/cuadros-estadisticos-indice-de-tabulados-sobre-los-datos-historicos-de-educacion-superior-a-nivel-nacional-incluye-registro-de-titulos-oferta-academica-matriculados-docentes-becas-y-cupos/, last accessed: 08.03.2019.

———. 2019b. *Total de becas internacionales por año de adjudicación, según tipo de beca y campo amplio*. Quito: SENESCYT, https://www.educacionsuperior.gob.ec/cuadros-estadisticos-indice-de-tabulados-sobre-los-datos-historicos-de-educacion-superior-a-nivel-nacional-incluye-registro-de-titulos-oferta-academica-matriculados-docentes-becas-y-cupos/, last accessed: 08.03.2019.

SENPLADES (Secretaría Nacional de Planificación y Desarrollo). 2013. *Plan Nacional para el Buen Vivir 2013-2017*. Quito: SENPLADES.

———. 2012. *Transformación de la Matriz Productiva*. Quito: SENPLADES.

———. 2009. *Plan Nacional para el Buen Vivir 2009-2013*. Quito: SENPLADES.

———. 2007. *Plan Nacional de Desarrollo 2007-2010*. Quito: SENPLADES.

Singer, Hans. 1950. "The Distribution of Gains between Investing and Borrowing Countries." *The American Economic Review*, Papers and Proceedings of the Sixty-second Annual Meeting of the American Economic Association 40 (2): 473–485.

Sinnott, Emily, John Nash, and Augusto de la Torre. 2010. *Natural Resources in Latin America and the Caribbean: Beyond Booms and Busts?*. Washington D.C.: World Bank.

Smith, Adam. 2007 (1776). *An Inquiry into the Nature and Causes of the Wealth of Nations*. Amsterdam: Metalibri.

Solíz, María Fernanda. 2019. "Extractivismo, cambio de la matriz productiva y violencia política." In *Ecuador: Balance de una década. Crisis socioambiental, extractivismo, política e integración*, edited by César Montúfar, 255–284. Quito: Universidad Andina Simón Bolívar sede Ecuador.

Solow, Robert. 1957. "Technical Change and the Aggregate Production Function." *The Review of Economics and Statistics* 39 (3): 312–320.

Sotelo, Adrián. 2005. *América Latina: de crisis y paradigmas. La teoría de la dependencia en el siglo XXI*. México D.F.: Plaza y Valdés.

Stavenhagen, Rodolfo. 1979 (1971). *Sociología y subdesarrollo*. Fifth edition. México D.F.: Nuestro Tiempo.

Stutzman, Ronald. 1981. "El mestizaje: an all-inclusive ideology of exclusion." In *Cultural transformations and ethnicity in modern Ecuador*, edited by Norman Whitten, 45–94. Urbana: University of Illinois Press.

Sunkel, Osvaldo. 2006. "En busca del desarrollo perdido." *Problemas del Desarrollo. Revista Latinoamericana de Economía* 37 (147): 13–44.

———. 1976. "The Development of Development Thinking." *The IDS Bulletin* 8 (3): 6–11.

Svampa, Maristella. 2016. "América Latina: Fin de ciclo y populismos de alta intensidad." In *Rescatar la esperanza. Más allá del neoliberalismo y el progresismo*, edited by Entrepueblos 63–90. Barcelona: Entrepueblos.

———. 2013. "«Consenso de los commodities» y lenguajes de valoración en América Latina." *Nueva Sociedad* 244: 30–46.

Stubbs, Richard. 2009. "What ever happened to the East Asian Developmental State? The unfolding debate." *The Pacific Review* 22 (1): 1–22.

Thurbon, Elizabeth, and Linda Weiss. 2016. "The developmental state in the late twentieth century." In *Handbook of Alternative Theories of Economic Development*, edited by Erik Reinert, Jayati Ghosh, and Rainer Kattel, 637–650. Cheltenham: Edward Elgar.

Tibán, Lourdes. 2018. *Tatay Correa: Cronología de la persecución y criminalización durante el correísmo. Ecuador 2007-2017*. Quito: CACS.

Tilly, Charles. 1985. "War making and state making as organized crime." In *Bringing the state back in*, edited by Peter Evans, Dietrich Rueschmeyer, and Theda Skocpol 169–187. Cambridge: Cambridge University Press.

Todaro, Michael, and Stephen Smith. 2012. *Economic Development*. Eleventh edition. Boston: Addison-Wesley.

Ulrichsen, Kristian. 2017. "Post-Rentier Economic Challenges." *India Quarterly* 73 (2): 210–226.

UNCTAD (United Nations Conference on Trade and Development). 2019. *Commodity Dependence: A Twenty-Year Perspective*. Geneva: UNCTAD.

———. 2017. *Commodities and Development Report 2017: Commodity Markets, Economic Growth, and Development*. New York: UNCTAD and FAO.

———. 2014. *UNCTAD at 50: A Short History*. Geneva: United Nations.

UNDP (United Nations Development Programme). 2013. *Human Development Report 2013. The Rise of the South: Human Progress in a Diverse World*. New York: UNDP.

———. 2010. *Ecuador Yasuni ITT Trust Fund: Terms of Reference*. 28.7.2010, http://mdtf.undp.org/document/download/4492, last accessed: 02.03.2018

United Nations. 1998. *Kyoto Protocol To the United Nations Framework Convention on Climate Change. United Nations*. https://unfccc.int/resource/docs/convkp/kpeng.pdf, last accessed: 02.03.2018.

———. 1992. *United Nations Conference on Environment and Development. Agenda 21*. https://sustainabledevelopment.un.org/content/documents/Agenda21.pdf, last accessed: 02.03.2018.

———. 1987. *Report of the World Commission on Environment and Development: Our Common Future*. http://www.un-documents.net/our-common-future.pdf, last accessed: 02.03.2018.

———. 1972. *Declaration of the United Nations Conference on the Human Environment*. http://www.un-documents.net/unchedec.htm, last accessed: 02.03.2018.

Uslar Pietri, Arturo. 1936. "Sembrar el petróleo." *Ahora*, July 14.

Vallejo, Ivette, Natalia Valdivieso, Cristina Cielo, and Fernando García. 2016. "Ciudades del Milenio: ¿Inclusión o exclusión en una nueva Amazonía?" In *Nada dura para siempre. Neo-extractivismo tras el boom de las materias primas*, edited by Hans-Jürgen Burchardt, Rafael Domínguez, Carlos Larrea, and Stefan Peters, 281–316. Quito: Universidad Andina Simón Bolívar sede Ecuador, International Center for Development and Decent Work.

van Dijk, Teun. 1999. *Análisis del discurso social y político*. Quito: Abya Yala.

Velasco, Fernando. 1981. *Ecuador: subdesarrollo y dependencia*. Quito: El Conejo.

———. 1979. *La dependencia, el imperialismo y las empresas transnacionales*. Quito: El Conejo.

Vera, María Pía. 2013. *Más vale pájaro en mano: crisis bancaria, ahorro y clases medias*. Quito: Flacso sede Ecuador.

Villavicencio, Arturo. 2019. "La magna obra pública del gobierno de la revolución ciudadana." In *Ecuador: Balance de una década. Crisis socioambiental, extractivismo, política e integración*, edited by César Montúfar, 93–118. Quito: Universidad Andina Simón Bolívar sede Ecuador.

———. 2014. "Un cambio neodesarrollista de la matriz energética. Lecturas críticas." In *La restauración conservadora del correísmo*, edited by Juan Cuvi, 267–88. Quito: Montecristi Vive.

Villavicencio, Fernando. 2017. *El feriado petrolero*. Quito: Focus.

Vos, Rob. 1987. *Industrialización, empleo y necesidades básicas en el Ecuador*. Quito: Corporación Editora Nacional.

Wade, Robert. 2018. "The Developmental State: Dead or Alive?." *Development and Change* 49 (2): 518–546.

———. 1990. *Governing the Market: Economic Theory and the Role of Government in East Asian Industrialization*. Princeton: Princeton University Press.

Wilcock, Neil, Corina Scholz, and Hartmut Eisenhans. 2016. *Hartmut Elsenhans and a Critique of Capitalism: Conversations on Theory and Policy Implications*. Basingstoke: Palgrave Macmillan.

Williamson, John. 1993. "Democracy and the 'Washington Consensus'." *World Development* 21 (8): 1329–1336.

Wilson, Jeffrey. 2015. "Understanding resource nationalism: Economic dynamics and political institutions." *Contemporary Politics* 21 (4): 399–416.

World Bank. 2019a. *External debt stocks*. Washington D.C.: World Bank, https://data.worldbank.org/indicator/DT.DOD.DECT.GN.ZS?end=2016&locations=EC&start=1970&view=chart, last accessed: 13.02.2019.

———. 2019b. *Household final consumption expenditure*. Washington D.C.: World Bank, https://data.worldbank.org/indicator/NE.CON.PRVT.CD?end=2017&locations=EC&start=1960, last accessed: 13.02.2019.

———. 2019c. *Manufacturing, value added (% of GDP)*. Washington D.C.: World Bank, https://data.worldbank.org/indicator/NV.IND.MANF.ZS?end=2002&locations=EC&start=1971, last accessed: 13.02.2019.

———. 2019d. *Oil rents (% of GDP)*. Washington D.C.: World Bank, https://data.worldbank.org/indicator/NY.GDP.PETR.RT.ZS?end=2017&locations=EC&start=1960, last accessed: 13.09.2019.

———. 2019e. *Total debt service (% of GNI)*. Washington D.C.: World Bank, https://data.worldbank.org/indicator/DT.TDS.DECT.GN.ZS?end=2016&locations=EC&start=1970&view=chart, last accessed: 13.07.2019.

———. 2019f. *Personal remittances, received (current US$)*. Washington D.C.: World Bank, https://data.worldbank.org/indicator/BX.TRF.PWKR.CD.DT?end=2002&locations=EC&start=1971, last accessed: 13.02.2019.

———. 2019g. *School enrollment, tertiary (% gross)*. Washington D.C.: World Bank, https://data.worldbank.org/indicator/SE.TER.ENRR?end=2016&locations=EC&start=1970&view=chart, last accessed: 13.02.2019.

———. 2019h. *GDP growth (annual %)*. Washington D.C.: World Bank, https://data.worldbank.org/indicator/NY.GDP.MKTP.KD.ZG?locations=EC, last accessed: 13.02.2019.

———. 2019j. *Inflation, consumer prices (annual %)*. Washington D.C.: World Bank, https://data.worldbank.org/indicator/FP.CPI.TOTL.ZG?end=2018&locations=EC&start=1970, last accessed: 13.02.2019.

———. 2019k. *Mineral rents (% of GDP)*. Washington D.C.: World Bank, https://da ta.worldbank.org/indicator/NY.GDP.MINR.RT.ZS?locations=EC, last accessed: 13.09.2019.

———. 2018. *Global Economic Prospects: Broad-Based Upturn, but for How Long?* Washington D.C.: World Bank.

———. 2013. *China 2030: Building a Modern, Harmonious, and Creative Society*. Washington D.C.: World Bank.

———. 1980. *Ecuador: problemas y perspectivas de desarrollo*. Washington D.C.: World Bank.

Wright, Erik Olin. 2009. "Understanding Class. Towards an Integrated Analytical Approach." *New Left Review* 60: 101–116.

———. 1996. "The Continuing Relevance of Class Analysis – Comments." *Theory and Society* 25: 693–716.

———. 1987. "Reflections on Classes." *Berkeley Journal of Sociology* 32: 19–49.

———. 1985. *Classes*. London: Verso.

WTO (World Trade Organization). 2014. *World Trade Report 2014. Trade and Development: Recent Trends and the Role of the WTO*. Geneva: WTO.

Yanza, Luis. 2004. "El juicio a Chevron Texaco". In *Petróleo y desarrollo sostenible en el Ecuador: las* apuestas, coordinated by Guillaume Fontaine, 37–44. Quito: Flacso sede Ecuador, FES-ILDIS, Petrobras.

Zamosc, Leon. 1994. "Agrarian Protest and the Indian Movement in the Ecuadorian Highlands." *Latin American Research Review* 29 (3): 37–69.

Zapata, Ximena, Diana Castro, and Daniele Benzi. 2018. "Las relaciones sino-ecuatorianas en la época de la 'revolución ciudadana'." *Enfoques Multidisciplinarios (REDCAEM)* 5: 4–27.

Newspaper Articles

Astudillo, Giovanni, and Lineida Castillo. 2019. "150 obras fueron financiadas con las regalías anticipadas." *El Comercio*, July 23.

Astudillo, Giovanni. 2019. "Régimen afianzará minería como eje fundamental de la economía." *El Comercio*, June 5. https://www.elcomercio.com/actualidad/regi men-afianza-mineria-economia-ecuador.html, last accessed: 06.06.2019.

Brooke, James. 1993. "Oil and Tourism Don't Mix, Inciting Amazon Battle." *The New York Times*, September 26. https://www.nytimes.com/1993/09/26/world/oil-and-tourism-don-t-mix-inciting-amazon-battle.html, last accessed: 12.03.2019.

Daily El Comercio. 2019. *El IVA no sube y se liberan los precios de gasolinas y diésel*. Quito, October 2.

———. 2019. *Ecuador logra récord en extracción de petróleo en zona protegida de Amazonía, según Petroamazonas*. Quito, August 17. https://www.elcomercio.com/actu alidad/ecuador-record-extraccion-petroleo-yasuni.html, last accessed: 17.08.2019.

———. 2019. *En julio, el déficit presupuestario se incrementó en USD 500 millones*. Quito, August 4.

―――. 2019. *Gobierno: 11 820 funcionarios públicos fueron despedidos desde diciembre*. Quito, March 13. https://www.elcomercio.com/actualidad/trabajadores-desvi nculados-sector-publico-ecuador.html, last accessed: 03.09.2019.

―――. 2018. *Créditos quirografarios se usan para pagar deudas*. Quito, May 26. https://www.elcomercio.com/actualidad/creditos-quirografarios-pagar-deudas-biess.ht ml, last accessed: 03.03.2019.

―――. 2018. *El reajuste de una obra con sello asiático*. Quito, April 6. https://especial es.elcomercio.com/2017/10/yachay/#, last accessed: 12.03.2019.

―――. 2015. *El Régimen aplicó salvaguardias de hasta el 45% a las importaciones*. Quito, March 6. https://www.elcomercio.com/actualidad/negocios-salvaguardias -productos-comercio-exterior.html, last accessed: 02.03.2018.

Daily El Telégrafo. 2016. *En enero de 2016 el Biess desembolsó $ 99 millones en 1.932 operaciones crediticias*. Guayaquil, February 11. https://www.eltelegrafo.com.ec/n oticias/politica/3/en-enero-de-2016-el-biess-desembolso-99-millones-en-1-932-ope raciones-crediticias, last accessed: 03.09.2019.

Daily El Universo. 2019. *Ecuador dejará la OPEP en 2020*. Guayaquil, October 1. https://www.eluniverso.com/noticias/2019/10/01/nota/7543135/gobierno-decide-salida-ecuador-opep-partir-2020, last accessed: 01.10.2019.

―――. 2018. *Contraloría realiza 14 exámenes por Yachay*. Quito, February 8. https://www.eluniverso.com/noticias/2018/02/09/nota/6616348/contraloria-realiza-14-ex amenes-yachay, last accessed: 12.03.2019.

―――. 2013. *Ivonne Baki despidió el proyecto Yasuní, pero buscará que se proteja*. Guayaquil, August 22. https://www.eluniverso.com/noticias/2013/08/22/nota/13 27846/ivonne-baki-despidio-proyecto-yasuni-buscara-que-se-proteja, last accessed: 12.03.2019.

Daily La Razón. 2019. *Gasolina del país, de las más baratas del mundo*. México D.F., April 17. https://www.razon.com.mx/negocios/gasolina-del-pais-de-las-mas-barat as-del-mundo/, last accessed: 18.04.2019.

González, Patricia. 2018. "El Biess aumentó la entrega de créditos quirografarios en el 2017." *El Comercio*, January 7. https://www.elcomercio.com/actualidad/biess-e ntrega-creditosquirografarios-afiliados-financiamiento.html, last accessed: 12.03.2019.

Griswold, Eliza. 2012. "How 'Silent Spring' Ignited the Environmental Movement." *The New York Times*. September 21. https://www.nytimes.com/2012/09/2 3/magazine/how-silent-spring-ignited-the-environmental-movement.html, last accessed: 12.03.2019.

Heredia, Valeria. 2018. "Informe final de la Contraloría establece responsabilidades penales en contratos para cinco edificaciones de Yachay." *El Comercio*, April 6. https://www.elcomercio.com/actualidad/yachay-contraloria-perjuicio-informe-pe nal.html, last accessed: 12.03.2019.

Kaufmann, Stephan. 2019. "Keine Krankheit, nur ein Symptom." *Neues Deutschland*, July 20. https://www.neues-deutschland.de/artikel/1123102.korruption-kei ne-krankheit-nur-ein-symptom.html, last accessed: 10.08.2019.

Kraus, Clifford. 2013. "Plan to Ban Oil Drilling in Amazon is Dropped." *The New York Times*. August 17. https://www.nytimes.com/2013/08/17/business/energy-en vironment/ecuador-drops-plan-to-ban-drilling-in-jungle.html, last accessed: 12.03.2019.

Long, Gideon. 2019. "Ecuador ends fuel subsidies to keep $4.2bn IMF programme on track." *Financial Times*. October 2. https://www.ft.com/content/69bed0ce-e52 b-11e9-9743-db5a370481bc, last accessed: 05.10.2019.

Maidenberg, H. J. 1971. "Oil Companies Find Ecuador's Long-Sought Eldorado." *The New York Times*, July 18. https://www.nytimes.com/1971/07/18/archives/oil-c ompanies-find-ecuadors-longsought-eldorado-tuna-fish-however.html, last accessed: 12.03.2019.

Montenegro, Javier. 2019. "La nómina continúa obesa." *El Expreso*, September 20. https://www.expreso.ec/actualidad/nomina-empresas-publicas-estado-empleados-KI3138491, last accessed: 20.09.2019.

Orozco, Mónica. 2018. "Ecuador vendió incluso el petróleo que no tenía en 2016." *El Comercio*, February 14. https://www.elcomercio.com/actualidad/ecuador-venta -petroleo-petrotailandia-petroecuador.html, last accessed: 12.03.2019.

Pacheco, Mayra. 2019. "10 avatares del fallido proyecto de la Refinería del Pacífi-co." *El Comercio*, August 28. https://www.elcomercio.com/actualidad/ecuador-pe troleo-refineria-pacifico-financiamiento.html, last accessed: 29.08.2019.

Reuters. 2019. "Ecuador declares state of emergency as protesters decry end to fuel subsidies." *The Guardian*, October 3. https://www.theguardian.com/world/2019/ oct/03/ecuador-state-of-emergency-fuel-subsidies-protest, last accessed: 05.10.2019.

———. 2006. "Ecuador Cancels an Oil Deal with Occidental Petroleum." *The New York Times*, May 17. https://www.nytimes.com/2006/05/17/business/worldbusine ss/17oil.html, last accessed: 12.03.2019.

Revista Líderes. 2017. *Las salvaguardias aplicadas en el 2015 terminan*. Quito, May 31. https://www.revistalideres.ec/lideres/economia-ecuador-salvaguardias-aplicad as-terminan.html, last accessed: 12.03.2019.

Rohter, Larry. 2000. "Ecuador Decides to Wean Military from Oil Riches." *The New York Times*, December 22. https://www.nytimes.com/2000/12/22/world/ecu ador-decides-to-wean-military-from-oil-riches.html, last accessed: 12.03.2019.

Standing, Guy. 2016. "The Five Lies of Rentier Capitalism." *Social Europe. Politics, Economy, and Employment & Labour*. October 27. https://eprints.soas.ac.uk/24833 /1/five-lies-rentier-capitalism, last accessed: 12.03.2018.

Tapia, Evelyn. 2019. "Finanzas defiende actividad minera legal y dice que generará USD 3,800 millones de inversión hasta el 2021." *El Comercio*, June 20. https://w ww.elcomercio.com/actualidad/finanzas-defiende-mineria-legal-inversiones.htm l, last accessed: 21.06.2019.

———. 2018. "5 empresas públicas que se liquidan este 2018 registran 1373 em-pleados." *El Comercio*, April 13. https://www.elcomercio.com/actualidad/ecuado r-empresas-liquidacion-planeconomico-empleadospublicos.html, last accessed: 21.06.2019.

References

The Guardian. 2013. *Ecuador election: Rafael Correa set to win despite fossil fuel fears.* London, February 14. https://www.theguardian.com/world/2013/feb/14/ecuador -election-president-rafael-correa, last accessed: 11.09.2018.

United Press International. 1975. "Ecuador Crushes Revolt by Troops." *The New York Times*, September 1. https://www.nytimes.com/1975/09/02/archives/ecuador -crushes-revolt-by-troops.html, last accessed: 12.03.2019.

Valencia, Alexandra. 2017. "Ecuador seeks renegotiation of China oil sales, loans." *Reuters*. October 24. https://www.reuters.com/article/ecuador-oil/ecuador-seeks-r enegotiation-of-china-oil-sales-loans-idUSL2N1MZ1G5, last accessed: 12.03.2019.

———. 2016. "Ecuador to pay $980 million to Occidental for asset seizure." *Reuters*. January 13. https://www.reuters.com/article/ecuador-occidental/ecuador -to-pay-980-million-to-occidental-for-asset-seizure-idUSL2N14X0U420160113, last accessed: 12.03.2019.

———. 2015. "UPDATE 1-Ecuador signs $2.5 bln oil supply deal with Thailand." *Reuters*. July 31. https://www.reuters.com/article/ecuador-petroecuador/update-1- ecuador-signs-2-5-bln-oil-supply-deal-with-thailand-idUSL1N10B2TA20150731, last accessed: 12.03.2019.

Official Documents

Executive Order No. 23. Official Gazette No. 223, Quito, May 26, 1961

Supreme Order No. 1459. Official Gazette No. 322, Quito, October 1, 1971.

Supreme Order No. 1447-C. Official Gazette No. 325, Quito, October 6, 1971.

Supreme Order No. 430, Quito, June 6, 1972.

Supreme Order No. 522. Official Gazette No. 88, Quito, June 26, 1972.

Supreme Order No. 1048. Official Gazette No. 145, Quito, September 15, 1972.

Supreme Order No. 162. Official Gazette No. 253, Quito, February 23, 1973.

Supreme Order No. 374, Quito April 5, 1973.

Supreme Order No. 1172. Official Gazette No. 410. Quito, October 15, 1973.

Agreement of Lima, Lima, November 2, 1973.

Supreme Order No. 1393, Quito, December 14, 1973.

Supreme Order No. 995. Official Gazette No. 239, Quito, November 23, 1976.

Supreme Order No. 2400. Official Gazette No. 564, Quito, April 12, 1978.

Supreme Order No. 2450. Official Gazette No. 579, Quito, May 4, 1978.

Supreme Order No. 2625. Official Gazette No. 624, Quito, July 7, 1978.

Supreme Order No. 3289. Official Gazette No. 792, Quito, March 15, 1979.

Executive Order No. 1802. Official Gazette No. 456, Quito, June 7, 1994.

Executive Order No. 967. Official Gazette No. 223, Quito, December 26, 1997.

Executive Order No. 197. Official Gazette No. 47, Quito, October 15, 1998.

Executive Order No. 685. Official Gazette No. 149, Quito, March 16, 1999.

Executive Order No. 1583. Official Gazette No. 302 (Supplement II), Quito, June 29, 2006.

Executive Order No. 1672. Official Gazette No. 312 (Supplement), Quito, July 13, 2006.

Executive Order No. 2. Official Gazette No. 8, Quito, January 25, 2007.

Executive Order No. 103. Official Gazette No. 26, Quito, February 22, 2007.

Executive Order No. 117-A. Official Gazette No. 33. Quito, March 5, 2007.

Resolution No. 25DIR-2007-03-30. Empresa Pública de Hidrocarburos del Ecuador (PETROECUADOR). Quito, March 30, 2007.

Executive Order No. 263. Official Gazette No. 67. Quito, April 19, 2007.

Executive Order No. 475. Official Gazette No. 132, Quito, July 23, 2007.

Executive Order No. 662. Official Gazette No. 193. Quito, October 18, 2007.

Executive Order No. 766. Official Gazette No. 231, Quito, December 13, 2007.

Executive Order No. 847. Official Gazette No. 253, Quito, January 16, 2008.

Executive Order No. 882. Official Gazette No. 269, Quito, February 9, 2008.

Executive Order No. 1227. Official Gazette No. 401, Quito, August 12, 2008.

Executive Order No. 1572. Official Gazette No. 530, Quito, February 17, 2009.

Executive Order No. 1116. Official Gazette No. 359, Quito, May 4, 2009.

Executive Order No. 241. Official Gazette No. 132, Quito, February 19, 2010.

Executive Order No. 314. Official Gazette No. 171, Quito, April 14, 2010.

Executive Order No. 315. Official Gazette No. 171, Quito, April 14, 2010.

Executive Order No. 596. Official Gazette No. 356, Quito, January 6, 2011.

Executive Order No. 648. Official Gazette No. 391, Quito, February 23, 2011.

Executive Order No. 870. Official Gazette No. 534, Quito, September 14, 2011.

Executive Order No. 1030. Official Gazette No. 637, Quito, February 9, 2012.

Executive Order No. 1135. Official Gazette No. 699 (Supplement), Quito, May 9, 2012.

Resolution No. RPC-SO-037-265-2012. Consejo de Educación Superior (CES). Quito, October 31, 2012.

Executive Order No. 1457. Official Gazette No. 922, Quito, March 28, 2013.

Executive Order No. 74. Official Gazette No. 72 (Supplement II), Quito, September 3, 2013.

Resolution of the National Assembly. Quito, October 3, 2013.

Executive Order No. 578. Official Gazette No. 448, Quito, February 28, 2015.

Executive Order No. 753. Official Gazette No. 573, Quito, August 26, 2015.

Executive Order No. 1004. Official Gazette No. 760, Quito, May 23, 2016.

Executive Order No. 7, Quito, May 24, 2017.

Executive Order No. 399, Quito, May 15, 2018.

Executive Order No. 732, Quito, May 13, 2019.

Executive Order No. 883, Quito, October 1, 2019.

Quoted Interviews

Interview with Augusto Tandazo, former Executive Secretary of the Latin American Energy Organization (OLADE), Quito, September 18, 2015.

Interview with retired professional, former adviser to President Alfredo Palacio, Quito, September 18, 2015.

Interview with former Minister of Coordination of Economic Policy, Quito, October 7, 2015.

Interview with Alberto Acosta, former President of the Constituent Assembly, former Minister of Energy and Mines, Quito, February 12, 2016.

Interview with Pato Chávez, spokesperson Yasunidos, Quito, April 13, 2016.

Interview with Fernando Fajardo, member of Yasunidos, Quito, May 6, 2016.

Interview with Víctor Bretón, lecturer at the Universitat de Lleida and FLACSO Ecuador, Quito, August 8, 2016.

Interview with retired professional, former official of the Consejo Nacional de Desarrollo (CONADE), Quito, January 9, 2017.

Interview with María Augusta Espín, Vice President of Academic Affairs at the Central University of Ecuador, Quito, March 8, 2019.

Interview with former consultant at Secretaría Nacional de Planificación y Desarrollo (SENPLADES), Quito, March 16, 2017.

Interview with former Deputy Secretary of the Ecuadorian Secretariat of Higher Education (SENESCYT), Quito, July 6, 2017.

Interview with Ana Cevallos, retired professional, relative of a high-ranking officer involved in the 1975 military revolt, Quito, September 19, 2017.

Interview with Fabián Alarcón, retired professional, former staff member at General Motors del Ecuador, Quito, September 19, 2017.

Interview with former scholarship holder of the Ecuadorian government, Quito, August 8, 2018.

Interview with former consultant at Yachay EP, Quito, September 16, 2018.

Interview with Javier Espín, retired professional, Quito, October 10, 2018.

Interview with Ximena Estévez, retired professional, Quito, October 10, 2018.

Interview with Pepe Vásquez, mechanical engineer and state's contractor, Quito, October 11, 2018.

Interview with Jessica López Pérez, Director of Climate Change Projects at the Consorcio de Gobiernos Autónomos Provinciales del Ecuador (CONGOPE), Quito, November 13, 2018.

Interview with Javier Espín, retired professional, Quito, November 14, 2018.

Interview with Synneva Geithus Laastad, PhD candidate at the Department of Sociology and Human Geography of the University of Oslo, Quito, December 6, 2018.

Interview with Luis Manzano, former Director of Renewable Energy at the Ministry of Electricity and Renewable Energy, Quito, January 23, 2019.

Interview with lecturer at private university in Quito, Quito, January 24, 2019.

Other Quoted Interviews

Interview with Wilson Pástor, former head of Petroamazonas. Interview by Alonso Soto and Alexandra Valencia, Reuters, December 18, 2007. https://www.reuters.com/article/petroecuador-occidentalidUSN1852864120071218, last accessed: 12.03.2019.

Interview with Pablo Ortiz, former General Manager of Ecuador Estratégico. Interview by Dr. Stefan Peters, Lago Agrio, September 8, 2015.

Interview with Eduardo Cadena, former Executive Director of the Quito Chamber of Commerce (Cámara de Comercio de Quito, CCQ). Interview by Dr. Stefan Peters, Quito, September 14, 2015.

Interview with Ángel Sallo, former head of Ecuador Estratégico in Sucumbíos. Interview by Dr. Stefan Peters, Lago Agrio, September 18, 2015.

Interview with Ivette Vallejo, lecturer at FLACSO Ecuador, Interview by Dr. Stefan Peters, Quito, September 22, 2015.

Interview with Sergio Sáenz, former Communication Director at the Pichincha Chamber of Small and Medium-Sized Enterprises (Cámara de la Pequeña y Mediana Empresa de Pichincha, CAPEIPI). Interview by Dr. Stefan Peters, Quito, September 14, 2016.

Interview with Pablo Lucio Paredes, former member of the Asamblea Constituyente, lecturer at USFQ Ecuador. Interview by Dr. Stefan Peters, Quito, September 21, 2016.

Interview with Jaime Vargas, President of the Confederation of Indigenous Nationalities of Ecuador, CONAIE. Interview by Gloria Muñoz Ramírez, La Jornada – Ojarasca, January, 2020. https://www.jornada.com.mx/2020/01/11/ojarasca273.pdf?fbclid=IwAR2A3AZaHqgS9MbDYf07llCZgHexR_q8b2zPvHOnYVRkpUaaO28anfFUgyo, last accessed: 12.01.2019.